Italy in EMU

Also by Marco Buti:

Anne Brunila, Marco Buti and Daniele Franco (editors)
THE STABILITY AND GROWTH PACT: THE ARCHITECTURE OF FISCAL POLICY IN EMU

Marco Buti, Jürgen von Hagen and Carlos Martinez-Mongay (editors)
THE BEHAVIOUR OF FISCAL AUTHORITIES: STABILIZATION, GROWTH AND INSTITUTIONS

Marco Buti and Daniele Franco
FISCAL POLICY IN ECONOMIC AND MONETARY UNION: THEORY, EVIDENCE AND INSTITUTIONS

Marco Buti (editor)
MONETARY AND FISCAL POLICIES IN EMU: INTERACTIONS AND COORDINATION

Marco Buti and André Sapir (editors)
EMU AND ECONOMIC POLICY IN EUROPE: THE CHALLENGE OF THE EARLY YEARS

Marco Buti, Paolo Sestito and Hans Wijkander (editors)
TAXATION, WELFARE AND THE CRISIS OF UNEMPLOYMENT IN EUROPE

Marco Buti, Daniele Franco and Lucio R. Pench (editors)
THE WELFARE STATE IN EUROPE: CHALLENGES AND REFORMS

Marco Buti and André Sapir (editors)
ECONOMIC POLICY IN EMU: A STUDY BY THE EUROPEAN COMMISSION SERVICES

Italy in EMU

The Challenges of Adjustment and Growth

Edited by

Marco Buti

palgrave
macmillan

First published 2009 by
PALGRAVE MACMILLAN

Palgrave Macmillan in the UK is an imprint of Macmillan Publishers Limited, registered in England, company number 785998, of Houndmills, Basingstoke, Hampshire RG21 6XS.

Palgrave Macmillan in the US is a division of St Martin's Press LLC, 175 Fifth Avenue, New York, NY 10010.

Palgrave Macmillan is the global academic imprint of the above companies and has companies and representatives throughout the world.

Palgrave® and Macmillan® are registered trademarks in the United States, the United Kingdom, Europe and other countries.

ISBN-13: 978–0–230–22335–6 hardback
ISBN-10: 0–230–22335–4 hardback

This book is printed on paper suitable for recycling and made from fully managed and sustained forest sources. Logging, pulping and manufacturing processes are expected to conform to the environmental regulations of the country of origin.

A catalogue record for this book is available from the British Library.

Library of Congress Cataloging-in-Publication Data

Italy in EMU : the challenges of adjustment and growth / edited by
Marco Buti.
p. cm.
Includes bibliographical references and index.
ISBN 978–0–230–22335–6 (alk. paper)
1. European Union—Italy. 2. Italy—Economic policy. 3. Monetary policy—Italy. 4. Economic and Monetary Union. I. Buti, Marco.
HC240.25.I81847 2008
332.4'940945–dc22 2008024817

10 9 8 7 6 5 4 3 2 1
18 17 16 15 14 13 12 11 10 09

Printed and bound in Great Britain by
CPI Antony Rowe, Chippenham and Eastbourne

Dedicated to the memory of
Riccardo Faini, fellow economist and friend

Contents

Acknowledgements

This book is dedicated to Riccardo Faini, an outstanding Italian economist who suddenly passed away on 20 January 2007. Riccardo, probably more than any other economist, looked at the Italian economy through 'European eyes', seeing European integration as a real opportunity to modernise Italy's economic policy – indeed, policy *tout court*. As President Ciampi says in his foreword, Riccardo's qualities went far beyond his outstanding academic and cultural stature as an economist. Many of the contributors to this volume worked with him and became personal friends. All of us appreciated his insight, wit and human warmth. His comprehensive and acute analysis of the Italian economy is an invaluable legacy that inspires this book.

The book is the fruit of the concerted effort of many players. I would like to thank, first and foremost, all the contributors for complying graciously with my repeated and pressing requests. My thanks also go to Laura Bardone, Lucia Piana and Vito Ernesto Reitano, who have helped right from the start in the conception, shaping and finalisation of the book. Without their relentless efforts, it simply would not have seen the light of day. Alessandro Turrini provided valuable comments and insights. Thanks also go to Sophie Bland for editorial help and to Carmen Zammit for her work on layout throughout the preparation of the book.

Marco Buti

Contributors

Marco Buti, editor	**Deputy Director General, Directorate-General for Economic and Financial Affairs, European Commission**
Laura Bardone	Directorate-General for Economic and Financial Affairs, European Commission
Alexandra Bibbee	Senior Economist, Economics Department, Organisation for Economic Cooperation and Development
Tito Boeri	Professor, Universitá Bocconi, Milan
Eric Chaney	Chief Economist for Europe, Morgan Stanley
Carlo Azeglio Ciampi	President of the Italian Republic from 1999 to 2006
Lorenzo Codogno	Director of Economic and Financial Analysis, Italian Ministry of Economy and Finance
Daniele Franco	Head of the Structural Studies Department, Bank of Italy
Vittorio Grilli	Director General of the Treasury, Italian Ministry of Economy and Finance
Daniel Gros	Director, Centre for European Policy Studies
Martin Larch	Directorate-General for Economic and Financial Affairs, European Commission
Alessandro Leipold	Deputy Director of the European Department, International Monetary Fund
Lucia Piana	Directorate-General for Economic and Financial Affairs, European Commission
Vito Ernesto Reitano	Directorate-General for Economic and Financial Affairs, European Commission
Pietro Rizza	Structural Studies Department, Banca d'Italia
André Sapir	Professor, Université Libre de Bruxelles
Vito Tanzi	Former director of the Fiscal Affairs Department of the International Monetary Fund and former Under-Secretary of State, Italian Ministry of Economy and Finance

Tables

Figures

Foreword: In Memory of Riccardo Faini, Economist and Gentleman

Carlo Azeglio Ciampi
Former President of the Italian Republic

The painful memory of that Saturday 20 January 2007 on which Riccardo Faini died is still fresh in my mind and that alone would be sufficient to make me want to write about someone who was both a friend and a colleague, almost as if doing so could somehow bring him back among us, discussing his latest findings, planning further research – possibly in the light of those discussions – ceaselessly driven both by a desire to go the extra distance and add to mankind's collective knowledge and by the feeling of dissatisfaction that inhabits the mind and, even more so, the spirit of every genuine researcher.

In the context of the topics on which Faini's research had most recently been focused – a task which, at the cost of some sacrifice on his part, he managed to combine with the demanding work he was assigned by the Ministry of Economic Affairs – this collection of essays is a continuation of a dialogue that was all too suddenly interrupted. In a way, the essays can allow their authors to maintain a link with a friend who has been taken from their midst.

I shall in these few lines attempt to distil my memories of a person I had perhaps not known as long as had some of his fellow economists but with whom there was an immediate and close rapport, a sense of being 'on the same wavelength', that can transcend any difference in age, experience or career paths.

I first met Riccardo Faini in 1995 when I was asked by President Santer to chair the newly created European Competitiveness Advisory Group. At the time, I was looking for someone who could first and foremost deliver sound scientific expertise. Of no less importance to me was that I should be able to count on someone who was driven by ideals. In other words, I was looking not just for an outstanding economist; my remit meant that I needed someone with a strong sense of the role and importance of the institutions, someone who, motivated by deep-rooted personal feelings rather than as a result of a scientific and simply methodical approach, could pay attention to the social aspects. As I saw it, all this was indispensable to being in tune with what had driven the Essen European Council in February 1995 and had led to the creation of the Advisory Group.

The European Council's decision had stemmed from the fact that loss of competitiveness, and its consequences in terms of development and employment, was the most difficult challenge facing Europe at the end of the 20th century and the beginning of the third millennium. It was a problem that was both old and new and required a complex mix of traditional, non-traditional, short-term and long-term measures. That was how I saw it. At the time, there was not yet full awareness of the implications of globalisation and the entry into the world market of the two new major Asian economies: China and India. I took the view that, when dealing with such serious and complex issues, the only way of arriving at a common understanding lay in dialogue and negotiation.

My right-hand man accordingly had to be someone who was bold and open-minded, rigorous and flexible, and both an idealist and a pragmatist. This, in my mind's eye, was the profile of the person I was looking for.

Faini's scientific and academic profile, and his career path generally, convinced me that I had found the right man. And of course so he was. Throughout my time as chairman of the Group, I knew I could count on a highly fruitful collaboration on both a professional and a human plane. Working closely with Faini provided confirmation of his scientific and cultural stature as an economist. In Faini as a person I also saw a number of traits which have become somewhat rare in an age in which people think they can convince others by shouting, in which aggressiveness is often seen as a quality and in which strength of character has been replaced by arrogance. Young though he was, Faini was also mild-mannered, and courteous, a gentleman of the old school.

Later, when I was in charge of the Treasury Ministry, designating Faini as Italy's representative at the IMF was of course a perfectly logical choice, a decision that could be made both easily and rapidly and that immediately met with the approval of academic and institutional circles. During his time at the IMF he was the subject of widespread and unreserved appreciation. The sadness with which his death was greeted in some way provides further confirmation that that choice was the right one.

On the day after he died I read and heard many messages of condolence from colleagues, friends and students and, while they occasionally differed in tone, perhaps reflecting how closely the person concerned knew Faini, it was clear to see that he was the subject of a great deal of admiration and respect.

I recognised in those tributes many of the brushstrokes which, more than a decade ago, I had included in my portrait of what an ideal collaborator should be, a profile which Faini easily matched with, as an added bonus, his kindness, warmth and wit, all this accompanied by a modesty which was all the more surprising given his scientific and intellectual stature. Among those many messages there was one which I found particularly striking and which gives a true picture of Riccardo Faini the academic, the man and his personality. It refers to a quality of his which I found particularly valuable in the course of our work on the Competitiveness Group. This is what I read:

> He saw complexity simply as a challenge to his intellect, an incentive to gaining a grasp of a given situation. While economic theory lay at the heart of his analyses it was by no means the only instrument he used.

Introduction

Marco Buti
European Commission

Setting the scene

Italy's adoption of the euro in 1999 was a major political achievement that served to rehabilitate Italy's economic policy governance in the eyes of the international community. The country's fulfilment of the Maastricht criteria defied the scepticism of many observers and policy-makers outside Italy, who often saw these criteria as a useful screening device to keep the under-performers out of the virtuous club.

Indeed, the discussion on the viability and desirability of Italy's membership was the magnified reflection of the debate on whether the single currency was practicable or worthwhile in the first place. Some predicted a bumpy start for the euro or even a collapse, with Italy – a repeated fiscal offender – actually most likely to trigger such a crisis. Others saw the common currency as a great opportunity to bring about long-term gains in trade and growth thanks to the elimination of exchange rate uncertainty, falling risk premia and a reduction of transaction costs so as to become major players in the global economy.

Within national borders, there were strong political economy arguments in favour of the euro adoption. Indeed, most Italian economic policy actors agreed that there was little alternative for Italy: in the run up to the euro the markets largely demonstrated that any attempt to peg the lira to the single currency would be frustrated by recurrent speculative attacks and volatile capital movements. At the same time, going back to full exchange rate flexibility would have meant losing the external anchor that had helped orientate Italy's economic policy in the previous two decades. The euro was seized upon by policy-makers as an opportunity to strengthen such a constraint so as to impose domestic discipline and secure reforms that would have been difficult to achieve otherwise in the face of institutional weaknesses and policy failure at home. But while the single currency was acknowledged as bringing valuable potential benefits, it was also clear that it would carry significant challenges. Losing the use of exchange rate devaluations as a quick fix in the event of competitiveness losses would force the Italian national authorities to accept their responsibility to come up with adequate policy responses to tackle the long-standing structural weaknesses of the economy.

Ten years into its existence, the euro has proved to be a clear success.[1] The single currency has ensured macroeconomic stability and boosted cross-border trade, financial integration and investment. It has spurred the economic integration of Europe – not least through its successive enlargements – increased its resilience to adverse shocks and made it a regional and global pole of stability. Given its long-standing macroeconomic and fiscal imbalances, Italy benefited proportionately more than other euro-area members from the stability-oriented framework of the Economic and Monetary Union. The steep fall in inflation recorded by the euro area as it approached the euro adoption, and its stabilisation thereafter, was particularly impressive in Italy. Euro-area entry also reduced the risk premia incorporated in interest rates to a greater extent than on average in the euro area. This, in turn, helped public finances through the reduction of the servicing costs of the very high government debt.

While clearly a success, so far the euro has fallen short of some initial expectations and there remains potential to reap its benefits further. To start with, growth performance has been subdued in several euro-area countries – but particularly in Italy. Labour markets in the euro area and in Italy have also shared common trends. The substantial improvement in the euro area's labour market position has been accompanied by a fairly sustained decline in labour productivity and in many cases a deepening of the divide between core and 'marginal' workers, with an increasing number of flexible temporary contracts existing side-by-side with rigid permanent contracts. Once again, this development has been particularly evident in Italy. In the area of public finances, while many euro-area countries have made significant steps to meet the ageing challenge and substantially reduced deficits and debt, they have also struggled to comply with the Stability and Growth Pact (SGP) requirements, with a number of them recording a general government deficit above the 3 per cent of GDP threshold established in the Treaty. Italy's difficulties with fiscal consolidation have been long-standing and came to the forefront again when it was placed under the Excessive Deficit Procedure (EDP) in July 2005. As in most other euro-area countries, Italy's fiscal position improved in the years 2006–7 and eventually the EDP was abrogated in 2008. With the highest public debt ratio among euro-area countries, the Italian public finance situation remains, however, fragile. And finally, although the euro-area member states have embarked on substantive structural reforms within the so-called Lisbon process to tackle their economic challenges, the reform agenda has not yet been completed. This, too, is especially true for Italy.

Finally, a number of new developments such as globalisation, ageing, climate change and the spectacular development of new communication technologies are significantly changing the economic environment faced by all euro-area countries, offering new opportunities but also posing important challenges. Some of these trends are hitting Italy especially hard, owing to its particular production framework and demographic structures.

With these parallel paths in mind, this book sets out to assess Italy's experience in EMU as a paradigm of a country featuring important structural shortcomings that decides to relinquish monetary independence. The book highlights challenges ahead and outlines some of the key policy issues that will need to be tackled in the coming years. It comprises contributions from academics and policy-makers who have been closely following economic and policy developments in Italy in the past decade or who have been directly involved in the policy-making process. The analysis focuses on three main issues: i) Italy's growth and productivity performance; ii) macroeconomic adjustment in the monetary union; and iii) budgetary consolidation and the sustainability of public finances.

Italy in EMU: the challenges of adjustment and growth

The new policy environment created by the euro

As foreseen at the onset of the third stage of EMU, by joining the single currency, the risk premia paid on liabilities issued by the Italian government and private agents fell considerably and durably as a result of the elimination of the exchange rate risk. Reduced interest expenditure helped adjust government budget balances and put the debt-to-GDP ratio on a downward trajectory. Inflation remained only slightly above the price stability objective of the European Central Bank. Reduced transaction costs, enhanced price transparency and the lower uncertainty brought about by the single currency were also expected to raise growth, both by improving resource allocation and by fostering investment.

On the other hand, euro-area participation was challenging in two major respects. First, the irrevocable fixing of the exchange rate parity would mean that competitiveness losses could no longer be recovered in the easy (but unsustainable) option offered by a devaluation of the nominal exchange rate. Second, the framework for budgetary discipline of the SGP would impose a persistent constraint on debt accumulation and eliminate the possibility of carrying out large fiscal expansions.

Thus, while the new policy environment created by the monetary union provided ample opportunities, it also required the necessary structural reforms to improve price and wage responsiveness for an efficient and smooth adjustment, and further fiscal consolidation to create sufficient room in the government accounts to let automatic stabilisers play freely and cope with the budgetary pressures related to ageing. Indeed, in line with some views in the academic literature, the single currency was expected to produce incentives for governments to undertake structural reform in the pursuit of market flexibility. The *ex-ante* views on fiscal adjustment were mixed, with many identifying the surveillance once in the euro area as less effective than in the run-up to the euro adoption.

On balance, how has the Italian economy fared in the above respects ten years down the road?

Living with the euro: a bird's eye view of the first ten years

A look back over the last ten years shows that Italy's experience in EMU has been mixed. The euro is often used as a scapegoat to explain the rather disappointing overall performance of the Italian economy, but, in reality, a full assessment of how Italy would have fared outside of EMU would most probably conclude that the EMU-related benefits associated with a stable macro-financial environment largely outweigh the costs of losing monetary policy autonomy. The underperformance of the Italian economy results from inappropriate economic policies at the national level, in particular as they have not been able to fully reap the opportunities offered by its participation in EMU.

There is a broad consensus that the major problem that the Italian economy encountered in the past decade was the pronounced and protracted *potential growth* gap *vis-à-vis* the rest of the euro area, in the order of 0.75 percentage points per year (i.e., just above 1.25 per cent and 2 per cent in Italy and the euro area, respectively). The diagnosis of this malaise is still broadly similar to that arrived at in a review of the Italian economy published by the European Commission in 1999.[2] Only with respect to one of the specific weaknesses that had emerged at the time of that review has there been a good deal of progress – namely, Italy's inability to fully exploit its existing labour potential. While the country's growth performance may have been disappointing, it has been much more successful in terms of job creation, thanks, *inter alia*, to reforms making the labour market more flexible, notably as concerns new hires.

Unfortunately, the flipside of this development has been a significant slowdown in productivity, with growth in output per hour down from 1.5 per cent on average per year in the period 1992–8 to just 0.5 per cent over 1999–2008. The positive employment performance could be at the origin of the labour productivity slowdown, at least in the short run. However, the evidence shows that the main culprit was the sharp and prolonged slowdown in total factor productivity (TFP) growth. This is the economic growth component usually associated with a more productive use of production factors, achieved by reallocating resources towards high-growth sectors and activities, absorbing any slack in the use of factors of production, better exploiting economies of scale and innovating more. The slowdown in Italian TFP compared with other euro-area countries can hardly be attributed to the single currency, which, on the contrary, should have helped to boost it by contributing to better functioning markets and stronger competition.[3] At most, it can be argued that the new policy environment created by the euro brought to light the structural weaknesses underlying this development.

The picture described above, which emerges at the level of the national economy when looking at aggregated data, hides a sharp regional split, with marked and persistent regional disparities between the Centre/North and the South. The South's sorry performance compared to the Centre/North but also, and more visibly, compared to the other regions of the EU, is still very largely due to its inability to exploit its existing labour potential. Raising the growth potential of the whole country will crucially depend on the southern regions catching up.

The constraints imposed by the EMU macroeconomic policy framework highlights the need for a different macroeconomic *adjustment* paradigm, which depends crucially on the adjustment of intra-area real exchange rates and factor mobility. Some of the risks related to adjustment that were looming when the euro was created did not materialise, or at least they have not yet had the time to manifest themselves fully. Despite the persistent growth gap of the Italian economy with the rest of the euro area, cyclical developments in Italy followed those of the rest of the euro area quite closely. Indeed, during the past decade, Italy has been hit by relatively mild asymmetric shocks or, rather, the shocks went in opposite directions, thus largely offsetting each other and leaving Italy subject to the same common shocks that hit the whole of the euro area.

The sharp drop in risk premia triggered by participation in the euro area, from which Italy benefited to a larger extent than the euro-area average, acted as a positive temporary shock on the demand side. On the supply side, the deceleration in TFP was offset by high labour accumulation, leaving potential growth largely unchanged. Finally, Italy experienced a marked loss of export competitiveness, due to the abrupt deceleration in productivity and the steep increase in competition from low-wage exporters. Although the latter was in principle a common shock affecting the whole euro area, it had a largely asymmetric impact on the Italian economy, because of Italy's particular trade specialisation. The loss of external competitiveness translated into a negative contribution of net exports to growth, thereby widening the growth gap compared with the rest of the euro area.

Looking ahead, macroeconomic adjustment for the Italian economy is likely to be longer and more painful than for many other euro-area members. As the positive impact of falling real interest rates has vanished, the Italian economy is left to cope with the (persistent) negative shocks to which it has so far failed to adjust. In particular, slow TFP growth and market share erosion by low-wage competitors are steadily reducing Italian competitiveness (both within and outside the euro area), whereas efficient adjustment within the euro area would instead require an improvement in the country's competitiveness compared with its euro-area partners.

Regarding *public finances*, the story of Italy's first ten years in the euro area is mainly one of missed opportunities. In the run-up to euro adoption, it achieved impressive fiscal consolidation and important reforms with the objective of containing growth in pension-related liabilities to ensure sustainable public finances in the long term. But once the 'carrot' of euro-area participation had vanished, consolidation fatigue set in. Thus, the EMU dividend in terms of lower interest expenditure was not used to create and maintain a budgetary position conducive to sound public finances, nor was the high-growth period at the turn of the century used to carry out a counter-cyclical structural adjustment in the budget. Since potential growth did not pick up as the government had envisaged, the deficit grew again, and broke through the 3 per cent Treaty ceiling already in 2001. It was brought back within that limit only after a largely revenue-based adjustment implemented over 2006–7, under the 'stick' of the Excessive Debt Procedure.

Finally, concerning the pace of *structural reform*, the run-up to the euro was characterised by significant steps towards reforming the labour market, liberalising protected sectors, privatising state-owned companies and removing the excessive regulatory burden. In the labour market, the reform process started with the incomes' policy agreement of July 1993 that effectively contributed to wage moderation and the structural reduction of inflation in Italy. Further reforms have been undertaken since 1997 along the lines of targeting flexibility of work contracts for new entrants, thus significantly reducing hiring and firing costs at the margin. A rather impressive record was achieved in the reduction of the direct role of the State in the economy, and the reform of corporate governance regulations in 1998 added an important building block to the modernisation and liberalisation of the economic system. In the aftermath of the euro adoption, however, the drive for structural reforms decelerated, probably also because the 'monetary convergence bonus' of falling risk premia reduced the urgency of adjustment. Two major exceptions concerned the labour market, where the reform process was brought forward with the so-called Biagi law, and the financial sector, where the Bank of Italy has been promoting important regulatory reforms that are conducive to greater contestability in the system. In other areas, many reforms often remained at an early stage of implementation (like the reform of the public administration) or followed a piecemeal, rather than comprehensive approach (like the liberalisation process in services and products markets in 2006–7). On the long-term sustainability of public finances, the reform record has been mixed. For instance, there has been some backtracking in the pension-reform process.

Challenges ahead and open questions

Looking ahead, the Italian economy still faces daunting challenges. First, there is a need to increase Italy's growth potential in line with the performance of the rest of the euro area, which itself needs to be improved. Second, the conditions for competitiveness to act as an effective channel of adjustment should be strengthened. Third, public finances need to be put firmly on a sustainable footing by reaching and maintaining a sound budgetary position over the medium term and ensuring that the evolution of age-related expenditure is compatible with converging debt developments.

Achieving these goals is not just important for the Italian economy, but it is also in the interest of EMU as a whole. Italy, by virtue of its sheer size, accounts for a large share of the drop in the euro area's potential growth compared with that of the US observed from the early 1990s. The Italian government debt represents around 27 per cent of total euro-area gross debt of the government sector.

Since complementarities and synergies are likely to be strong in the policy approaches needed to tackle the above challenges, there are good arguments in favour of simultaneous actions. Re-launching TFP growth is a key precondition for the competitiveness channel to work effectively for intra-area adjustment. At the same time, moving production patterns towards high-value-added, technologically intensive sectors and market segments would shelter Italy from the pressures of competition from low-wage economies and help raise TFP growth. This requires a comprehensive policy approach, which focuses both on the supply of the production factors needed to move up the technological ladder, namely human capital, and the framework conditions for stimulating investment in new sectors and activities. While the manufacturing sector is already undergoing some degree of spontaneous restructuring in response to this challenge, by repositioning itself in the higher market segments, this process cannot be completed without also involving the non-tradable sectors of the economy. As for public finances, reaching a sound medium-term budgetary objective is key to keeping a fiscal stance compatible with the free operation of automatic stabilisers and catering for the age-related budgetary pressures. Moreover, by entailing a durable reduction in interest expenditure, it would also allow budgetary policy to make the necessary contribution to re-launching potential growth via appropriate revenue and expenditure policies.

A number of structural weaknesses in the Italian economy, many of which are deeply rooted in the lagging South, represent serious obstacles to achieving the above objectives. These are:

- Product and factor markets still present rigidities that are not consistent with a swift reallocation of resources towards high-growth sectors and activities. The non-tradable sector appears to be characterised by a relatively high degree of price stickiness, which hampers adjustment through the competitiveness channel in response to asymmetric shocks.
- While over the past decade much improvement has been recorded in the labour market, resulting in robust employment growth and a steep fall in the unemployment rate to below the EU average, employment and participation rates in Italy remain low by international standards, particularly for women, youth and older workers. At the same time, the Italian welfare system largely fails on both redistribution and efficiency. Its heavy bias towards pension spending and a patchy protection provided to the unemployed are not supportive

of an active permanence in the market of working-age individuals, particularly the older ones, nor of labour mobility.

- Italy's corporate governance and corporate culture contribute to maintaining highly fragmented industry structures with a prevalence of small-sized firms, which are not very conducive to investment in innovation and research. Financial markets, notably the segments that provide financial resources to risky innovative activities, are not as well developed as in countries scoring better in terms of TFP growth and innovative performance.
- The high public-debt ratio continues to exert a drag on long-term economic growth. In particular, the government sector seems to lack the degree of control over public expenditure in a medium-term perspective achieved by other EU countries which have managed to durably improve their public accounts.
- There is also a widespread perception that the quality of public finances is inadequate. The composition of public expenditure is biased towards a high cost of servicing the debt and pension spending. This takes its toll on more productive expenditure as well as on other social spending and is a major factor in the overall high rigidity of Italy's public spending. There is also evidence that the quality of services provided by the public sector needs to be improved. Notably, the supply of education, in terms of both quantity and quality, is lagging behind that of partner countries with a more satisfactory potential growth performance. Similarly, an inefficient judicial system certainly has a role to play in creating an unfavourable business environment.

While there is broad agreement on the need to overcome these structural weaknesses, there are some issues which raise some policy dilemmas or where the policy answers are not so obvious.

First, a prerequisite for Italy to regain competitiveness on international markets is that productivity growth outpaces wage developments. In principle, this could be achieved through wage restraint. However, as the prolonged stagnation of real wages in the private sector since the beginning of the 1990s has already affected households' disposable incomes, such a policy stance appears socially and politically unpalatable. The key policy challenge for Italy is therefore to attain a swift and durable recovery in productivity growth: ultimately, it is only by boosting productivity that higher wages can be combined with increased employment opportunities. Still, there remains scope for better balancing wage coordination at the national level with the need to make appropriate wage adjustment at firm and/or local levels, so as to allow a better alignment of wage and productivity developments. This move would help improve incentives in the labour market, loosen regional imbalances and sustain private investment already in the short term. In addition, the public sector has a model role to play: wage moderation and differentiation in the government sector would not only help contain public expenditure growth but it would also avoid encouraging unsustainable demonstration effects in the private sector.

Second, the rules-based framework of the Treaty and SGP is conducive to the objective of a sound and sustainable medium-term budgetary position for the Italian public finances. However, EU rules can be effective only if there is a conviction on the side of the political establishment and public opinion that they are necessary. In a country traditionally characterised by a fragmented political system, strengthening national budgetary rules and institutions is crucial to ensure fiscal discipline.

Finally, there is the overarching issue of how to overcome the resistance to structural reforms that may temporarily reduce rents accruing to protected positions but which are key to creating the conditions for recovering competitiveness. This is particularly true for strongly regulated product and services markets. Although there is no easy way to counter vested interests, national governments and European institutions should make it a priority to raise public awareness of the stakes involved in reforms and the costs of maintaining the status quo. In this respect, the Lisbon strategy, which seeks to accelerate structural reform through greater policy coordination, open advocacy of benefit reforms and peer pressure, should be used to maximum effect by Italian policy-makers as a vehicle to carry the reform process forward.

The book

This book features a comprehensive analysis of situation, challenges and prospects facing the Italian economy after a decade in the euro area, with a view to allowing a better understanding of the factors underlying Italy's growth performance *vis-à-vis* the other euro-area countries and identifying policy priority areas.

Chapter 1 by Riccardo Faini, to whose memory this book is dedicated, and André Sapir (Université Libre de Bruxelles) sets the scene for a better understanding of the growth malaise of the Italian economy, its determinants and the priorities for action. After providing a broad picture of economic developments over the decade 1995–2005, the article considers possible reasons for the steady loss of competitiveness experienced by the Italian economy, concentrating on its specialisation model. A comparative analysis highlights the fact that, unlike other industrialised countries, Italian exports are heavily based on traditional low-skill products, which are more and more exposed to competition from emerging markets. This is reflected in a human capital gap *vis-à-vis* the other industrialised countries that is persistently high or even, in some cases, opening up. The authors argue that overcoming the obsolete model of Italy's industrial specialisation requires first and foremost an upgrading of human capital with a view to creating the appropriate conditions to make the specialisation pattern conducive to higher productivity and growth. This implies improving formal education, from compulsory to the tertiary level, but also promoting investment in research and development and strengthening lifelong-learning education. It is also necessary to enhance mobility of resources from the declining sectors to the expanding ones, and to put in place a modern system of unemployment benefits that can reduce resistance to change.

Chapter 2 by Laura Bardone and Vito Ernesto Reitano (European Commission) traces a retrospective analysis of Italy's economic performance since it entered the euro area and investigates how macroeconomic adjustment has been proceeding under the new policy environment created by the euro. The two main channels of market-based adjustment are considered, i.e. the real interest channel and the competitiveness channel. The analysis also attempts to understand how market-based adjustment in Italy was influenced by the interaction of policy initiatives affecting, in particular, wages and prices. It is argued that the major problem that afflicted the Italian economy in the past decade was the pronounced and protracted slowdown in productivity, widespread to most sectors of the economy. Primarily due to this, the Italian economy has so far failed to adjust smoothly and efficiently through the adjustment channels that are available in the context of a monetary union. The productivity slowdown has deep-seated structural roots, which with the loss of monetary independence came forcibly to light through their impact on both domestic demand and external competitiveness. In order to ensure that the market channels of adjustment unfold in a smoother and timelier manner, Italy has no choice other than to use structural reforms to improve the functioning of labour, product and services markets so as to boost competition and the capacity of firms to innovate. More rapid changes in price and wage competitiveness would also be desirable, especially where the wage response to firm- or sector-specific shocks is concerned.

Vittorio Grilli (Italian Ministry of Economy and Finance) largely confirms the findings in Chapter 2. While acknowledging the ongoing restructuring process in the tradable sector in response to globalisation, he argues that more time and evidence are needed to reach more solid conclusions on the extent of this process and warns that competition from emerging markets could also 'upgrade' very soon.

In his comment to Chapter 2, Daniel Gros (Centre for European Policy Studies, Brussels) observes that the loss of competitiveness experienced by Italy, as serious as it is, does not feature prominently in the public debate. This is in sharp contrast with the situation in Germany, where competitiveness has dominated policy-making. One reason might be that the Italian economy is much less open than that of Germany, so that it is more difficult to find a constituency that supports the necessary adjustment. In the absence of any pressure for reforms coming from international trade, there is a risk that the gap between Italy and its major trading partners will continue widening.

Chapter 3 by Lorenzo Codogno (Italian Ministry of Economy and Finance) focuses on two apparent puzzles displayed by the Italian economy since the euro adoption: i) how can an extremely poor performance in productivity growth be combined with strong employment growth?; and ii) how can a sharp decline in competitiveness come along with higher export prices and a general situation for exporters that looks far from desperate? The author provides some possible explanations for these puzzles. Special factors such as the regularisation of the immigrant workforce and the entry of low-skilled workers into the labour market may have contributed to depressing measured productivity and overestimate the loss in competitiveness. Against the backdrop of Italy's structural problems, the chapter addresses the question of whether the Italian economy can adjust and grow. The answer in the chapter is that, notwithstanding the fact that medium-term prospects for the Italian economy remain challenging, as export market shares are still being lost and TFP growth is still disappointing, there are some encouraging signs of improvement. Notably, the labour market has performed strongly and some adjustment appears to have taken place in the exposed sectors in response to pressure from intense competition.

Commenting on Chapter 3, Tito Boeri (Università Bocconi, Milan) argues that the move from a model of 'jobless growth' in the early 1990s to one of 'growthless job creation' in the past decade is common to many euro-area countries rather than being specific to Italy. In his view, the apparent trade-off between employment and productivity growth is ultimately due to the fact that we are still in the middle of the river in reforming labour markets and largely unprepared to manage migration. The author also warns against the increasing divide that characterises the Italian labour market. This divide keeps many workers segregated from mainstream employment in marginal jobs offering little incentive for human capital investment and highly exposed to labour market risk.

Sergio de Nardis (Istituto di Studi e Analisi Economica (ISAE), Rome) provides further insights into some of the aspects discussed in Chapter 3. Regarding the labour market, he argues that labour market reforms produced modifications in agents' behaviour both on the demand and the supply side of the labour market. Overall, these policy changes delivered a better functioning of the labour market. In particular, wage responsiveness to labour market imbalances increased since the mid-nineties. As for the behaviour of firms in response to the globalisation challenge, the author brings evidence that a spontaneous reallocation process in the tradable sector, within sectors rather than across sectors, has taken place. Policy-makers are now confronted with the difficult task of promoting the needed structural reforms to improve the rest of the economy, that is, the non-tradable sectors.

Chapter 4 by Daniele Franco and Pietro Rizza (Bank of Italy) reviews the tormented history of the Italian public finances. Their chapter examines the factors underlying the recurrent fiscal imbalances as well as the medium- and long-term prospects of the Italian public finances, which have to cope with an economic environment characterised by persistently low growth. It is argued that Italy's fiscal consolidation effort has been largely successful but it is not yet complete. The worsening of the fiscal situation in the first years of the new century shows that there is no room for complacency and illustrates the difficulty of containing expenditure growth. The length of the consolidation process reflects the size of the imbalances, unsatisfactory macroeconomic developments, as well as inadequate fiscal institutions. According to the authors, the challenges facing fiscal policy in the coming years, notably the need to cope with the ageing population, are largely shared by most other developed countries. But there are also country-specific challenges stemming from the high debt ratio, the size of the irregular economy, the unbalanced structure of social protection and the sizeable income differences between regions. The authors also consider some problematic aspects of fiscal policy governance.

This latter aspect is taken up by Martin Larch and Lucia Piana (European Commission) in their comment to Chapter 4. They take a closer look at how Italy compares with the rest of the euro area along four different dimensions of fiscal governance: fiscal rules in general, expenditure rules, budgetary procedures and the quality of medium-term budgetary frameworks. Italy fares below the euro-area average in these respects, but the fiscal consolidation efforts undertaken in the context of the EDP procedure have started to address these shortcomings. However, past experience shows that once the external pressure is no longer there, risks are high that Italy's fiscal policy returns to a short-term focus. According to the authors, taking additional initiatives to improve Italian fiscal governance is crucial to avoid the risk of a painful, but cathartic, crisis.

Vito Tanzi retraces the events described in Chapter 4 against the background of his experience at the International Monetary Fund and as policy-maker in Italy for some years. He also discusses reforms that are in his view needed to improve fiscal policy governance. He highlights how the unrelenting growth in public spending that characterised the Italian public finances over most of the past decade dates from the 1970s and 1980s, when successive governments attempted to expand the role of the public sector without providing for adequate financing. This created legal and political 'entitlements' that made it extremely difficult for later governments to curb primary spending growth, especially as those governments themselves were aggregations of many groups, each reflecting particular constituencies and vested interests. He then identifies the public sector, largely oversized and lacking the necessary culture of austerity, as an area in need of reform.

The final section of the book is devoted to how Italy is viewed by external observers such as the International Monetary Fund (IMF), the Organisation for Economic Cooperation and Development (OECD) and the market. Both the IMF and the OECD carry out regular country-specific analysis of economic developments and issue policy recommendations. In doing so, they influence the policy debate at national level. The 'market', here represented by the investment bank Morgan Stanley, follows economic and policy developments at country-specific level with a view to informing clients about investment opportunities.

In her contribution, Alexandra Bibbee (OECD) concentrates on key supply-side issues in Italy. She argues that boosting productivity growth and increasing participation in the labour market are the core challenges for Italy. While acknowledging the signs of adjustment in the tradable sector, she propounds more thoroughgoing structural reforms – which will need vigorous public advocacy to be accepted. Her contribution also discusses the large underground economy and the persistent North-South gap that still characterises the Italian economy. Effectively tackling these two issues would unleash great potential for the whole economy, by improving on the use of the existing labour resources.

Alessandro Leipold (IMF) briefly discusses Italy's growth challenge, in particular advocating broad-based liberalisation as key to address it. Promoting economic pedagogy (i.e., educating society about a country's economic challenges and solutions) and improving implementation capacity are highlighted as two important aspects to advancing the reform agenda. The author recalls that in both aspects, Riccardo Faini played a vital role. He then concentrates the rest of his contribution on public finances. Reforming budgetary procedures and addressing the rigidities and misplaced incentives in public employment would in his view allow taming public spending with the aim of achieving a durable fiscal consolidation, alleviating a stifling tax burden and redirecting resources to more productive uses. Public administration reform is also seen as sorely needed to deliver more efficient public services and to attract and retain the talent required for carrying reforms forward.

Finally, Eric Chaney (Morgan Stanley) challenges the view of those who believe that Italy could be the first casualty of an ill-concieved monetary union. While acknowledging many of the structural problems that still seriously hamper Italy's growth, he sees Italy as being on the mend and likely to attract more foreign capital than it has done in the past. He points out that the performance of the Italian financial markets has been rather positive *vis-à-vis* other euro-area countries, especially in risk-adjusted terms.

Notes

1. European Commission (2008)
2. European Commission (1999)
3. See footnote 1 and Barrell *et al.* (2008)

1

An Obsolete Model? Growth and Specialisation in the Italian Economy*

*Riccardo Faini***
and
André Sapir
Université Libre de Bruxelles

1.1 Introduction

In only 30 years, from 1950 to 1980, the gap in income separating Italy from the rest of Europe was completely eliminated. The ratio of per capita income in Italy to that in Europe grew almost without interruption from 75 per cent in 1950 to 99.6 per cent in 1980. During that period, even the extent to which development lagged behind the United States was cut, from 35 per cent to 70 per cent.[1] Of course, during those years of rapid growth, there were times when the Italian economy suffered slowdowns, in some cases protracted. All of these could basically be put down to supply-side shocks, deriving from sharp increases in salaries or increased prices for imported raw materials. The first significant halt in the process of growth, in 1964, and the next one, in 1969, coincided

* The present chapter is an English translation of 'Un Modello Obsoleto? Crescita e Specializzazione dell'Economia Italiana', in Boeri *et al.* (2005), pp. 19–77. Thanks to publishers Il Mulino of Bologna for permission to reprint this article.

** Riccardo Faini died on 20 January 2007. He was Professor of Economics at the University of Rome 'Tor Vergata', Chief Economic Adviser to the Minister of Economy and Finance of Italy, Tommaso Padoa-Schioppa, Co-Director of the CEPR programme on International Trade and Member of the Presidential Council of the *Società Italiana degli Economisti*. He was Director General for Economic Analysis at the Italian Treasury between 2001 and 2003, Executive Director at the International Monetary Fund between 1998 and 2001 and he worked in the Trade Policy Division at the World Bank 1985–8. He had a PhD in Economics from the Massachusetts Institute of Technology and a degree in Economics from Universitá Bocconi, Milan. He published extensively in the areas of development, migration, international trade and investment decisions of firms.

with a deterioration in labour relations and substantial salary increases. In both cases, to the impact on supply of increased labour costs must be added that demand imposed by a restrictive economic policy which sought to moderate inflationary pressures and limit the deterioration in the balance of payments. In 1974 first of all and later in 1979 the oil shocks had a negative effect on incomes.

Over the next 25 years the economic landscape of Italy changed fundamentally. After disappearing for a while, the gap with Europe remained stable before widening again in the early 1990s. Likewise the process of convergence with the United States stopped and then went into reverse. Finally, over the four years from 2001 the economy stagnated.[2] By contrast with the pattern in the past, the abrupt halt in the Italian economy has not coincided with a period of heavy wage increases or significant supply-side shocks. Quite the contrary: the last decade has seen very pronounced moderation in wage increases. The increase in oil prices is too recent to have affected the growth process in this part of the century, nor does it appear, at least at the moment, that it will significantly affect future developments. Nor can the unsatisfactory trend of incomes in Italy be put down to the general trend of the world economy. Over the three years up to 2005 average growth in the international economy has been higher than in the period from the early 1990s onwards.

The basic question we are asking in this chapter is whether the slowdown in the Italian economy in recent years reflects cyclical factors, in which case it will be short-lived, or structural problems, the size and impact of which have worsened recently.

In the first section we review Italy's economic performance indicators. The latest data on income, duly corrected for differences in purchasing power, and the penetration of Italian goods on world markets, highlight a significant deterioration in its economic position. Data on salaries and distribution of wealth confirm that these trends have not resulted in an increase in the purchasing power of salaries – quite the contrary. To underline the basically structural nature of the problems of the Italian economy it is enough to look at the figures on productivity trends which, after falling for several decades, are now in negative territory and well below those of the other industrialised countries.

In the next part we consider possible reasons for the Italian economy's loss of competitiveness, something frequently blamed on membership of the European Monetary Union, which prevents a devaluation of the exchange rate to boost the economy. If this were the case, Italy's economic difficulties, particularly the most recent ones, should coincide with a period of increases in the real exchange rate, leading to loss of competitiveness on international and domestic markets. But a medium-term analysis of the trend of the real exchange rate does not reveal a movement of this kind. The revaluation from 1995 was merely a partial correction of an overshoot, the excessive devaluation from 1992 to 1995. From 1998 to the present the real exchange rate has stood at levels lower than those prevailing over the medium term, but has also fluctuated less. Greater exchange-rate stability should have favoured economic growth. Nor can the euro be blamed for the structural fall in the productivity rate. Joining the euro does not therefore provide an adequate explanation for the difficulties which the Italian economy is experiencing.

We then go on to look at the role of more structural factors, concentrating in particular on the specialisation model of the Italian economy at international level. A comparative analysis demonstrates how the sectoral structure of Italy's exports has remained basically unchanged, particularly as compared with that of the other industrialised countries. This means that Italian exports are even more skewed than in the past towards traditional sectors, which are increasingly exposed to competition from developing countries. In the post-war period, Italy enjoyed a relatively advantageous position: the liberalisation of international trade had been limited almost entirely to the industrialised countries, at the expense of the developing countries. This meant that the Italian economy could maintain and even increase its comparative advantage over the other industrialised countries in the traditional sectors with low human capital intensity. This strength was, however, gradually eroded by the growing integration of the developing countries into the world economy and, above all, by the Italian economy's inability to adapt the structure of its own comparative advantages to the new situation. An analysis of the human capital endowment demonstrates that the gap separating Italy from the other industrialised countries in this respect not only did not diminish but sometimes widened. In such circumstances, the call to promote the growth of new sectors, particularly high-technology sectors making relatively more intensive use of human capital, appears quite futile unless it is accompanied by a determined effort to improve the education system at all levels.

In the final part, we examine the strategies used to stimulate the Italian economy. A number of authors (Allegra *et al.*, 2004; Grillo, 2004; Nardozzi, 2004) have drawn attention to the lack of competition from which the Italian economy suffers. Others have demonstrated the rigidities of the labour market or the lack of material and non-material infrastructures. Still others have pointed to the inadequate size structure of Italian firms. There can be no doubt that all these factors have hampered the growth of the economy. It nevertheless remains true that overcoming an obsolete specialisation model which is increasingly exposed to competition from emerging countries makes improving the human capital endowment, and so altering the structure of Italian comparative advantage, a matter of urgency. There is little point in setting ambitious R&D objectives if the country is still poor in those productive factors, principally a skilled labour force, which promote growth in the high-technology sectors with high intensity of human capital, that have benefited most from the growth in world trade.

Italy is a country which has so far invested comparatively little in its most valuable resource, its human capital. It is vital to reverse this trend and a first step would be to direct more resources towards the education system, in particular the universities. But this is not enough. These resources must be used judiciously, contrary to what has happened too often in the past; in particular Italy must create the conditions in which the expanded supply of skilled labour finds an appropriate counterpart in demand from the productive system. Hence demand requires a two-track approach, with horizontal policies to support innovation, training, and the internationalisation of small and medium-sized firms alongside measures on the supply of human capital through increased investment in education, particularly higher education. This is the only way of breaking the vicious circle of a lack of skilled labour perpetuating an obsolete specialisation model which in turn discourages demand for human resources.

Finally, it is essential to encourage the mobility of resources from sectors in decline to those which are expanding. As noted above, Italy is a country which has been unsuccessful in changing its specialisation model and adapting it to changed world economic conditions. That change requires more efficient capital markets, able to allocate savings to growth sectors, and a modern system of social shock absorbers, able to reduce resistance to change without introducing excessive distortions. Trade protectionism, by contrast, particularly when used against emerging countries, is not even an adequate short-term response in that it discourages the movement of resources to new sectors and devotes further resources to traditional sectors.

1.2 The data on decline: income, productivity and market shares

Decline is a relative concept. It can be measured using a variety of indicators, with reference to past trends or those in other countries. Below we shall look at movements in three performance indicators commonly used in the literature: per capita income, productivity and export market share.

1.2.1 Income trends

In the view of Ciocca (2003), for a country such as Italy, which suffers from deep structural imbalances and is always at risk of sliding into an economic recession, the comparison has to be with its own past. The data in this case are unequivocal: in per capita terms, the rate of growth of the Italian economy fell steadily from over 5 per cent in the 1960s to under 1.5 per cent in the last decade. But these figures are difficult to interpret, firstly because the most recent growth in the Italian economy, even if unsatisfactory in many ways, does not differ significantly from long-term historic trends, and still more so because it is not possible to ignore the fact that the vast majority of the industrialised countries saw a slackening in growth. Growth performance should therefore be measured with reference to other countries sufficiently similar to Italy as regards the initial and structural conditions. Accordingly, data which are comparable at international level will need to be used. In what follows, we shall refer to the data from the Conference Board and Groningen Growth and Development Centre (the Conference Board and GGDC) on trends in per capita income at purchasing power parities, using uniform methods of calculation and statistical conventions for the various countries. Three corrections – for population, purchasing power and uniformity of definitions – are all necessary. In studying growth in incomes, in fact, it is essential to start by taking account of the various demographic dynamics which, as argued elsewhere (Faini, 2004), have had a fairly pronounced impact on income growth in Europe, and particularly in Italy, compared with the United States. In comparing income levels, it is essential then to consider either differences in purchasing power resulting from varying price levels (even if expressed in a common currency) between countries or differences in the conventions and procedures for calculating income between the various countries.

The Conference Board and GGDC data (Figure 1.1) show that the process of convergence between Italy and the European Union went sharply into reverse from the second half of the 1990s. In only nine years, from 1995 to 2004, Italy's per capita income fell from 102.7 per cent of the European average to 97.4 per cent, i.e. by five percentage points. An analysis based on Eurostat data (Faini and Gagliarducci, 2005)[3] reaches similar conclusions. While data corrected for purchasing power parity should certainly be considered with some caution, avoiding the derivation of long-term trends from more recent information, it nevertheless remains the case that the widening of the divergence from the European average is too marked and above all too rapid to be ascribed simply to statistical problems. Figure 1.1 also shows the movement of the gap

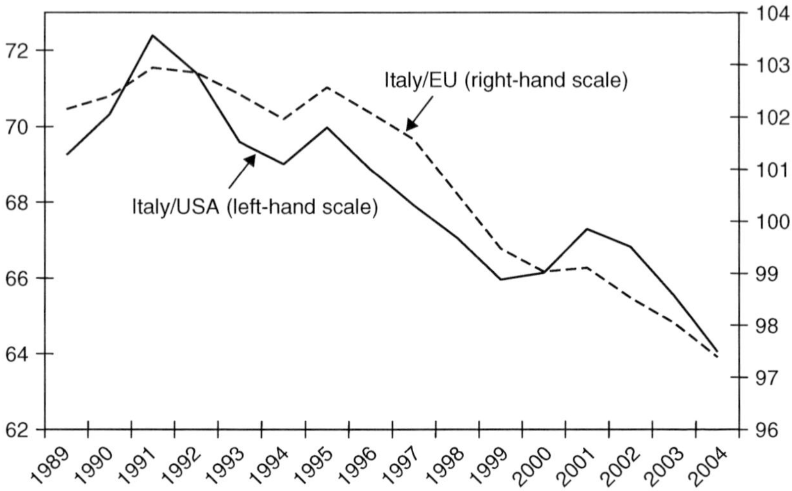

Figure 1.1 From convergence to divergence? Ratio of per capita incomes in purchasing power parities
Source: Conference Board and Groningen Growth and Development Centre.

vis-à-vis the United States. There are no significant differences compared with similar data for Europe, which demonstrates that over the 1990s the difference in income between Europe and the United States remained basically unchanged. The more rapid growth of the American economy is in fact almost entirely due to stronger demographic trends. In per capita terms, the income gap between Europe and the United States remained fundamentally constant.[4] It is no accident that the extent to which Italy fell behind the United States did not differ substantially from how it fell behind Europe (Figure 1.1).

1.2.2 Productivity and salaries

During the post-war period, the trend of wage rates played a decisive role in how the economic cycle developed and had a strong impact on the course of employment, incomes and inflation. The data for the last decade, however, no longer reveal a positive relationship between wage moderation and economic growth. Relatively restrained wage rises have undoubtedly promoted better performance in employment terms, but have been accompanied by a phase of stagnation in growth in national income. Between 1998 and 2002 the reduction in the rate of growth in

Table 1.1 Trend of real remunerations (annual growth rates)

	Contractual salaries	Actual salaries
1997–8	1.3	1.2
1999	0.1	−0.3
2000	0.6	−0.6
2001	−0.4	0.2
2002	−0.4	−0.2
2003	−0.5	−0.6

Source: ISTAT. The data on contractual and actual salaries (taken from the OROS data bank) have been deflated by the NIC index of consumer prices.

the economy was accompanied by a noticeable reduction in the trend of wage settlements.

The ISTAT survey on salaries (distributed from 1997) and data on contractual remuneration demonstrate stagnation in real wages. Table 1.1 compares the trend in annual changes in the ISTAT indicators for inflation and gross salaries per full-time equivalent of employed. The data show that between 1997 and 1999 salaries, whether contractual or actual, registered a modest but real increase in purchasing power. From 1999 onwards, this trend reversed and nominal salaries grew more slowly than consumer prices. From 1999 to 2003, the total loss of purchasing power of actual remunerations was 1.5 per cent measured on the NIC (general consumer price) index.

But what are the reasons behind this essentially downward trend? Sapir *et al.* (2004) highlight that, in the past, high salaries and high productivity in Europe were largely the reflection of the fact that less skilled and less productive workers remained marginal to and often excluded from the labour market, thus raising, but only artificially, the average level of remuneration and productivity. This may mean that the fall in real salaries recorded in recent years is no more than a reflection of the increased opportunities for access to the labour market of a less skilled or, if better educated, younger and so less expert and less productive, labour force. The data of the Banca d'Italia biennial survey of family budgets appears, however, to contradict this argument. While it is true that from 1995 onwards starting salaries fell by about 2 per cent on average, it is nevertheless the case that, over the same period, the remuneration profiles of those taking up subsequent jobs also fell in a very similar way, although over a rather different time span (Faini and Gagliarducci, 2005). It does not therefore appear that this argument can provide any more than a marginal explanation of wage trends in Italy. This is reinforced by the fact that Italy's employment performance is not particularly brilliant when compared with the rest of Europe. According to the OECD, the rate of employment for young people in the 15–24 age band fell by one point, from 27.8 per cent to 26.8 per cent between 2000 and 2003. By contrast, over that period it grew in EU–15 from 40.8 per cent to 42.6 per cent.

It should however be emphasised that, even if a growth in employment slanted towards less productive workers was the main reason for the slowdown in wage rates, we should also note an automatic speeding up of the rate of increase of incomes, driven by constantly rising rates of employment and activity. However, this is not the case, as we have seen. Income growth, whether compared with the past or with the other industrialised countries, actually fell. Not only did the renewed surge in employment growth not translate into a surge in incomes; it coincided with a slowdown in economic growth, which demonstrates that factors other than the make-up of employment growth are needed to explain the falling behind of the Italian economy.

The striking fact is that the difficulties of the Italian economy are structural in origin. Figure 1.2 shows that the average productivity of the Italian labour force (measured as GDP per hours worked) fell drastically from the 1960s until recent years. Eliminating possible cyclical fluctuations (by means of the Hodrick-Prescott filter), the graph shows a gradual reduction in productivity growth which, in data not filtered for cyclical effects, actually becomes negative in 2002 and 2003. A comparison with

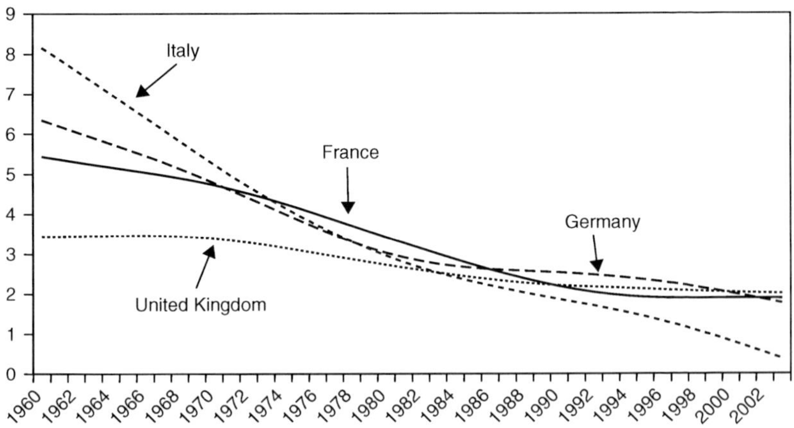

Figure 1.2 Productivity trend (growth rate, Hodrick-Preston filter)
Source: GGDC. The vertical axis shows percentage changes in the rate of growth of productivity.

other European countries shows that the fall in productivity is rather sharper in the case of Italy and, particularly, that in recent years productivity growth in Italy has remained at levels significantly below those of its European partners.

We can now understand better why the Italian economy has fallen behind. The slowdown, indeed the halt, in productivity growth goes a very long way to explaining wage stagnation. In a situation where labour productivity has difficulty in growing, real salaries cannot grow unless the economic system is to lose all competitiveness. In turn, the feeble growth of labour productivity is attributed to the collapse in total factor productivity rather than to a reduction in capital intensity (Brandolini and Cipollone, 2003). In the 1990s, investment and the stock of capital grew quite rapidly, even compared with the other industrialised countries, driven by a tax system which was fairly favourable to the accumulation of capital (Faini, 2004). If this trend were to continue over the medium term, it would call into question the possibility of sustained growth in either salaries or incomes as a whole.

1.2.3 The trend in market share of Italian exports

The collapse of productivity is inevitably reflected in the competitiveness of Italy's exports on world markets, where their share fell from 4.7 per cent in 1996 to 4 per cent in 2001. Elsewhere, one of the authors (Faini, 2004) has shown how the declining position of Italian exports over that period can be entirely attributed to cyclical factors (the real revaluation of the lira in response to the overshooting of the exchange rate in the previous three years) and above all to market effects (the strength of the dollar and the increase in oil prices which swelled the value of world trade outside Europe). In the same period, it was no accident that Germany and France likewise noted a strong fall in their positions on international markets, from 9.7 per cent to 9.2 per cent and from 5.7 per cent to 5.3 per cent respectively. It nevertheless remains the case that when, in subsequent years, the impact of both factors was no longer felt – the lira ceased to appreciate in real terms in 1998 and, more importantly, the dollar fell against European currencies from 2001 – Italy's share continued to fall (finally reaching 3.8 per cent in 2004), while France and, still more so, Germany saw their exports recover their share of world markets. In particular, Germany's share of world exports was estimated to have gone back up to 10 per cent in 2004 (Figure 1.3). To sum up, therefore, the loss of position of Italy's exports cannot be attributed solely to market factors – if it were so, Italy's share would have recovered – it was due mainly to structural problems.

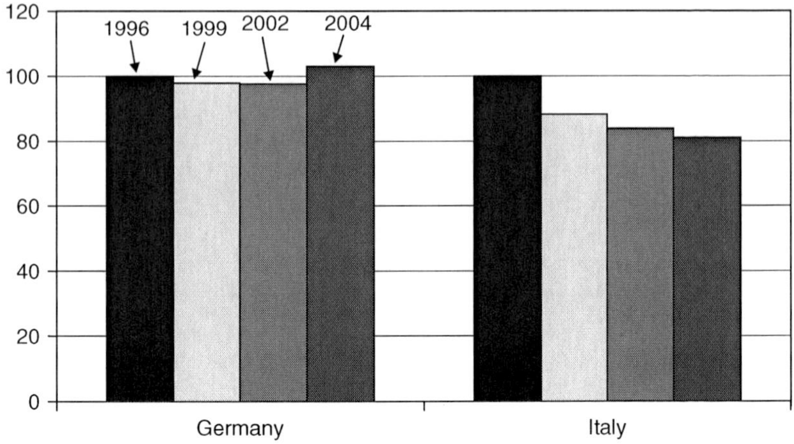

Figure 1.3 Market share of world exports (1996 = 100)
Source: Prepared from GGDC data.

1.3 But is it the fault of the euro?

The fact that the trend of productivity began to fall off in the 1970s demonstrates that the problems of the Italian economy are not recent in origin. This phenomenon cannot be explained away by an alleged downturn in the world economy (which is not supported by the data), nor movements in raw materials prices (which rose too recently to have influenced the trend of incomes in Italy over the last decade), nor still less the direction of economic policies (real interest rates are at historic lows and European fiscal policy has been expansionary in recent years). Above all, the structural difficulties of the Italian economy cannot be laid at the door of membership of the European Monetary Union and adoption of the single currency, the euro. This is confirmed by the fact noted above that other countries which adopted the European currency did not suffer a similar downturn in productivity growth.

It would, however, be possible to argue that the fixing in 1999 of rigid parities between the lira and the other European currencies deprived the Italian economy of a safety valve which in the past had allowed it to overcome – even if only temporarily – its own structural weaknesses. Since the collapse of the Bretton Woods system of fixed exchange rates in 1974, and the arrival of an era of floating exchange rates, Italy had regularly devalued its exchange rate to offset the competitive disadvantages of its economy. Entry into the euro eliminated that possibility and,

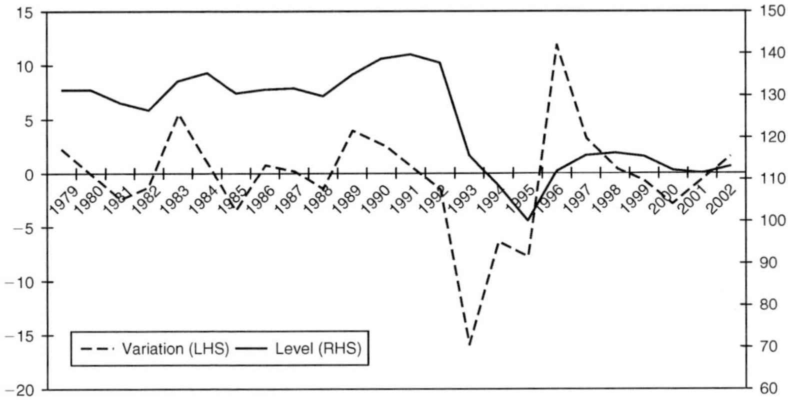

Figure 1.4 The real exchange rate: level and fluctuations
Source: International Monetary Fund.

as Grillo (2004) notes, 1995, the year in which Italian exports began to lose ground on world markets, was also the year which saw the last devaluation of the lira.

The link between short-term growth and exchange-rate changes can be seen on several occasions in the recent economic history of Italy. The rise in the nominal exchange rate[5] between 1988 and 1991 coincided with a fairly pronounced fall in growth. The spurt in the Italian economy in 1994 was helped by the sharp devaluation of the nominal exchange rate which began at the end of 1992 and continued until 1995. Even subsequently, the profile of growth appears to correlate closely with changes in the exchange rate.

The stimulus given to the economy by devaluing the nominal exchange rate is, however, almost always short-lived. In particular, the nominal exchange rate is not a valid indicator of the degree of competitiveness of a country's economy. Devaluations of the nominal exchange rate may, as regularly happened in Italy, reflect a positive gap in inflation which makes a country's exports less competitive. If we correct changes in the nominal exchange rate by changes in relative prices (or average unit labour costs) we obtain a measure of the real exchange rate (Figure 1.4). This series reveals two elements. First of all, from 1993 the real exchange rate was at a historically very low level. The revaluation between 1995 and 1997 did no more than correct the excessive devaluation which occurred in 1995. It should also be noted that from 1998 to 2000 the real exchange rate continued to fall, reflecting the strength of the dollar during that period. The structural difficulties of the Italian economy cannot, therefore, be ascribed to the rigidity of the nominal exchange rate after adoption of the euro or to a supposed revaluation of the real exchange rate for which the data provide no evidence. The second point of interest is the diminishing volatility of the real exchange rate following entry into the European Monetary Union. From 1998 to 2002 the (uncorrected) volatility of the real exchange rate fell markedly (Figure 1.4). If we then calculate the volatility of the real exchange corrected for variations in the terms of trade, the result is the same.[6] Lower volatility in the real exchange rate, and hence in the competitiveness of production, should boost international trade (Rose, 2000; Micco *et al.*, 2003) while also encouraging investment by risk-averse firms or, more generally, those concerned that the preselected level of productivity capacity is out of line because of unexpected variations in the real exchange rate.

To sum up, adoption of the euro did not coincide with an erosion in competitiveness of the economy and of Italian exports. From 1993 the real exchange rate was in fact at a historically very low level and fell further after 1998. Joining the European Monetary Union resulted principally in a sharp reduction in the volatility of the real exchange rate and hence in greater stability in the competitiveness of the Italian economy. In turn, greater stability in Italy's competitive situation should encourage business investment. The euro may be blamed for many things (certainly too many), but definitely not for having undermined the competitiveness of the economy.

1.4 Italy's specialisation model

Italy's comparative advantage lies predominantly in traditional sectors, with a low intensity of skilled labour, as has been noted repeatedly by studies of the country's specialisation model (Bugamelli, 2001; Chiarlone and Helg, 2002). As Bugamelli (2001) points out, Italy demonstrates a high degree of polarisation, with a strong comparative advantage in certain sectors and a similarly marked comparative disadvantage in others. Finally, there is no proof that Italy's specialisation model aligned itself more closely with that of the rest of Europe between 1987 and 1997.

In the past, a specialisation model skewed towards sectors with a high intensity of relatively unskilled labour did not handicap Italy. In the post-war period, in fact, Italy enjoyed a very advantageous position in so far as the process of liberalising international trade concerned the industrialised countries virtually exclusively (Subramanian and Wei, 2003) and

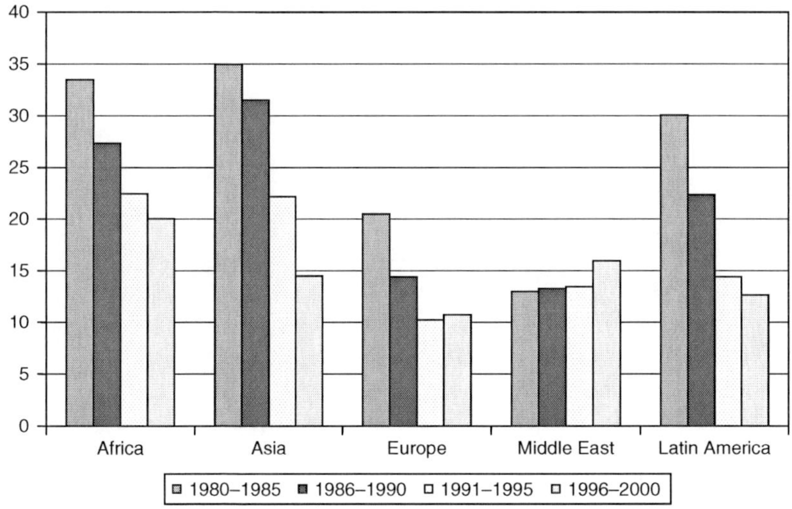

Figure 1.5 Average duties on imports
Source: Ng (2004).

left out (partly at their own choice) the developing countries. Hence, the economy was able to retain its comparative advantage *vis-à-vis* other industrialised countries in traditional non-labour-intensive sectors. This advantage was, however, gradually eroded by the increasing integration of the developing countries into the world economy resulting both from the gradual (but fairly slow) removal of trade barriers against those countries by the industrialised nations and from the process of trade liberalisation implemented often unilaterally by the emerging countries. Figure 1.5 shows how tariff barriers have gradually been reduced over the last 30 years in all parts of the third world, with the sole and partial exception of the Middle East. This has meant that the developing countries, particularly those in Asia, have accounted for an increasing share of world exports (Figure 1.6).

We shall look below at the structure of Italy's comparative advantage over the period from 1970 to 2002,[7] which makes it possible to include even long-term trends and exclude cyclical events. As an indicator of comparative advantage, we shall use the Balassa index (*B*), defined as the ratio between Italy's share of world exports in a given sector and Italy's share of total world exports. A figure greater than 100 shows that Italy has a comparative advantage in that sector. The Balassa index is made homogenous, by eliminating the country's exports from the world

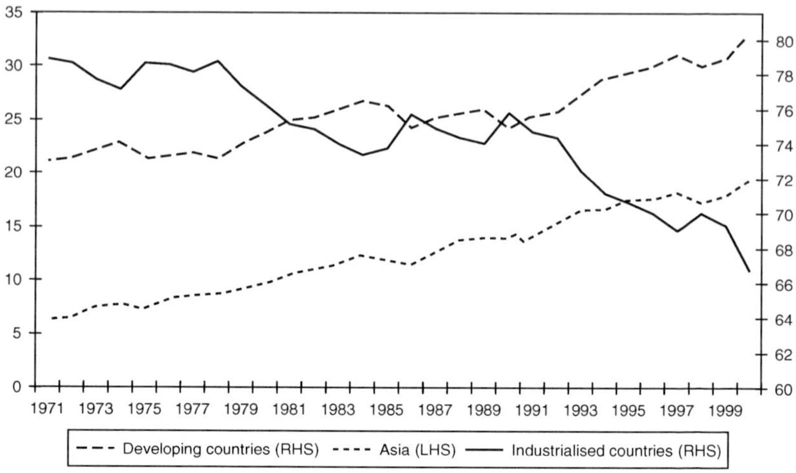

Figure 1.6 Share of world non-oil exports
Source: World Trade Organisation.

aggregate, and symmetrical, by considering a simple transformation with $B^* = (B - 1)/(B + 1)$ so that B^* varies from +100 to −100.[8]

Table 1.A3 (see Appendix, p. 33), gives the values of the Balassa index for Italy from 1970 to 2002, essentially confirming the result that the sectors where Italy's comparative advantage is greatest are the traditional ones (leather goods, textiles, footwear, clothing and furniture) and engineering. For the more advanced sectors (office equipment, equipment for telecommunications and the electronic processing of information, and precision instruments) the Balassa index is negative, often markedly so, which again demonstrates the country's lack of comparative advantage in goods of this type.

Of particular interest is the change over time in the structure of comparative advantage. There are two main points. Firstly, Italy's comparative advantage has increased in traditional sectors (Figure 1.7), such as textiles, non-metallic mineral products, furniture and clothing, all increasingly exposed to competition from the emerging countries. Secondly, many sectors have moved from a situation of virtual balance or even a comparative advantage in 1970 to one of pronounced despecialisation which has grown steadily over time. This is true of motor vehicles, but also of office and electrical equipment (Figure 1.8). Taken together, these trends show that Italy's position has deteriorated sharply even in a sector of great importance for its economy, engineering.

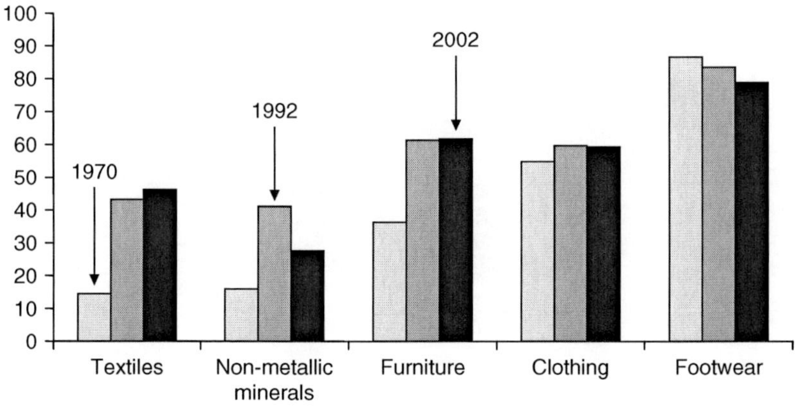

Figure 1.7 Trend of Italy's comparative advantage in traditional sectors (Balassa index)

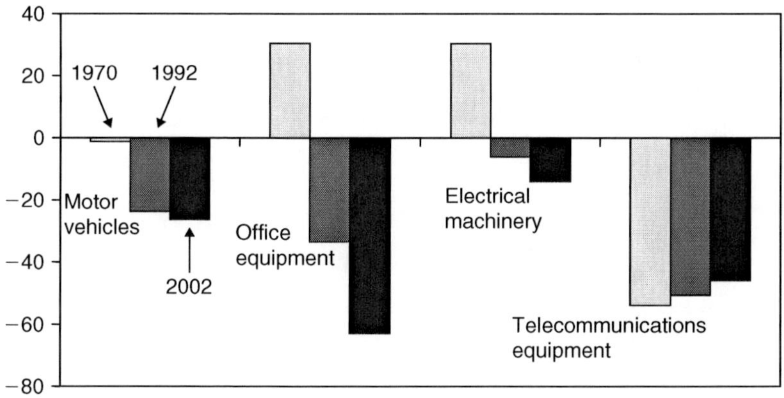

Figure 1.8 Italy's comparative advantage in advanced sectors (Balassa index)

Another striking fact is the stability of Italy's specialisation model. There are few sectors where the sign of the indicator of comparative advantage has changed over the last 40 years. Nor is there the slightest suggestion of any convergence between Italy's specialisation model and those of other countries. Faini and Gagliarducci (2005) have calculated a dissimilarity index designed to measure the difference in the structure of Italy's comparative advantages compared with the average of a highly representative sample of industrialised countries (which, besides Italy,

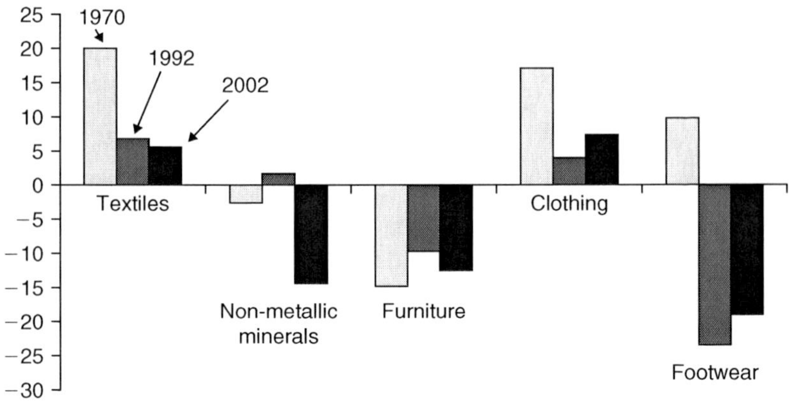

Figure 1.9 France's comparative advantage in traditional sectors

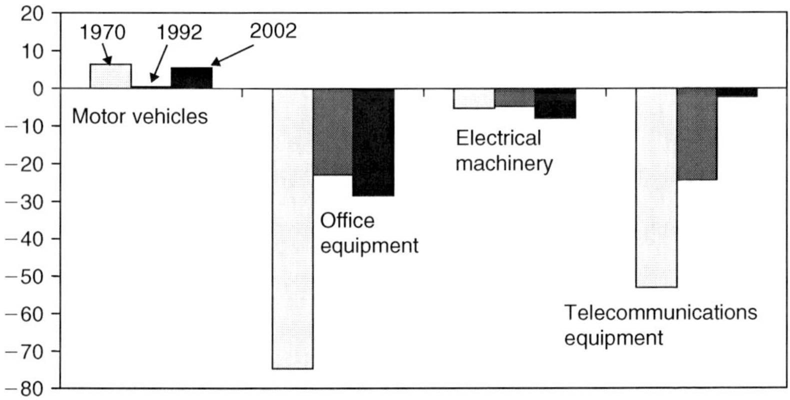

Figure 1.10 France's comparative advantage in advanced sectors

include France, Germany and the United States).[9] Between 1964 and 2002, all the countries, with the sole exception of Italy, showed a significant reduction in dissimilarities in the specialisation model, witnessing to the existence of a process of convergence.

Setting the trend of France's comparative advantages against that of Italy is even more telling. Table 1.A4 (Appendix, p. 34) shows in detail the movements of the Balassa index for France from 1970 to 2002. There are at least two key points, set out in the above diagrams (Figures 1.9 and 1.10). The first is that France, unlike Italy, is losing ground in the traditional sectors, leather goods, textiles, non-metallic mineral products, furniture, clothing and footwear (Figure 1.9). Secondly, France, again unlike Italy, is reducing its comparative disadvantage in sectors such as office equipment, telecommunications equipment and road vehicles (Figure 1.10). These diverging trends suggest in turn a high degree of divergence in the structure of the specialisation model of the two countries: the dissimilarity coefficient, which in 1980 stood at a relatively low level (2.5), grew almost steadily to reach 16.2 in 2002.

The indicators of comparative advantage set out in these figures use the standard international trade classification (SITC2). One advantage of this classification is that it can be used to go back in time, at least as far as 1970, and provides a long-term picture of changes in trade flows and the structure of the comparative advantage of a given economy. Its disadvantage, however, is that it does not permit relating trade data to data on production, making it impossible therefore to study the bases of comparative advantage in terms of factor intensity and factor endowment. What follows will supplement the study carried out so far by using international trade data using the international standard industrial classification (ISIC3). We use OECD data, specifically the STAN database, which refers to all industrialised countries. We then calculate the Balassa index, but only for the industrialised countries and the manufacturing sector. Details of this calculation for the 23 sectors of the industrial classification are shown in the Appendix.[10]

The results for Italy for 1980–2002 are given in Table 1.A3 (p. 33). Essentially, these confirm the results of the study based on the international trade classification, which demonstrate the rigidity of Italy's specialisation model and the substantial and growing weight of the traditional sectors.[11]

The STAN database was used not simply because of a desire to confirm the results obtained with the foreign trade classification but, as already noted, because of the need to look at the sectoral structure of comparative advantage with factor intensities for the various sectors. Unfortunately, not even the STAN database contains measurements of the intensity of human capital which are totally adequate and comparable at international level. To remedy this shortcoming, Bugamelli (2001) uses data from the INPS (Italian social security) archive on the ratio between workers and other employees in the various sectors in Italy and presumes that the same factor intensities also apply in the other countries. We shall use a different strategy below and measure the intensity in the use of skilled labour with the ratio between employees engaged in research and development and total employment in the individual sectors. This information is provided by the STAN database and allows the various countries in question to be compared. One disadvantage of this definition is that it includes only part of skilled labour, that component engaged in research. We are implicitly assuming that there is a proportional relationship between total skilled labour and labour engaged in R&D.

The next step in our study was to calculate, in the best tradition of international trade theory, the coefficient of correlation between Italy's human capital intensity index – HCI, the ratio between those engaged in research and development and the total number of people employed in the sector as a whole – and the Balassa index of comparative advantage, RCA. The calculation was repeated, for each year from 1980 to 2002, for five other countries: France, Germany, the United Kingdom, the United States and Spain. The results are given in Table 1.2 opposite. The main points may be summarised as follows:

- Italy's comparative advantage over the other industrialised countries lies in the sectors with low human capital intensity. The coefficient of correlation between the comparative advantage index and the human capital index is negative over the whole period;
- Italy's comparative advantage in the sectors with low human capital intensity grew throughout the period, in sharp contrast to the other industrialised countries. Italy is the only country where a coefficient of correlation between RCA and HCI becoming increasingly negative;
- Italy's specialisation model diverges not only from that of countries with a longer industrial tradition, such as France, Germany, the United Kingdom and the United States, but also from that of Spain. In the early 1980s the coefficient of correlation between RCA and HCI in the two countries was very similar, –0.50 for Italy and –0.45 for Spain. In Italy, however, this coefficient increased steadily (in absolute terms) from 1980 to 2001, reaching –0.65 in 2001. By contrast, in Spain the coefficient fell, reaching –0.25 in that year, showing that there the specialisation model was placing less and less emphasis on sectors with a low human capital intensity.

To put it succinctly, the failure of the Italian economy to converge on the specialisation model of the other industrialised countries and the essential stability of the structure of comparative advantages in sectors with a high intensity of low skilled labour reveals a peculiarity, if not an anomaly, in Italy's development process.

Table 1.2 Comparative advantage and intensity of human capital (correlation coefficients)

	Germany	Spain	France	Italy	UK	USA
1980	n.a.*	n.a.	n.a.	n.a.	n.a.	n.a.
1981	n.a.	−0.38	n.a.	−0.49	n.a.	0.54
1982	n.a.	−0.50	n.a.	−0.49	n.a.	0.63
1983	n.a.	−0.40	n.a.	−0.51	n.a.	0.64
1984	n.a.	−0.43	n.a.	−0.48	n.a.	0.67
1985	n.a.	−0.44	n.a.	−0.50	n.a.	0.66
1986	n.a.	−0.38	n.a.	−0.51	n.a.	0.65
1987	n.a.	−0.34	n.a.	−0.50	n.a.	0.59
1988	n.a.	−0.33	n.a.	−0.56	0.38	0.56
1989	n.a.	−0.29	n.a.	−0.57	0.36	0.56
1990	n.a.	−0.28	0.08	−0.57	0.38	0.56
1991	0.13	−0.32	0.15	−0.59	0.39	0.54
1992	0.12	−0.21	0.12	−0.55	0.31	0.53
1993	0.11	−0.23	0.15	−0.58	0.37	0.49
1994	n.a.	−0.19	0.20	−0.61	0.47	0.53
1995	0.09	−0.22	0.17	−0.63	0.34	0.57
1996	0.05	−0.18	0.19	−0.62	0.41	0.55
1997	0.02	−0.16	0.27	−0.64	0.36	0.56
1998	−0.02	−0.17	0.30	−0.64	0.38	0.55
1999	0.01	−0.18	0.28	−0.66	0.42	0.57
2000	0.01	−0.21	0.18	−0.64	0.45	0.54
2001	0.04	−0.25	0.15	−0.66	0.47	n.a.
2002	n.a.	n.a.	0.15	n.a.	n.a.	n.a.

*Not available.
Source: Prepared from OECD-STAN data.

Here it is essential to check to what extent these trends have affected the prospects for growth in Italy's exports and eroded the competitive position of the economy. To do this, we have calculated the coefficient of correlation between the sectoral index of Italy's comparative advantage in a given year and growth in sectoral exports at world level over the following five years. A positive coefficient shows that Italy's comparative advantage is greater in sectors which are relatively dynamic at world level and therefore that Italy is well placed to benefit from the growth of international trade. A negative coefficient, on the other hand, shows that the prospects for growth in Italian exports are poor. We also made the same calculation for France, Germany, the United Kingdom and Spain. The results are shown in Figure 1.11. In the case of Italy, the coefficient of correlation between sectoral comparative advantage and export growth reveals the continuing deterioration in the country's competitive position. The coefficient, which was positive and quite high in the second half of the 1980s, fell below zero in the early 1990s and became negative at the end of the period.[12] Germany's competitive position deteriorated too but, unlike in Italy, the process appears to have halted from the early 1990s. In sharp contrast to the Italian economy, France, Spain and the United Kingdom improved the capacity of their specialisation models to benefit to the greatest possible extent from structural changes in world trade.

The results of Figure 1.11 are confirmed by a simple shift-share analysis of export values for Italy. Table 1.3 shows the structural effect, which measures what the rate of growth of Italian exports would have been had they grown, at sectoral level, at the same pace as at world level.

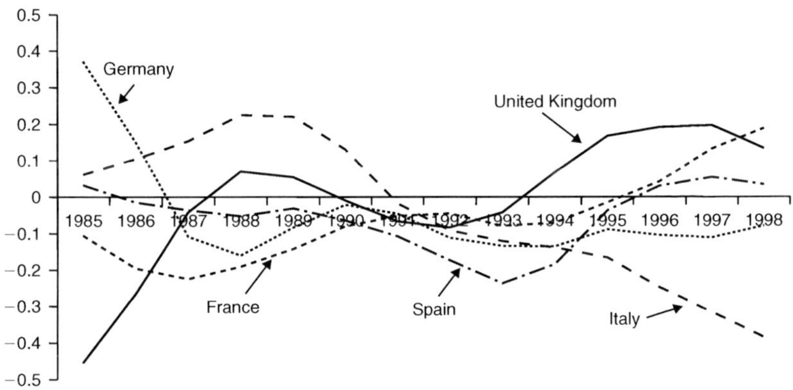

Figure 1.11 An obsolete specialisation model? (Correlation of sectoral indices of comparative advantages with sectoral growth in world exports)

Table 1.3 Effect of the sectoral structure on growth in total exports and manufacturing exports

	Total		Manufacturing	
	1987–1992	1997–2002	1987–1992	1997–2002
France	2.43	1.72	3.18	2.13
Germany	−1.89	2.46	−0.49	3.68
Italy	2.61	−0.89	2.92	−0.63
United Kingdom	−0.02	1.27	0.14	1.12
Spain	0.66	−0.53	0.98	−0.03

Source: Prepared from CEPII data.

This confirms that up to the second half of the 1980s Italy was relatively well placed – the structural effect is positive and quantitatively significant – to take appropriate advantage of the growth in international trade. Over the next decade, however, the ability of the Italian specialisation model to take full advantage of trends in world exports fell sharply. Spain too, a country which, as we have seen, shared with Italy a comparative advantage in production with low intensity of skilled labour, suffered a setback, but on a somewhat smaller scale than Italy, presumably reflecting the fact that, as shown by Table 1.2, it had been more successful than Italy in gradually altering its specialisation model.

In conclusion, the results set out so far demonstrate an anomaly peculiar to Italy. Unlike other industrialised countries, Italy's specialisation model has a relatively stable structure which, even over a comparatively long period of time, has not succeeded in adapting the structure of its comparative advantages to the changed conditions of the world economy.

1.5 The main features of the specialisation model

The pattern of specialisation of a country reflects, to a large extent, its factor endowment. Italy is a country where, at least since the Second World War, the human capital endowment has been relatively weak.

The message of the data is very clear. Let us take (Table 1.4) what is perhaps the simplest measure of a country's level of education, the average number of school years completed by the population of working age.

Table 1.4 Average number of school years completed – population 15+

	1960	1965	1970	1975	1980	1985	1990	1995	2000
Levels									
Italy	4.70	4.99	5.51	5.65	5.89	6.16	6.49	6.85	7.18
EU–11	5.73	5.89	6.29	6.42	7.02	7.35	7.81	8.13	8.45
US	8.49	9.09	9.53	9.69	11.86	11.57	11.74	11.89	12.05
Gap									
EU–Italy	1.03	0.90	0.78	0.77	1.13	1.19	1.32	1.28	1.27
US–Italy	3.79	4.10	4.02	4.04	5.97	5.41	5.25	5.05	4.87

Source: Estimates taken from Barro and Lee (2000) prepared from Unesco data. Figures for 2000 are projections. Average number of years adjusted for the different length of educational cycles.

Table 1.5 Persons having obtained a degree in post-secondary education – % population 25+

	1960 (%)	1965 (%)	1970 (%)	1975 (%)	1980 (%)	1985 (%)	1990 (%)	1995 (%)	2000 (%)
Italy	1.20	1.50	1.50	2.40	2.30	3.80	5.10	6.50	8.30
EU–11	1.30	1.70	2.00	3.00	4.00	4.90	6.50	8.20	10.10
US	10.00	11.00	12.90	15.30	18.00	20.40	27.30	28.10	30.30

Source: Estimates taken from Barro and Lee (2000) prepared from Unesco data. Data for 2000 are projections. Post-secondary education means all tertiary level (Isced definitions), whether university or not.

The average level of education in Italy is systematically below that of other countries in the euro area and, to a still greater degree, the United States. But what is even worse is that the gap between Italy and the other industrialised countries not only does not narrow but actually widens, at least until 1980. After that date, the gap has continued to widen, albeit only slightly, in relation to the euro area, and narrowed in relation to the United States, without, however, returning to the level recorded at the beginning of the period.

Another indicator of the extent to which Italy's accumulated human capital is lagging behind other countries is the percentage of individuals who have completed post-secondary training courses, whether or not at university (Table 1.5). In an economy which is increasingly oriented towards productive systems making intensive use of technology, university-type education is the most important productive factor for those sectors with a high intensity of R&D and an essential condition for making profitable use of technologies developed in other countries.

Here, too, the gap with the other industrialised countries, particularly the United States, has tended to grow.

These data relate to the population as a whole. If we focus on only the employed labour force, the picture does not change substantially; if anything, it worsens further (Faini and Gagliarducci, 2005). The percentage of the labour force which is highly skilled is half that of France and Germany and only a third of that in the United States.

To sum up, there can be no doubt, as ISTAT stressed in its last report, that over the last 40 years the average level of education of the Italian population has improved. But this does not mean that the gap with the other industrialised countries has narrowed – on the contrary, it has continued to widen in terms both of average years of education and university education. Nor does the quality of education appear to favour

Table 1.6 Results of the 2003 PISA tests

	Mathematics	Science	Reading
France	511	496	511
Germany	503	491	502
Italy	466	476	486
Spain	485	481	487
OECD total	500	494	500

Source: OECD.

Italy. The data from an international test (Programme for International Student Assessment: PISA) of mathematical, scientific and reading skills shows that 15-year-olds in Italy lag well behind their contemporaries in the other countries (Table 1.6).

It is therefore not surprising that Italy's comparative advantage lies mainly in the sectors with a low intensity of human capital. The fact that its shortfall in terms of human capital endowment is increasing is enough in itself to explain why its specialisation model is continuing to diverge from those of the other industrialised countries.

We should not, however, ignore the fact that the level of education of the population and of the labour force is itself an endogenous phenomenon. We have stressed that the poor supply of skilled labour results in an obsolete specialisation model but it is also true that the sectoral and dimensional structure of the economy depresses demand for better-educated workers. If only supply-side factors entered into the equation, the situation would show excess demand for educated workers and we would expect a high degree of willingness to invest in education, which the data do not reveal. Similarly, the rate of return of investment in education should be higher in Italy than in other countries where the supply of educated labour is relatively greater. Again, the data do not confirm this hypothesis. The OECD (2001) found that the rate of return of university education was 6.5 per cent in Italy, but 9.1 per cent in Germany, 14.3 per cent in France and 18.5 per cent in the United Kingdom. Finally, if the scarcity of supply were the only constraint, we should expect a substantial flow of skilled immigrants from abroad. But Italy does not seem able to attract significant flows of skilled and educated labour from elsewhere: only 12 per cent of immigrants have an advanced diploma, against 22 per cent in the European Union in general and 44 per cent in the United States. Similarly, the percentage of Italian graduates living and working abroad remains relatively high (7 per cent, compared with 3.9 per cent in France and 2.6 per cent in Spain).[13]

This shows that supply of and demand for human capital are not independent. It is possible that a vicious circle has taken hold, where the poor supply of human capital generates a development model based on small sizes and traditional sectors with a high intensity of poorly skilled labour which in turn discourages investment in education. The system is one of equilibrium, or rather stagnation, at a level lower than that where an abundant supply of human capital would encourage the more technologically advanced sectors, which in turn would increase demand for highly skilled labour. This unfavourable equilibrium has been considered in the literature on growth, which shows that a condition for a situation of this type is the existence of externalities in human capital investment. In Acemoglu (1996), for example, investments in physical and human capital are complementary and, where labour markets are imperfect, this generates a positive externality for investment in human capital.[14] Aghion, Meghir and Vandenbussche (2005) reach basically similar conclusions by looking at the relationship of complementarity between human capital and technological progress. In Acemoglu (2003) the development of new technologies and their use for productive purposes are influenced by the level of specialisation of productive factors (specifically the labour force), which itself influences the degree of progress in the training process and determines demand for it. This process may tend towards equilibrium at a high level of scientific development and training, as seems to have happened in the United States over the last decade, but may also fall dangerously into a vicious circle resulting in a lower equilibrium in terms of both human capital and technological endowment, as seems to have happened in Italy.

1.6 Beyond decline? The crucial role of economic policy

Because of its specialisation model, Italy has to cope with ever-increasing competition from the emerging countries, with lower salaries and an increasingly skilled labour force, which are eroding the comparative advantage the country still possesses in higher quality segments within the traditional sectors. Furthermore, the sectors where Italy has a comparative advantage are those where world demand tends to increase quite slowly. Its current specialisation therefore seems inappropriate to its aspiration to maintain its present relative standard of living, in a world where technological change is rapid and competition stiff.

How can Italy diversify its economy and create new areas of comparative advantage? At first sight the answer seems quite simple. Italy's comparative advantage is excessively skewed, particularly in relation to the other industrialised countries, towards sectors which make relatively greater use of poorly skilled labour and invest relatively less in research and development. In turn, the development of sectors which carry out little research and make relatively less intensive use of better-educated labour reflects the relatively fairly scarce supply of educated workers which, as we have seen, is a feature of the Italian economy. R&D activity also suffers from the lack of highly skilled workers. There is no doubt that the weak propensity of Italian firms to invest in R&D reflects either the sectoral structure of the economy – which, as we have seen, penalises the sectors with a high intensity of R&D – or the size of Italian firms, which even in the same sector tend to be comparatively smaller and so invest relatively less in R&D. But in turn both the weight of the traditional sectors in the Italian economy and the small size of firms reflect the scarcity of skilled labour. We have clearly shown in this article that there is a close relationship between the structure of the comparative advantages of Italy's exports and the scarcity of supply of better skilled labour. It is well known that the demand for skilled labour grows with the size of firms (Fabiani, Schivardi and Trento, 2003). The scarcity of skilled labour is a further brake on the growth of Italian firms.

Action on the supply side of the education equation is therefore essential to overcome the stagnation and inadequacies of Italy's specialisation model. But it is not enough, as we have seen. It is also necessary to break the vicious circle of poor supply of skilled labour leading to an obsolete specialisation model while at the same time the sectoral and dimensional structure of the Italian economy depresses demand for better-educated workers.

To escape from this trap, Italy[15] must therefore act simultaneously on two fronts. Firstly, it must make significant improvements in its education system and increase the supply of graduates, particularly in science and technology. Secondly, its public policy must encourage demand for education by the private sector by promoting innovation and intervening in the mechanisms which still discourage investment in education and training on the labour market.

The need to reform the education system, particularly at university level, is indisputable. It is notable that the reform model proposed by the present government, which brings forward in time the professional choices made by students, does not meet the need for training which, in a globalised world subject to constant technological and economic shocks, should stress general preparation allowing the individual to adapt to changed market circumstances without excessive cost or difficulty. The works of Krueger and Kumar (2003a, 2003b) demonstrate in this regard how the German training system, which stresses the professional rather than the general aspect, achieved better results than the more generalist American system in the 1950s and 1960s, a time of less marked technological change, but proved fairly inadequate when faced with the constant changes in economic and technological conditions which have been the hallmark of the last 15 years.

The outline of an effective university reform is certainly complex and lies beyond the scope of this chapter. Suffice it to note that thorough and courageous proposals to reform the university system have already been put forward by Rossi and Toniolo (2004). Nevertheless, it is essential to stress that in financing research the creation of centres of excellence and criteria for distributing funds solely on merit should receive top priority. In Italy, and elsewhere in Europe, any increase in finance for research should be accompanied by a system of *ex ante* or *ex post* assessment of the quality of the research through a bottom-up approach employing peer review and setting excellence as the sole criterion for allocating resources.

Still more complex is the role of economic policy in encouraging demand for human capital by the private sector and promoting investment in R&D. Should the public authorities concentrate on measures of a horizontal nature or should they encourage certain sectors regarded as particularly promising because of their economic and industrial spin-offs? The opposition between horizontal measures and sectoral polices is a central element in the debate on industrial policy, whether at political or academic level. But this is not a new debate – the subject was discussed at length from the mid-1980s onwards, when the programme to liberalise the internal market was launched and the European Community's competition policy was significantly strengthened, particularly as regards state aid and M&A (mergers and acquisitions) control.

This raised the question of whether the loss by the member states of their power over industrial policy should be offset by greater powers in this field for the Community authorities. Two positions were in contention at the time, the first favouring a European industrial policy which was sectoral, designed to create 'European champions', while the second sought an industrial policy strictly limited to horizontal measures, without distinguishing between the individual sectors.

The debate closed in November 1990 with the Commission's communication to the Council and to the European Parliament entitled 'Industrial Policy in an Open and Competitive Environment'. The communication, tabled by a German member of the Commission, Martin Bangemann, clearly favoured the horizontal approach. Its introduction summarises the underlying philosophy well: 'The role of public authorities is first and foremost to act as a catalyst and inspiration for innovation. The main responsibility for industrial competitiveness must lie with firms, but they have the right to expect from the public authorities an environment and prospects for their activities that are clear and predictable.' Hence, 'a programme which seeks to complete the internal market may be regarded as an industrial policy par excellence'.

The choice in favour of the horizontal approach is almost unanimously supported by the economics literature. Even Dani Rodrik, who certainly cannot be suspected of supporting a neoliberal ideology and often advocates a high-profile role of the state in the economy, came out firmly against purely sectoral measures. In a recent paper, Rodrik (2004) put forward various principles which public authorities should follow in defining industrial policy strategies. One principle states that public intervention should target activities, rather than sectors. This makes it possible to correct specific market failures which affect a number of sectors at the same time. Another principle is that activities which are subsidised must have a clear potential for technological (or other) spillovers. One activity that obviously meets this requirement, and therefore deserves public support, is R&D.

Horizontal policies have further significant advantages over sectoral assistance. Firstly, firms and entrepreneurs have better guarantees, in that the opportunities for being eligible for the benefits of industrial policies depend less on pressure by sectoral lobbies, whose power to exert influence risks varying to degrees which are often significant and does not always depend on exclusively economic considerations. Secondly, the selection of the sectors to assist is not left to the public sector, which in the past has not shown great skill in this area, but to the free operation of market forces. Thirdly, the frame of reference for the incentive process is inevitably more stable in a context where horizontal policies prevail, so providing further encouragement for investments with a longer time horizon.

To sum up, a policy designed to overcome stagnation and the inadequacy of the specialisation model must have several objectives: a) directing a greater flow of resources towards education and research; b) ensuring that these resources are used as efficiently as possible; c) promoting appropriate horizontal policies; and d) creating a stable framework of incentives.

We have already looked, albeit only briefly, at the need to increase the resources going to education, which are quite limited in Italy, particularly when compared with those of the other industrialised countries.

As regards the financing of research, it should be remembered that, at least in Italy, private research lacks resources in quantitative terms even more than public research. In terms of GDP, spending on public research in Italy is only slightly below that elsewhere: public spending on R&D in Italy stands at 0.5 per cent of GDP, compared with 0.6 per cent in Japan, 0.7 per cent in the United States and 1.1 per cent in the European Union. The gap is much wider for private spending on R&D, which stands at 0.5 per cent of GDP in Italy, against 2.4 per cent in Japan, 2 per cent in the United States and 1.1 per cent in the European Union. The problem therefore lies not solely with public spending but to a greater extent with private spending.

It is somewhat doubtful therefore whether massive public programmes of investment in R&D would satisfy the requirements of the Italian economy. But serious consideration should be given to the possibility of introducing a tax credit system for investment in R&D, as suggested by virtually all writers (Bloom, Griffith and van Reenen, 2002). Such a system should be permanent, unlike the measures introduced by the current Italian parliament, which have simply affected the time profile of expenditures that would have been undertaken anyway. The tax credit should mainly favour small start-ups. Finally, amendments to the European rules on state aid could also help revive investment in R&D as would the European patent system, provided that it does not impose excessive costs on small and medium-sized firms.

To sum up, the aim of acting on the demand for, and not just the supply of, skilled labour cannot be achieved by adopting policies designed to favour certain sectors at the expense of others. The latter is simply too difficult a task for policy-makers with a fairly limited ability to select winning sectors and in particular to resist pressures from sectoral lobbies. Preference should be given instead to horizontal policies which can correct market distortions by internalising externalities (as in the case of R&D) and to the provision by firms of training for their workers. A stable regulatory and financial framework should also be ensured. Consolidation of public finances is an obvious priority in this regard. As well, a stable system of incentives for investment in R&D and in training by firms responds to the same need.

1.7 Conclusions

This chapter has sought to establish whether the recent slowdown in the Italian economy reflects cyclical, short-term phenomena, or structural problems, the size and impact of which have grown in recent years.

The figures on the penetration of Italian goods on world markets have indicated a significant deterioration in Italy's economic position. The data on salaries and the distribution of incomes also shows that this trend has not coincided with an increase in the purchasing power of salaries or with a redistribution of income and wealth in favour of those less well off – quite the contrary, in fact.

This led us to examine the possible causes of the loss of competitiveness of the Italian economy. Particularly of late, this has been blamed on membership of the European Monetary Union, which makes it impossible to use devaluation of the exchange rate to boost the economy, although this is not backed up by a medium-term analysis of exchange-rate movements. Between 1998 and the present the real exchange rate has fallen below its trend level. The main change following the introduction of the euro was a reduced volatility of the real exchange rate. Membership of the euro does not therefore provide an adequate explanation of the difficulties from which the Italian economy is suffering. Other authors have pointed to the lack of competition, to rigidities in the labour market and to shortcomings in the financial markets. But these factors are present, sometimes to a greater degree, in other countries whose economies have performed better than Italy's and so do not explain in full the current disappointing performance.

The real weakness of the Italian economy is its pattern of international specialisation. The analysis in this chapter shows how in recent years the sectoral structure of Italian exports has remained substantially unchanged, particularly when compared with that of other industrialised countries, and remains skewed towards the traditional sectors, which are increasingly exposed to competition from developing countries. A further source of worry comes from the results of a detailed study of the human capital endowment, which indicate that, far from narrowing, the gap between Italy and other industrialised countries, particularly the United States, has in some cases widened. The data on investment in education, in terms both of expenditure and attainment in tertiary education, do not suggest that the gap will soon be reduced.

The 1990s saw a double shock, commercial and technological. On the one hand, developing countries, after leaving behind trade protectionism, partly at the behest of the industrial countries themselves, began to assume an increasingly higher profile in international trade. On the other, the information and communication technology revolution opened up new productive horizons. On both counts, Italy was in a weak position, which made it difficult to take advantage of the opportunities offered by these changes. The poor availability of human capital made Italian products more vulnerable to competition from the emerging countries and highlighted the obsolescence of Italy's specialisation model. At the same time, the scarcity of skilled labour made it difficult to take advantage of the new technological opportunities since even imitation requires an adequate supply of skills (Aghion *et al.*, 2005).

In such a situation there is no sense in setting ambitious R&D targets for a country that still lacks in those productive factors, primarily a highly skilled labour force, which promote the growth of the high-tech sectors. What is needed is a way of breaking the vicious circle where poor supply of human capital leads to a low-tech specialisation model, which in turn discourages demand for that same human capital. This requires a double action: on the demand side, with horizontal policies to support innovation, training and the internationalisation of small firms; and on the supply side, to increase human capital by boosting investment in education, especially at the tertiary level.

The inevitable changes to the structure of the Italian economy will require a further contraction in traditional sectors, and hence in demand for labour from the less educated strata. At the same time fresh resources will have to be directed to the sectors in which Italy manages to secure a position of comparative advantage. It is therefore essential to promote the mobility of resources from declining to expanding sectors. This will be assisted by more efficient capital markets, which can allocate savings to growth areas, and a modern system of social shock absorbers, able to reduce resistance to change without generating excessive distortions. Trade protectionism, by contrast, would discourage the movement of resources to the new sectors, encourage a shift of further resources to the traditional sectors and, in the last analysis, consign the Italian economy to further decline.

Appendix

Table 1.A1 gives the Balassa indices of comparative advantage (non symmetrical) for Italy's manufacturing sector from 1980 to 2002. They substantially confirm the results of the analysis carried out on the basis of the international trade classification set out in the text in Table 1.A2.

1. Italy's specialisation model has not changed over the years. The coefficient of correlation between the index of comparative advantage in 1980 and that in 2002 is 0.88. Of the eight sectors where Italian exports enjoyed a comparative advantage in 1980, seven reappear 22 years later. The only sector where Italy loses a position of comparative

Table 1.A1 Revealed comparative advantage for Italy, ISIC3 Manufacturing, 1980–2002

	15+ 16	17 to 19	20	21+ 22	23	24– 2423	2423	25	26	271+ 2731	272+ 2732	28	29	30	31	32	33	34	351	353	352+ 359	36+ 37
1980	0.60	2.68	0.51	0.45	1.27	0.61	0.79	1.47	2.47	0.90	0.29	1.33	1.37	0.92	0.73	0.41	0.46	0.69	0.33	0.29	1.09	2.15
1981	0.68	2.76	0.54	0.45	1.38	0.63	0.91	1.42	2.29	1.02	0.32	1.37	1.23	0.65	0.87	0.36	0.46	0.60	0.40	0.58	0.91	2.56
1982	0.66	2.91	0.46	0.46	1.34	0.66	0.74	1.46	2.15	1.01	0.32	1.32	1.27	0.65	0.86	0.40	0.46	0.52	0.30	0.56	0.83	2.73
1983	0.60	3.00	0.44	0.43	1.07	0.73	0.79	1.40	2.28	1.00	0.34	1.45	1.42	0.55	0.88	0.38	0.48	0.51	0.47	0.56	1.02	2.44
1984	0.68	3.12	0.43	0.48	0.97	0.71	0.85	1.40	2.31	0.97	0.35	1.38	1.48	0.50	0.83	0.38	0.50	0.48	0.27	0.65	0.97	2.61
1985	0.74	3.17	0.43	0.48	1.03	0.72	0.88	1.40	2.24	0.93	0.38	1.37	1.42	0.63	0.81	0.39	0.49	0.43	0.33	0.58	1.05	2.62
1986	0.66	3.21	0.44	0.48	0.99	0.67	0.78	1.39	2.23	0.93	0.40	1.45	1.46	0.57	0.79	0.38	0.49	0.47	0.27	0.55	1.06	2.51
1987	0.66	3.12	0.41	0.46	1.01	0.67	0.76	1.34	2.30	0.93	0.39	1.51	1.47	0.51	0.80	0.41	0.52	0.52	0.27	0.55	1.12	2.47
1988	0.68	3.18	0.45	0.48	0.83	0.66	0.72	1.31	2.42	0.90	0.42	1.51	1.48	0.54	0.84	0.41	0.50	0.55	0.39	0.51	1.27	2.47
1989	0.68	3.15	0.44	0.48	0.79	0.61	0.66	1.31	2.41	0.95	0.42	1.51	1.51	0.61	0.84	0.39	0.50	0.58	0.49	0.46	1.37	2.42
1990	0.68	3.10	0.45	0.48	0.86	0.54	0.65	1.27	2.35	1.01	0.43	1.45	1.49	0.56	0.82	0.38	0.55	0.60	0.44	0.54	1.41	2.38
1991	0.73	3.05	0.46	0.52	0.86	0.54	0.66	1.29	2.37	0.98	0.44	1.48	1.55	0.54	0.83	0.37	0.54	0.61	0.44	0.46	1.22	2.38
1992	0.76	3.00	0.44	0.52	0.96	0.56	0.79	1.29	2.38	1.05	0.44	1.51	1.55	0.49	0.83	0.40	0.55	0.53	0.31	0.51	1.39	2.38
1993	0.73	3.08	0.44	0.56	0.93	0.54	0.82	1.30	2.38	1.17	0.42	1.56	1.61	0.50	0.80	0.37	0.54	0.50	0.58	0.39	1.47	2.41
1994	0.72	3.21	0.45	0.55	0.87	0.54	0.80	1.32	2.44	1.13	0.47	1.58	1.59	0.47	0.79	0.35	0.54	0.54	0.46	0.41	1.47	2.47
1995	0.75	3.14	0.49	0.56	0.78	0.54	0.83	1.36	2.37	1.11	0.48	1.59	1.57	0.45	0.76	0.35	0.55	0.62	0.68	0.33	1.62	2.53
1996	0.76	3.12	0.46	0.58	0.65	0.53	0.83	1.30	2.29	1.07	0.45	1.59	1.63	0.38	0.77	0.34	0.56	0.59	0.96	0.35	1.73	2.44
1997	0.77	3.17	0.48	0.59	0.77	0.56	0.86	1.34	2.41	1.12	0.46	1.60	1.69	0.30	0.77	0.34	0.55	0.58	0.87	0.28	1.73	2.50
1998	0.81	3.08	0.51	0.60	0.80	0.56	0.80	1.32	2.44	1.11	0.48	1.60	1.69	0.29	0.80	0.35	0.54	0.59	1.55	0.35	1.67	2.44
1999	0.88	3.13	0.51	0.62	0.77	0.64	0.88	1.38	2.50	1.09	0.51	1.63	1.75	0.28	0.79	0.33	0.53	0.57	1.18	0.36	1.59	2.42
2000	0.90	3.39	0.54	0.63	0.90	0.65	0.99	1.38	2.50	1.21	0.53	1.62	1.69	0.25	0.76	0.32	0.51	0.59	1.40	0.46	1.69	2.47
2001	0.85	3.37	0.54	0.63	0.88	0.64	0.90	1.34	2.40	1.21	0.55	1.62	1.73	0.24	0.79	0.39	0.53	0.56	1.22	0.33	1.64	2.36
2002	0.93	3.21	0.52	0.65	0.78	0.59	0.86	1.32	2.41	1.16	0.58	1.62	1.76	0.23	0.82	0.36	0.54	0.53	1.48	0.44	1.68	2.32

Table 1.A2 Classification of manufacturing sectors in ISIC3

ISIC3	Description
15 – 437	TOTAL MANUFACTURING
15 + 16	Manufacture of food products, beverages and tobacco
17 to 19	Manufacture of textiles, wearing apparel, leather and leather products, footwear
20	Wood and products of wood
21 + 22	Paper and paper products, publishing, printing
23	Coke, petroleum products and nuclear fuel
24 – 2423	Chemical products (excluding pharmaceuticals)
2423	Pharmaceuticals
25	Rubber and plastics products
26	Manufacture of non-metallic mineral products
271 + 2731	Basic iron and steel
272 + 2732	Non-ferrous metals
28	Metal products, except machinery and equipment
29	Manufacture of machinery and equipment n.e.c.
30	Office, accounting and computing machinery
31	Electrical machinery and apparatus
32	Radio, television and communication equipment
33	Medical, precision and optical instruments
34	Motor vehicles, trailers and semi-trailers
351	Building and repairing of ships and boats
353	Aircraft
352 + 359	Railway and other transport equipment
36 + 37	Other manufacturing

advantage is fuel. The only sector to move out of a situation of comparative disadvantage is shipbuilding.

2. Nor does the ranking of the sectors where Italy has a comparative advantage change. The sectors where the comparative advantage is greatest are the same in 1980 and 2002: textiles and clothing (ISIC 17 and 19), manufacture of non-metallic mineral products (ISIC 26) and other manufacturing sectors (ISIC 36 and 37).
3. Similarly, the ranking of the sectors where Italy has a comparative disadvantage does not change either: in 2002 as in 1980 the lowest values for the Balassa index are in the telecommunications equipment (ISIC 32) and aircraft (ISIC 353) sectors. The severe loss of competitiveness in the office equipment sector is confirmed.

Table 1.A3 Balassa index (homogeneous and symmetrical) for Italy

	1970	1975	1980	1992	1997	2002
Foodstuffs	−7.4	−12.7	−25.8	−15.1	−15.8	−10.7
Non-edible raw materials	−54.2	−56.3	−61.1	−59.1	−57.1	−50.2
Fuel and lubricating oils	29.7	16.2	−13.4	−94.0	−94.5	−87.6
Chemical products and derivatives	−9.1	−11.6	−16.9	−16.7	−14.7	−12.7
Finished products classified on the basis of the raw material						
61 Leather and fur	34.4	46.1	48.4	72.8	79.4	84.0
62 Rubber	6.2	11.6	15.3	7.5	6.7	5.5
64 Paper	−43.8	−42.1	−37.7	−24.6	−17.0	−12.7
65 Yarn and textiles	14.5	15.9	26.6	43.2	44.5	46.2
66 Non-metallic minerals	16.0	17.7	23.0	41.1	32.0	27.6
67 Iron and steel	−24.1	7.3	−3.5	8.4	15.1	16.8
68 Non-ferrous metals	−54.7	−43.6	−49.9	−30.1	−29.1	−23.7
69 Metal	14.8	15.0	23.6	28.1	28.8	27.9
Transport machinery and equipment						
71 Generating machinery and engines	−93.4	−84.3	−14.2	−25.8	−18.3	−20.8
72 Specialised industrial machinery	20.6	13.6	12.4	28.7	31.6	32.9
73 Metal-working machinery	25.3	−7.0	17.2	22.3	23.9	26.7
74 Other industrial machinery	17.1	13.3	15.3	22.6	28.2	30.5
75 Office equipment	30.6	21.8	3.8	−33.5	−53.8	−62.9
76 Telecommunications equipment	−53.8	−36.5	−39.9	−50.6	−43.2	−45.9
77 Electrical machinery and apparatus	30.5	26.2	−2.6	−6.1	−16.1	−14.0
78 Road motor vehicles	−1.2	−1.9	−13.7	−23.8	−20.7	−26.4
79 Other transport equipment	−46.5	−71.5	−41.2	−32.4	−35.5	−13.3
Miscellaneous finished products						
82 Furniture and parts thereof	36.3	44.2	63.5	61.3	64.2	61.8
84 Clothing	54.9	53.2	63.1	59.7	59.1	59.3
85 Footwear	86.7	86.4	87.8	83.5	80.8	78.9
87 Professional, scientific and inspection instruments	−30.8	−38.7	−34.5	−32.0	−34.5	−35.7
88 Photographic and optical articles, n.e.a., watches	−17.0	−29.0	−35.5	−23.0	−12.5	−8.5

Table 1.A4 Balassa index (homogeneous and symmetrical) for France

	1970	1975	1980	1992	1997	2002
Foodstuffs	16.8	13.9	21.0	25.7	24.4	17.5
Non-edible raw materials	−25.9	−26.8	−27.0	−22.5	−26.4	−26.3
Fuel and lubricating oils	−23.8	−25.4	−29.1	−36.8	−16.3	−39.8
Chemical products and derivatives	10.9	8.2	11.7	16.8	10.5	8.3
Finished products classified on the basis of the raw material						
61 Leather and fur	28.3	6.9	2.4	−18.5	−20.8	−14.5
62 Rubber	11.4	15.3	39.3	23.8	25.0	18.7
64 Paper	−34.9	−25.7	−19.7	−7.8	−4.1	−4.0
65 Yarn and textiles	20.0	8.8	1.0	6.8	8.7	5.6
66 Non-metallic minerals	−2.6	−5.6	−14.6	1.7	−6.5	−14.4
67 Iron and steel	20.2	7.3	13.8	15.8	14.7	21.8
68 Non-ferrous metals	−25.8	−19.9	−10.3	−2.6	−6.2	−16.3
69 Metal	−0.1	6.4	4.7	0.4	0.4	0.9
Transport machinery and equipment						
71 Generating machinery and engines	−62.7	−62.5	−0.6	11.0	2.8	0.7
72 Specialised industrial machinery	−18.7	−12.3	−14.9	−24.3	−20.9	−17.4
73 Metal-working machinery	−8.1	−17.3	−19.1	−33.9	−34.4	−35.2
74 Other industrial machinery	−6.3	5.2	−1.7	−10.0	−4.4	−2.5
75 Office equipment	−74.8	−63.1	−11.4	−23.0	−17.3	−28.5
76 Telecommunications equipment	−53.1	−60.9	−35.6	−24.4	−7.8	−2.4
77 Electrical machinery and apparatus	−5.4	0.4	3.2	−9.5	−4.9	−8.0
78 Road motor vehicles	6.4	7.3	7.2	0.5	−0.1	5.5
79 Other transport equipment	−12.7	−11.4	4.2	19.0	33.4	33.0
Miscellaneous finished products						
82 Furniture and parts thereof	−14.8	−13.6	−14.1	−9.7	−12.8	−12.5
84 Clothing	17.1	18.2	13.7	4.0	0.1	7.4
85 Shoes	9.8	11.2	−0.7	−15.9	−23.5	−19.0
87 Professional, scientific and inspection instruments	−14.7	−9.1	−8.2	−16.7	−18.0	−14.3
88 Photographic and optical articles, n.e.a., watches	−10.8	−6.5	−13.3	−20.5	−21.2	−23.1

Notes

1. Data from the Conference Board and Groningen Growth and Development Centre. This is a project financed by the Conference Board and the European Commission which seeks to improve the comparability of macroeconomic and sectoral data using uniform methods of calculation and statistical conventions for the different countries. For further information, see: www.conference-board.org/economics
2. For an analysis of growth in Italy, see Ciocca (2004), Toniolo and Visco (2004), Nardozzi (2004), European Commission (1999) and OECD (2002).
3. It is important to note that the most recent revision by Eurostat to this series changed its trend considerably by introducing a significant deterioration in Italy's position which had not been clear from the earlier data. The series published by Eurostat early in 2003 showed that income in Italy increased from 104 in 1996 to 105 in 2001, leading one of the authors (Faini, 2004) to question whether Italy really had fallen behind.
4. It is true that the factors underlying this gap changed: a process of convergence of hourly productivity, at least until 1997, gave way to a wide gap in both occupation rates (until 1997) and in particular the number of hours worked per employed person (Blanchard, 2004).
5. The data is the effective nominal exchange rate, i.e., an average weighted by trade shares of the bilateral exchange rates between the lira and the currencies of Italy's main trading partners, as given by the International Monetary Fund.
6. See Faini and Gagliarducci (2005), where volatility is calculated using a Garch model in which the real exchange rate is also a function of the terms of trade.
7. For a full study of Italy's model of specialisation, see Onida (1999). Ice (2002) offers a decomposition of the factors which explain the trend of Italy's share of world exports.
8. The choice of the Balassa index rather than the Lafay index, which uses a transformation of the normalised trade balance and so takes account of the level of imports, is often justified on the grounds that overall exports are less distorted than import flows and so are relatively less affected by trade policies. Later reference will be made in every case to the Lafay index as well.
9. The dissimilarity index is simply the arithmetic mean of the squares of the differences between the Balassa index for a given country and its average value for all the countries considered.
10. Unlike in Tables 1.A2 and 1.A3, we give the non-symmetrical B index. A figure greater than 1 shows that the sector enjoys a comparative advantage.
11. Research using production data instead of foreign trade data gives similar results (ISAE, 2005).
12. The graph ends in 1998 in that it compares the comparative advantages of a given country in the year with growth in world exports between t and $t+5$.
13. See Docquier and Marfouk (2004) for further details of flows of highly skilled immigrants.
14. The decision by a subset of the labour force to increase its own human capital will lead firms to invest in physical capital. Since the process linking firms and workers is imperfect, even some workers who have not invested in their own training will nevertheless benefit from the greater physical capital.

15. The European Union can and must assist this process, principally by relaunching the Lisbon strategy. Developing the knowledge economy and strengthening the processes of innovation are in fact vital not just for Italy, but for the Union as a whole. At the same time, it must be recognised that this is an area where the role of national, and often even local, educational and innovation systems remain of crucial importance. As regards school systems in particular, primary responsibility remains entirely with the member state. Since these systems have developed over time and reflect deep-seated local and national traditions, it is neither desirable nor practicable to take steps at European level to improve them. In any case, Europe can play a complementary role in higher, and in particular post-graduate, education, where the link with research and innovation is strong, both because doctoral and post-doctoral programmes launch new avenues of research and because this is how the researchers of the future are trained in both the public and the private sectors.

2

Italy in the Euro Area: The Adjustment Challenge

*Laura Bardone and Vito Ernesto Reitano**
European Commission – Directorate-General for Economic and Financial Affairs

2.1 Introduction

Membership in a monetary union entails both benefits and challenges. The expected benefits are long-term gains in trade and growth due to the elimination of exchange rate uncertainty, falling risk premia and a reduction of transaction costs. The challenges are related to relinquished control of nominal interest and exchange rates as economic policy tools.

For Italy, the potential benefits and challenges of adopting the euro appeared of particular magnitude. Euro-area entry was expected to lower and stabilise inflation and reduce the risk premia incorporated in interest rates. This, in turn, would help consolidate public finances through the reduction of the servicing costs of the very high government debt. The stability-oriented framework of Economic and Monetary Union (EMU) was also expected to reduce uncertainty and enhance confidence, leading to a more efficient allocation of resources and higher potential growth. The changeover from prices expressed in the high denomination of the lira to prices expressed in the single currency would increase the transparency of relative prices across national borders, to the benefit of intra- as well as extra-euro area trade and investment. The challenge for Italy's participation in EMU was to move away from the tendency to recover competitiveness losses brought about by an inconsistent wage behaviour and the related price expectations through a devaluation of the exchange rate.

---

* We are grateful to Jürgen Kröger, Carlos Martinez-Mongay, Mary McCarthy and Alessandro Turrini for their helpful comments on earlier drafts of this chapter. The views expressed in this chapter are those of the authors alone. They do not necessarily represent the views and opinions of the European Commission.

Overall, there was confidence, at least among economic policy-makers, that the potential benefits to the Italian economy from the single currency membership could largely offset the related costs. First, it was acknowledged that competitive devaluations would trigger a vicious circle of inflationary pressures and further competitive devaluations. Second, the 1992 exchange rate crisis raised awareness of the unsustainable nature of an economic model dependent on large public sector deficits and a rapidly growing debt. There was, therefore, a strong political economy argument whereby the Italian government would happily tie its hands *vis-à-vis* domestic public opinion by a solemn commitment enshrined in the Treaty.

So far, however, the Italian economy has not had an easy ride in EMU. Growth performance has been rather disappointing, there has been a steady loss of external competitiveness and fiscal consolidation remains a challenge.

Building on the analytical framework developed in a review of adjustment dynamics in the euro area by the European Commission (2006), the present chapter investigates why the above expectations have not been fully met in the case of Italy. In particular, it analyses the performance of the Italian economy during the first decade in EMU and explores to what extent failings in the macroeconomic adjustment to asymmetric shocks are responsible for Italy's woes. The two main channels of market-based adjustment are considered: first, the real interest rate channel, which, by linking developments in the financial sector and the real economy, plays an important role in driving consumption and investment decisions; and, second, the competitiveness channel, i.e., changes in relative cost competitiveness based on wage and productivity developments. The analysis then attempts to understand how market-based adjustment in Italy was influenced by the interaction of policy initiatives affecting in particular wages and prices. There is indeed significant scope for fiscal and structural policies to raise the efficiency and speed of the adjustment process, the former primarily in its role of stabilisation tool and the latter in its capacity to improve the functioning of product, labour and financial markets so as to allow a smooth functioning of market adjustment channels. Thus, while tracing a retrospective analysis of how Italy fared during the first eight years in the euro area *vis-à-vis* the other euro-area countries, this chapter tries to identify possible policy lessons that can help ensure a more efficient functioning of the Italian economy and any other current or prospective euro-area member in the context of monetary union.

The chapter is organised as follows: Section 2.2 sets the scene by reviewing how real and nominal macroeconomic variables have evolved before and during monetary union, with an in-depth account of demand- and supply-side drivers of the output growth differential *vis-à-vis* the rest of the euro-area. In so doing, the relevant shocks that hit the Italian economy more than the rest of the euro-area countries are identified. Section 2.3 examines how the real interest rate and competitiveness adjustment channels worked in the EMU period and what factors, if any, hampered their smooth and efficient functioning. The roles of fiscal and structural policies in shaping the adjustment are examined in the subsequent section. The conclusions look at the prospects for the Italian economy.

Main findings

- Over the period 1999–2007, average annual growth of real GDP in Italy was among the lowest in the euro area. This negative growth differential, however, pre-dated the euro adoption. Potential growth is estimated to have fallen from above 2 per cent in the early 1990s to around 1.5 per cent between 1993 and 2007.
- The shock of the 1992 financial crisis and prospects of participation in EMU speeded up the inevitable adjustment of the Italian economy that had relied on unsustainable fiscal imbalances and competitive devaluations. After the disinflationary efforts during most of the 1990s, Italy benefited from the risk premia reduction significantly more than the rest of the euro area in the years immediately before and after the euro adoption. Other relevant factors, notably the substantial increase in households' financial wealth and confidence effects linked to the prospect of euro-area membership, supported domestic demand in the run-up to the euro and helped make the necessary Maastricht-induced adjustment less painful.
- After the adoption of the single currency, Italy did not close the growth gap with the rest of the euro area despite the larger reduction in the risk premia. The labour contribution to economic growth recovered substantially, also thanks to labour market reforms; however, total factor productivity (TFP) shrank dramatically. With the loss of monetary independence, the structural weaknesses hampering Italy's potential growth came forcibly to light through their impact on both domestic demand and external competitiveness.

- Moreover, with an export mix that competes with, rather than being complementary to, that of the emerging economies, Italy has been exposed more than other euro-area countries to increasing global competition.
- The more marked productivity slowdown and the impact of globalisation can be viewed as two negative asymmetric shocks relative to the rest of the euro area to which the Italian economy failed to respond efficiently through the channels that are available under monetary union. However, the fact that cyclical conditions in Italy did not significantly differ from those in the rest of the euro area suggests that there were little asymmetries in shocks or, rather, that asymmetries went in different directions, thus largely offsetting each other. Higher labour accumulation is one such offsetting factor. In addition, the sharp drop in risk premia triggered by the participation in EMU could be seen as a positive temporary shock on the demand side.
- Looking ahead, Italy has no choice other than to adjust via the competitiveness channel, as further support from significant decreases in real interest rates can no longer be expected.
- To restore competitiveness in international markets, productivity growth must outpace wage developments. Economic theory suggests that this can be promptly achieved only through wage restraint. However, as overall real wage growth in the private sector has already been relatively subdued for quite a long time, such a policy stance appears socially and politically unpalatable. Still, there remains scope for better balancing wage coordination at the national level with the need to make appropriate wage adjustment at firm and/or local levels, so as to allow a better alignment of wage and productivity developments. This move, which should concern the whole economy, including the public sector, would allow wages to better reflect productivity differentials across sectors and regions, thus helping loosen regional imbalances. It would also help sustain private investment already in the short run.
- The key policy challenge for Italy is to enable a swift and durable recovery in productivity growth. In this context, a policy strategy aimed at addressing the structural factors hampering productivity growth should be the cornerstone in the process of revamping Italy's competitiveness. Key policy requirements involve far-reaching structural reforms, including fostering internal competition, enhancing the business environment and developing a more dynamic financial sector. In this strategy, a permanent consolidation of public finances is a necessary prerequisite that would make room for the effective operation of the automatic stabilisers in the event of adverse economic

shocks. It would also create more favourable conditions for private and foreign investment and for enhanced expenditure on research and development, human capital and infrastructure.

- The run-up to the euro was characterised by significant steps towards reforming the labour market, liberalising protected sectors, privatising state-owned companies and removing the excessive regulatory burden. It also saw an impressive fiscal consolidation effort that allowed meeting the government deficit Maastricht criterion and put the debt ratio on a declining path. Since the euro adoption, however, the drive for structural reforms has decelerated, probably also because the 'monetary convergence bonus' of falling risk premia allayed the urgency of adjustment. Given the tradition of fragmented coalition governments and the difficulty of finding social consensus, the political economy for structural reform and healthy public finances must rely on raising public awareness of the related benefits.

2.2 Macroeconomic developments in EMU

After the adoption of the single currency, over the whole period 1999–2007 average annual growth of real GDP in Italy was among the lowest in the euro area (together with Germany and Portugal), 1.4 per cent per year as against 2.3 per cent in the rest of the area. However, the slowdown in real GDP growth predates euro-area accession, as the negative growth differential had already been above half a percentage point in the period 1992–8. This is reflected in the evolution of potential growth, which, in the aftermath of the 1992 financial crisis, is estimated to have fallen from above 2 per cent to around 1.5 per cent between 1993 and 2007.

Figure 2.1 shows the different performance of real GDP per capita growth since 1991 in cumulative percentage terms in the major euro-area countries, including Italy, and the rest of the euro area.

Italy, together with France and Germany, started exhibiting a visible growth gap relative to the other euro-area countries in the second half of the 1990s. The growth gap opened up further during the first half of the 2000s, as real GDP growth stagnated. In 2006, the Italian economy recorded a small economic rebound, but still underperformed most other euro-area countries. As a result, Italy's relative income position has deteriorated seriously: after peaking at almost 107 per cent in 1988, gross domestic product per capita, expressed in purchasing power standards and relative to the euro area, recorded a steep decline from 2000 onwards. It fell below the euro-area average in 2002 and decreased further thereafter. In 2007, it was around 92 per cent.

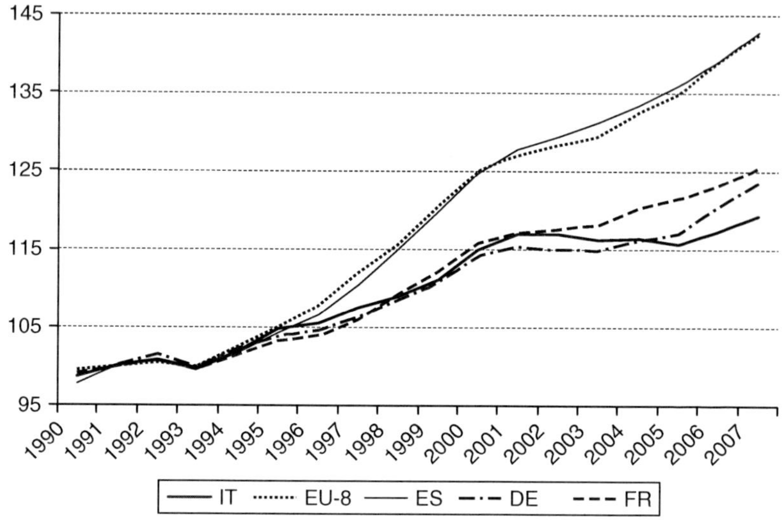

Figure 2.1 Real GDP per capita growth in Italy and the euro area
National currencies, 1991 = 100

Note: EU–8 refers to the euro area of 12 countries excluding Italy, Germany, France and Spain.
Source: Commission services.

Behind Italy's dismal growth performance still lies a huge geographic dualism, with marked and persistent regional disparities between the Centre/North and the South. In 2007, GDP per capita in the Southern regions was still less than 60 per cent that of the Centre/North, only marginally better than 50 years ago despite large public transfers in the intervening period. After a short period of catching up at the end of the 1990s and early 2000s, real GDP in the two macro regions grew at roughly the same pace; in 2007, real GDP growth in the South was again lower than in the Centre-North (0.9 per cent against 1.6 per cent). In a context where disparities in GDP per head between regions in the EU have narrowed markedly over the past decade, with growth in the least prosperous regions outstripping that elsewhere, the economy of the South of Italy is losing ground *vis-à-vis* the other poor regions of the EU.[1]

A review of the Italian economy published in 1999 by the European Commission[2] identified the drift of the Southern regions as one of three areas where specific weaknesses of the Italian economy had emerged at the time. The other two areas were the inability to fully exploit the existing labour potential and the impoverishment of capital endowment in construction (infrastructure as well as residential, industrial and other construction). In what follows, we attempt to update that analysis by including the period following the euro adoption. First, we compare the contributions of the various demand components to real GDP growth in Italy and in the euro area; we then use a growth-accounting exercise to dissect the supply-side determinants of growth.

2.2.1 Demand-side factors driving the persistent output growth differential

The Italian economy's underperformance *vis-à-vis* the rest of the euro area over 1999–2007 was due to both domestic and external demand (Figure 2.2, Panel A).

Although private consumption was a main driver of real GDP growth in Italy, its slower growth pace compared to that experienced in the rest of the euro area explains more than half of the growth gap *vis-à-vis* the latter. As for the other components of domestic demand, real public consumption and gross fixed capital formation provided a mildly positive contribution to real GDP growth, but the latter did slightly less so than in the other countries of the euro area. Finally, external demand deducted 0.2 of a percentage point per year on average from real GDP growth in the first nine years of euro-area membership, increasing the growth gap with the rest of the euro area by an average of almost half a percentage point per year. The difference is particularly striking when looking at the two components of the trade balance separately; the negative impact on growth of Italy's markedly worse performance of exports was partly stemmed by a more subdued dynamics of imports.

For both Italy and the rest of the euro area, Panel B of Figure 2.2 compares the demand composition of real GDP growth during euro-area years with that in the period preceding euro adoption, as a first step in attempting to identify the specific features of Italy's growth (under)performance since the loss of the exchange and interest rates as national monetary policy tools.

In Italy, the improvement in the contribution of domestic demand between the two periods was entirely due to public consumption and gross fixed capital formation, whereas the evolution of private consumption was broadly similar to that in the pre-1999 period. In particular, public consumption recovered pace over the euro-area years, after contracting in the previous sub-period to help meet the Maastricht criteria. As for gross fixed capital formation, it hardly contributed to GDP growth during the 1990s. The share of total investment in GDP over the 1990s declined in Italy from over 20 per cent of GDP to 17 per cent. The deterioration affected both construction and equipment, and originated in both the public and the private sectors. It was due to a variety of

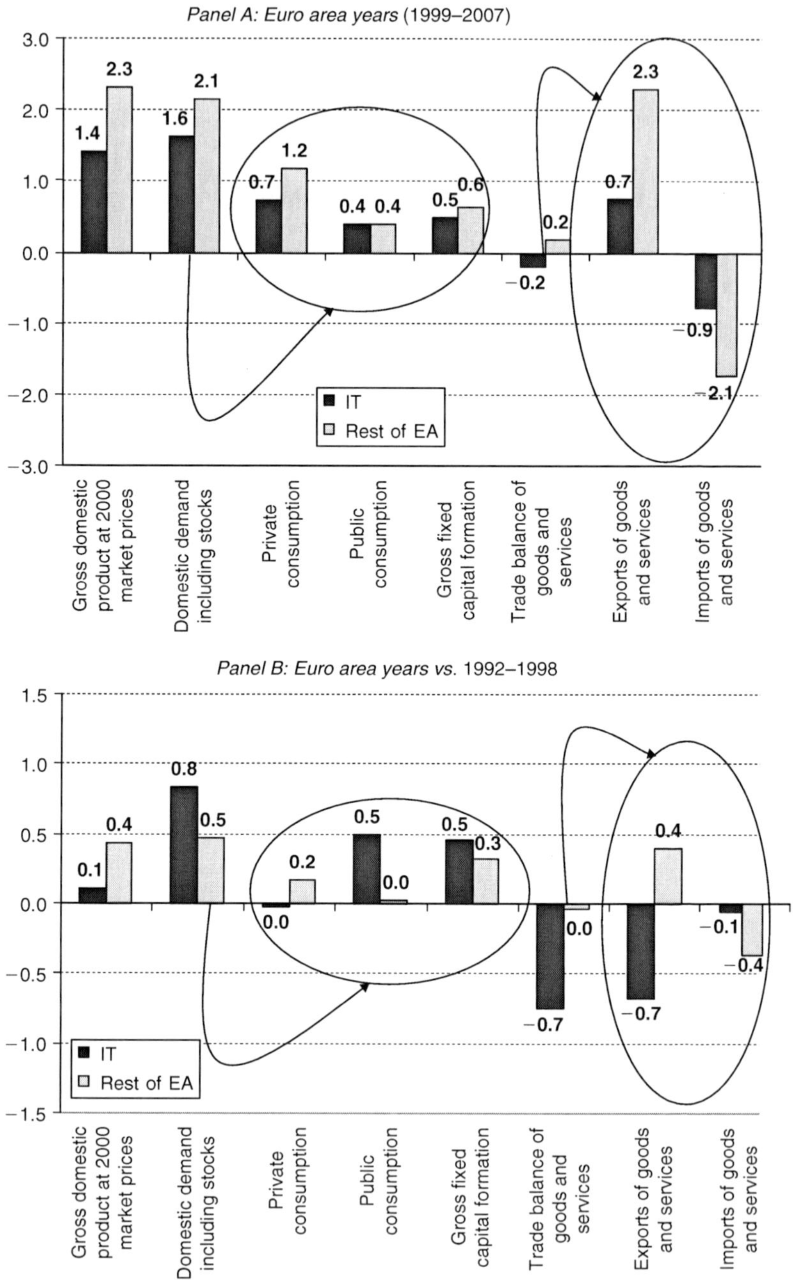

Figure 2.2 Real GDP growth and its demand-side contributions
Source: Commission services.

causes: the adverse business cycle after the 1992 financial crisis; the need to reduce the government budget deficit, which led to cuts in public investment (see Chapter 4); and the widespread judicial anti-corruption investigations, which led to a paralysis of local and central government decisions concerning building permits. In the second half of the past decade, it also reflected the substitution of labour for capital that was induced by the cheaper cost of labour (Bassanetti *et al.*, 2006). In an era of swift technological advance, this comparative lack of investment in the Italian economy is likely to have exacted its toll in terms of competitiveness and productivity. In the subsequent sub-period of euro-area years, private – mainly construction – investment recovered somewhat also thanks to historically low real interest rates.

However, for Italy, the most notable difference in terms of contributions to real GDP growth before and after the euro adoption concerns the marked deterioration of export performance, which was only partly offset by a slightly lower average growth of imports. Comparing the same two periods, the rest of the euro area recorded opposite developments: an improvement in the performance of exports coupled with a commensurate worsening of the contribution of imports to growth.

A key issue is whether this represented anything exceptional that can be traced back to the adoption of the euro or whether it reflects deep-seated problems in the country's ability to compete in the external markets that pre-dated the euro adoption. Particularly for Italy, answering this question must take into account the role of Italy's product specialisation in exposing the country to the impact of reduced barriers to trade and globalisation. This is a well-documented subject that is discussed in other chapters of this book (see chapters 1 and 3; Rae and Sollie, 2007). Italy's export shares in the most dynamic sectors of global trade are found to have been consistently lower than those of Germany, France and Spain since the early 1990s. Conversely, Italian foreign sales had and have maintained a comparative advantage in traditional, low-skilled and labour-intensive sectors for which competition from emerging economies is stronger. This is all the more true in Italy's Southern regions, which have therefore been affected even more severely than the rest of the country by the sharpening competition of the emerging economies (SVIMEZ, 2007). The situation appears to be markedly different in Germany, whose main competitors are largely located in Europe or the USA. Thus, with an export mix that competes with, rather than being complementary to, that of the emerging economies, Italy has been exposed more than other euro-area countries to increasing global competition. This can therefore be considered as an asymmetric shock for the Italian economy originating outside the euro area.

2.2.2 Supply-side determinants: a growth accounting exercise

A traditional growth accounting exercise that dissects the sources of Italy's growth gap *vis-à-vis* the euro area reveals the presence of structural problems in the Italian economy that the loss of national monetary independence probably just made more evident. In Panel A of Figure 2.3, the evolution of real GDP in Italy and in the rest of the euro area over the euro-area years is decomposed into six variables representing supply-side determinants of growth. The first two variables – TFP and capital deepening – measure labour productivity whereas the latter four – working age population, average hours worked, participation and unemployment rates – can be combined to measure total labour input.

Figure 2.3 highlights the TFP problem of the Italian economy that has attracted so much attention in the debate over Italy's economic malaise (see, for example, Chapter 1). While TFP has made a decisively positive contribution to growth in the euro area, this was hardly the case for Italy, where this variable explains most of the real GDP growth differential. On the other hand, Italy outperformed the euro area in terms of reduction in the unemployment rate and, to a lesser extent, the contraction in average hours worked more than offset the more subdued growth in working-age population. Panel B illustrates these developments by comparing them with the evolution of the same variables over the period preceding the euro adoption. The slowdown in TFP growth between 1999 and 2007 is common to both Italy and the rest of the euro area, but was much more marked in the former. For the purposes of our analysis, it can thus be viewed as an asymmetric (and endogenous) shock for the Italian economy. Capital deepening decelerated at about the same pace in the two areas, and has continued to be lower in Italy than elsewhere. On the other hand, Italy's secular decline in average hours worked, also observed in other euro-area countries, was offset by substantial improvements in the other determinants of labour input, and this to a greater extent than in the rest of the euro area.

As explained in greater detail in Section 2.4, a series of labour market policies and reforms in Italy helped to contain labour costs from the early 1990s onwards, while at the same time enhancing flexibility in the use of the labour input. As the successive reform steps took place, employment continued to grow, even in the face of sluggish economic activity, leading to a significant reduction in the Non-Accelerating Inflation Rate of Unemployment (NAIRU). By far the largest share of new jobs was created

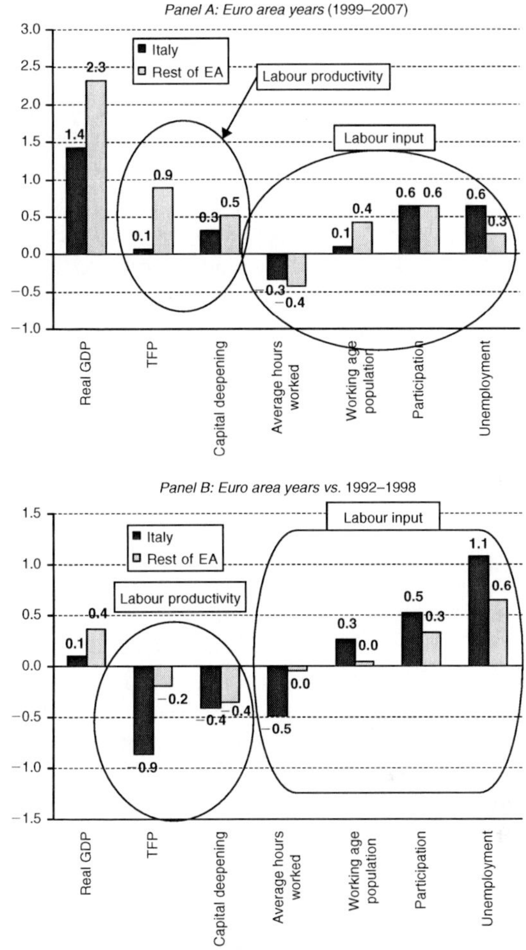

Figure 2.3 Real GDP growth and its supply-side determinants

Note: Assuming a Cobb-Douglas-production function $Y = A(L \cdot H)^{\alpha} K^{1-\alpha}$ where Y denotes the level of *GDP*, *L* employment, *H* the average hours worked per person employed, K the capital stock and α the labour share in income, real GDP can be written as

$$Y = \frac{Y}{H \cdot L} H \cdot L = A \cdot \left(\frac{K}{H \cdot L}\right)^{1-\alpha} H \cdot WP \cdot PART \cdot (1 - ur)$$

where *WP* stands for the working age population, *PART* denotes the participation ratio as a share of *WP* and *ur* the rate of unemployment. In terms of growth rates *g* this is:

$$g_Y = g_A + (1-\alpha)(g_K - g_L - g_H) + g_H + g_{WP} + g_{PART} - g_{ur} \cdot \frac{ur}{1-ur}$$

The expression $(g_K - g_L - g_H)$ is referred to as capital deepening, i.e. the increase in the capital labour ratio.

Source: Commission services' calculations.

in the services sector, but the effect of a more flexible labour market was strong enough to halt the negative employment trend in manufacturing. This is in clear contrast with the rest of the euro area where manufacturing firms increased the number of layoffs. It can be argued that there has been some trade-off between employment growth and labour productivity due to: i) an overall deceleration in capital deepening as labour became cheaper relative to capital and more flexible as a factor of production; and ii) the entry of low-skilled, low-productivity workers into the labour market, with the result of slowing down the rise in labour quality (see Chapter 3). However, while it is tempting to assume that the recent job 'miracle' itself caused the productivity slowdown, with the latter being the price to pay for the former, in the long run the decline in labour productivity growth cannot be explained without accounting for the decline in total factor productivity (European Commission, 2007b). At the same time, a more detailed growth accounting exercise carried out by European Commission Services shows that, even after taking account of variations in the quality of labour input, as measured by the level of educational attainment of workers, the big picture presented in Figure 2.3 does not significantly change. TFP still contracted in Italy during the euro-area years, in contrast with the experience of most other euro-area countries.[3]

In sum, the dismal growth performance recorded in the Italy in the euro-area years is mostly the result of a declining TFP. Overall, factor accumulation dynamics contributed very little. In particular, while capital deepening slowed, the Italian economy has made considerable progress in utilising the existing work potential over recent years. The exceptionally low TFP growth experienced by Italy over the last decade indicates a disappointing absorption of new technologies. A widely held view is that, in the new economic environment, structural factors that limit the organisational efficiency and ability to innovate by Italian industry, insufficient competition, including in the services sector, and low human capital accumulation are amongst the determinants of the marked slowdown in TFP in recent years (Larch, 2004).

The picture that emerges at the level of the national economy when looking at aggregated data needs to be qualified when considering data by sector or by macro-region. A more detailed analysis at sectoral level shows that the labour productivity slowdown in euro-area years has been widespread in all the economic sectors, both tradable and non-tradable, except utilities, financial intermediation and construction (which however account for just about 15 per cent of total value added in the economy). The slowdown was quite abrupt in the manufacturing sector,

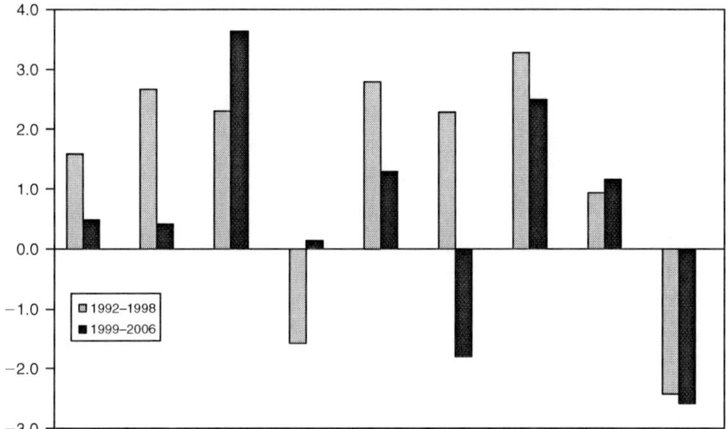

	Total - All NACE branches	Manufact. (D)	Electricity gas and water supply (E)	Construct. (F)	Wholesale and retail trade (J)	Hotels and restaurants (H)	Transport, storage and communic.(I)	Financial intermed. (J)	Business activities (K)
1992–1998	1.6	2.7	2.3	−1.6	2.8	2.3	3.3	0.9	−2.4
1999–2006	0.5	0.4	3.6	0.1	1.3	−1.8	2.5	1.2	−2.6
GVA share in 2006	100.0	18.1	2.0	6.1	11.5	3.8	7.7	4.9	22.2

Figure 2.4 Italy – Labour productivity in private sectors (*GVA per hour worked – annual average growth*)

Source: Commission services' calculations on national accounts data before the 2008 revisions.

but productivity in the services sector was also very disappointing. In particular, the large business services sector saw a continuation of a negative trend in labour productivity that, according to Daveri and Jona-Lasinio (2006), 'has the flavour of a missed opportunity' as the Italian services companies do not seem to have grabbed the opportunities offered by new technologies.

Looking at data by region, the South lags well behind the rest of the country in terms of labour market performance: in 2007, the employment and participation rates in the South were still at just 47 per cent and 53 per cent respectively, vs. around 65 per cent and 68 per cent in the Centre/North; unemployment in the South was about three times as high, well above the euro-area average. What is more, the regional divide in labour market performance widened between 2004 and 2007, as employment growth in the Southern regions was less than half that in the rest of the country and the participation rate even decreased. Overall, the labour input accounts for about two-thirds of the GDP per capita gap between the two macro-regions, whereas labour productivity accounts for the other third.

2.2.3 Nominal convergence: inflation developments

In a monetary union, the two main channels of monetary policy transmission are the exchange rate channel and the interest rate channel. Given identical nominal exchange and interest rates for all countries within a currency area, real exchange and interest rates may differ across countries, as a result of differences in their inflation rates. While Section 2.3 will examine specific developments in the two real rates, it is worth starting here with a look at inflation developments in Italy relative to the rest of the euro area.

The price-stability-oriented monetary policy stance followed during most of the 1990s to meet the Maastricht nominal convergence criteria successfully lowered inflation in Italy, as it did in all other high-inflation countries. From an annual average rate in excess of 6 per cent in the early 1990s, the inflation rate fell to just above 2 per cent in 1998. The period since the creation of the euro area saw a continuation of low core inflation in the area, in spite of sharp increases in oil prices and an initial sharp depreciation of the euro. However, Italy, like the other high-inflation countries, maintained a persistently positive inflation differential with the euro-area average until 2004.

Cyclical conditions do not seem to explain the persistent differential in price developments in euro-area years (Figure 2.5).[4] As discussed in more detail in the next section, it is more likely that structural factors played a role, in particular the lack of internal competition in the services sector and the more marked productivity slowdown experienced in Italy, which has resulted in higher unit labour costs.

2.3 Adjustment in EMU

2.3.1 The theoretical framework

Within a monetary union, an above-average increase in costs and prices in a country that is 'out of sync' with the euro-area business cycle, or as a result of structural factors, lowers the difference between the nominal interest rate and the inflation rate, i.e., the real interest rate. A lower real interest rate, however, makes it more attractive to advance investment and consumption via inter-temporal substitution and wealth effects, thereby stimulating economic activity. Thus, the adjustment through the real interest rate is potentially pro-cyclical. This has raised concerns about the possibly destabilising effect of adjustment through this channel that provides additional stimuli to countries that are already in a boom, and slows economic activity in countries that are lagging behind.

Under the impact of the competitiveness adjustment channel, the same country discussed above would record above-average demand that

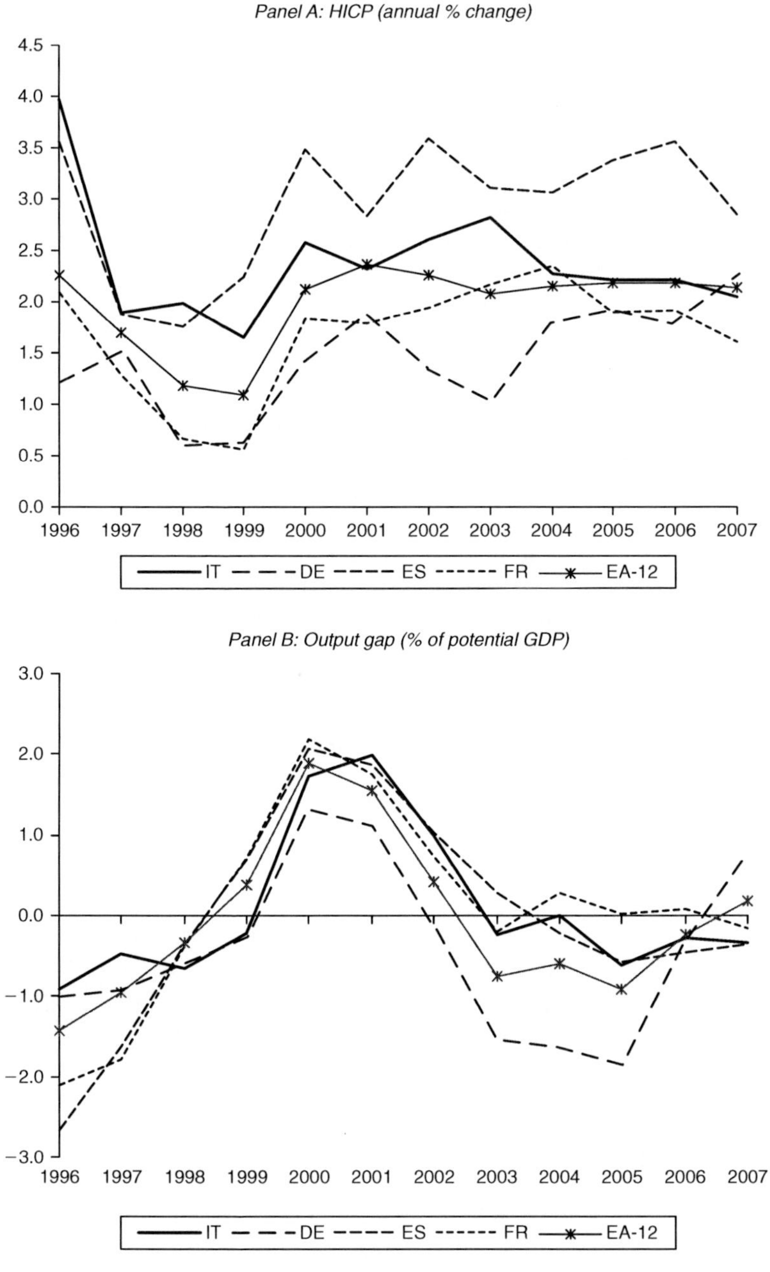

Figure 2.5 Consumer price inflation and output gap
Source: Commission services.

tends to push up costs and prices. The deterioration in the relative cost situation worsens that country's cost and price competitiveness and slows the pace of economic activity towards the euro-area average. Eventually, the induced slowdown would increase unemployment, ease wage pressures, reduce inflation and lead to a slowdown of domestic demand and to a recovery of competitiveness, which would boost growth through a better performance of the external sector. So, in principle, the competitiveness channel has a stabilising effect under different cyclical conditions within a monetary union.

A key conclusion of the review of adjustment dynamics in the euro area (European Commission, 2006) concerned the interaction between the potentially destabilising or pro-cyclical impact of the real interest rate channel and the stabilising impact of the real exchange rate/competitiveness channel. The report found that, while the impact of the former could be strong in the short run, the exchange rate impact tends to operate cumulatively and to dominate the process of economic adjustment in euro-area economies in the long run. In particular, to the extent that, in the context of increased economic, financial and monetary integration, economic agents base their decisions not only on national economic and financial developments but also take into account developments in other countries, the potentially destabilising effect of real interest rates is expected to become less important in a monetary union. The financial sector also plays a role, as the existence of credit constraints can affect the sensitivity of consumption and investment to the interest rate. Finally, the efficiency and speed of the adjustment via the competitiveness channel crucially depends on the degree of wage and price flexibility. Relatively slow responses run the risk that with movements in the intra-euro-area the real effective exchange rate may be prolonged, and that adjustment may be inefficient. A further element to be considered is the possibility of non-Keynesian responses to fiscal policy, especially in countries with a very high government debt like Italy. Overall, it is rather difficult to disentangle *ex-post* the relative importance of the real interest rate channel from that of these other factors.[5]

Starting from a more in-depth account of Italy's evolution of domestic demand and the disappointing developments of external demand during euro-area years, the next two sub-sections analyse the functioning of these two adjustment channels.

2.3.2 The monetary convergence bonus and adjustment through the real interest rate channel in Italy

The run-up to the creation of the euro area saw substantial convergence towards low nominal and real interest rates (Figure 2.6), reflecting

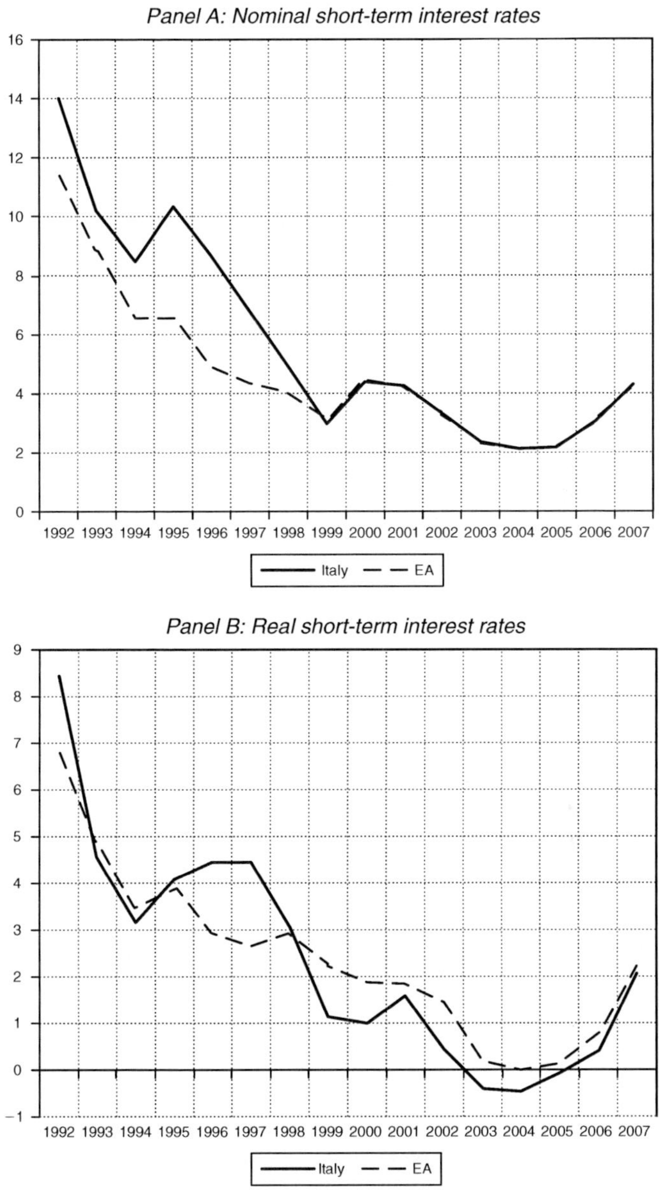

Figure 2.6 Nominal and real interest rates in Italy and the rest of the euro area
Source: Commission services.

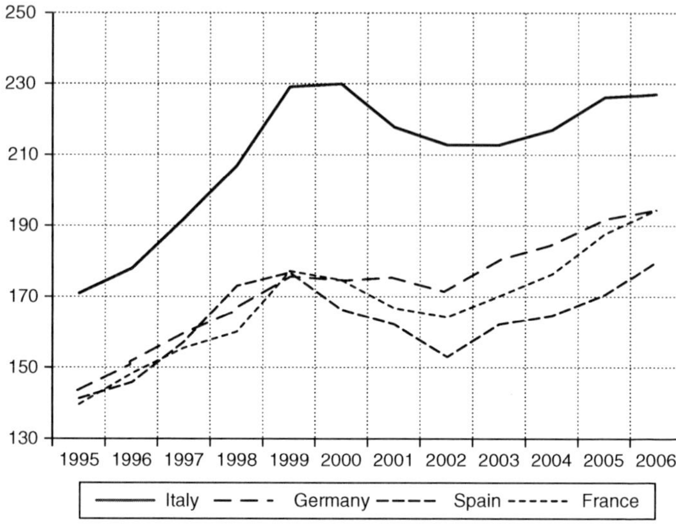

Figure 2.7 Financial assets of households and NPISH (% of GDP)
Source: Commission services.

progress towards low and stable inflation and the diminishing risk premia, as well as the substantial fiscal consolidation observed during the same time period. In Italy, the reduction in real interest rates between 1997 and 1999 was more pronounced than in the rest of the euro area, given Italy's higher starting position and the relatively restrictive monetary stance in previous years. The downward trend continued during euro-area years but at a slower pace and broadly in line with the euro-area average. In 2005, interest rates measured *ex-post* started increasing again, both in Italy and the rest of the euro area.[6]

Fostered by the fall in inflation and interest rates, the period leading to the euro adoption saw a substantial increase in households' financial wealth in most euro-area countries. This was true particularly in Italy where the value of financial assets held by households as a share of GDP was significantly higher than in the rest of the euro area (Figure 2.7), due, *inter alia*, to relatively restrictive mortgage markets, underdeveloped and/or inefficient insurance markets and the perception that large general government account imbalances would sooner or later have an impact on disposable income.

Thanks to the drop in real interest rates, the increase in financial wealth as well as possible non-Keynesian effects linked to the dramatic improvement of government accounts,[7] the household saving ratio dropped steadily in Italy[8] in the 1990s, by almost 1.5 per cent every year and especially in 1997 and 1998. The resulting increase in private consumption was, however, more muted, reflecting the contraction in real disposable income, which was in turn affected by stagnant real wages and declining employment, as well as, inevitably, the prolonged and severe fiscal adjustment needed to meet the Maastricht 3 per cent of GDP deficit criterion.[9] At 1.3 per cent per year on average between 1992 and 1998, growth of private consumption in Italy was half a percentage point (pp.) less than in the rest of the euro area.

The downward trend in the saving ratio reversed in 2001 and then broadly stabilised until 2005, as the wealth effect stemming from the appreciation of real assets, namely increasing house prices, was not strong enough to completely offset the loss of financial wealth that occurred in this period (Draghi, 2007).[10] In addition, any positive confidence effects linked to the prospect of a permanent improvement in public finances may have vanished in the 2000s with the re-emergence of fiscal imbalances and the uncertainty about the long-term sustainability of the pension system (see Chapter 4). As a result, private consumption increased in Italy by almost 1 pp. less than in the rest of the euro area, in line with subdued households' disposable income dynamics (Figure 2.8).

Investment, as we saw in the previous section, was relatively moderate in both the pre-1999 and the euro-area periods, and mainly driven by construction in the latter period. Indeed, the real interest rate channel seems to have substantially influenced households' investment decisions. After several years of contraction, housing investment has steadily increased since 1999, accompanied by a double-digit increase in mortgages. However, the significant growth of credit to households recorded in Italy has been substantially lower than in Spain (Figure 2.9), in spite of a similar reduction in the exchange rate risk premium. Overall, the indebtedness of Italian households remains well below that in the rest of the euro area. According to several studies, this is due to credit market imperfections. For example, high down-payment ratios for home purchase and slow financial innovation have been indicated as specific factors that affected the level of indebtedness of Italian households (Jappelli and Pistaferri, 2000). On the other hand, credit growth in Italy does not seem to be affected by a particularly high direct cost of borrowing, as interest rates attached to the same type of mortgages across euro-area countries are very similar (ECB, 2007). Thus, the observed higher interest rates on average prevailing in Italy during the euro period could be due to the product range offered by banks and the fact that Italian households seem to have a preference for mortgages with an initial longer

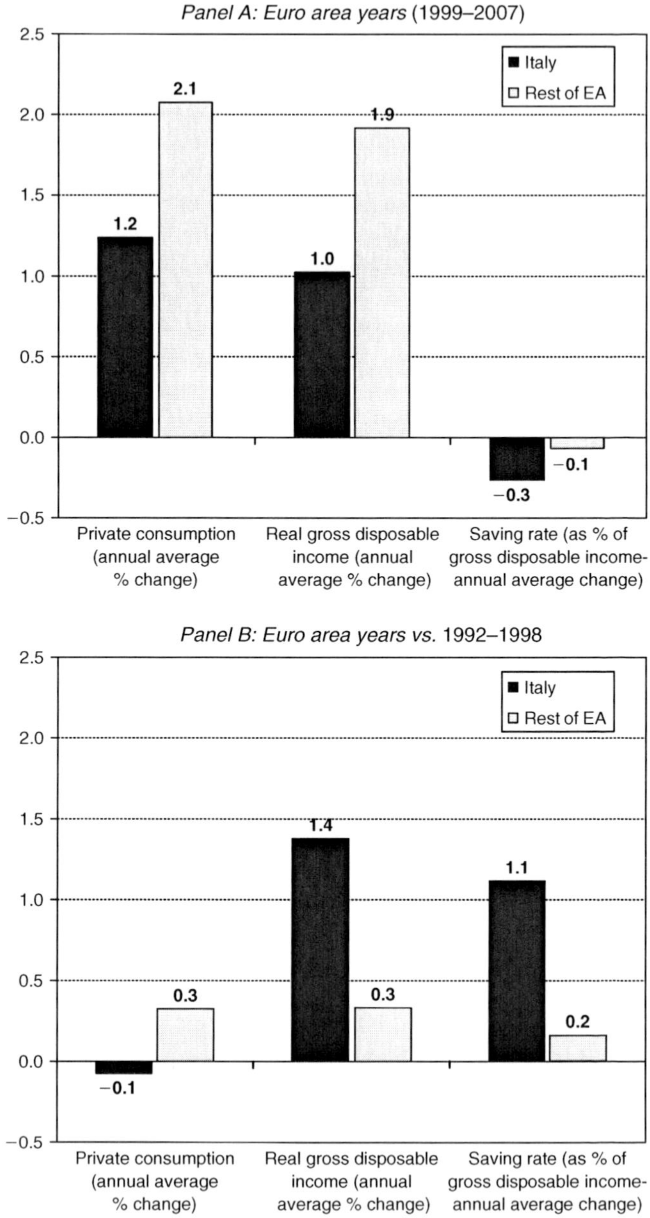

Figure 2.8 Private consumption expenditure and its main determinants

Note: For real gross disposable income and the saving rate, the figures for the rest of the euro area do not include Greece, Ireland and Luxembourg.

Source: Commission services.

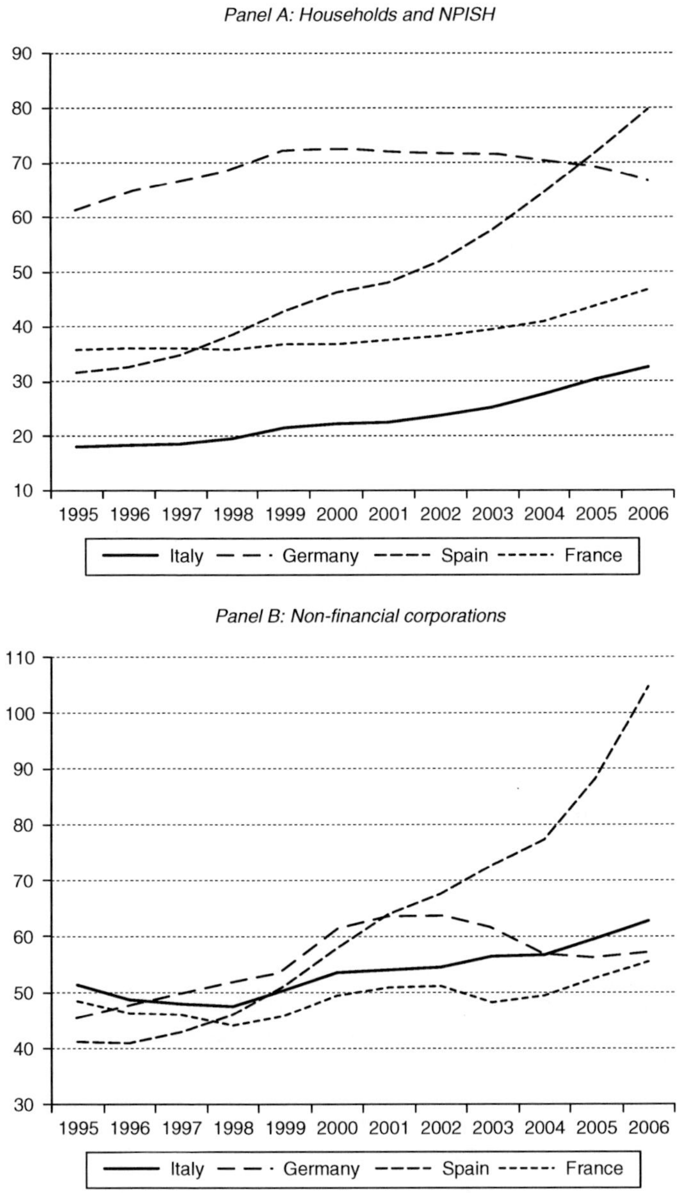

Figure 2.9 Loans (% of GDP)
Source: Commission services.

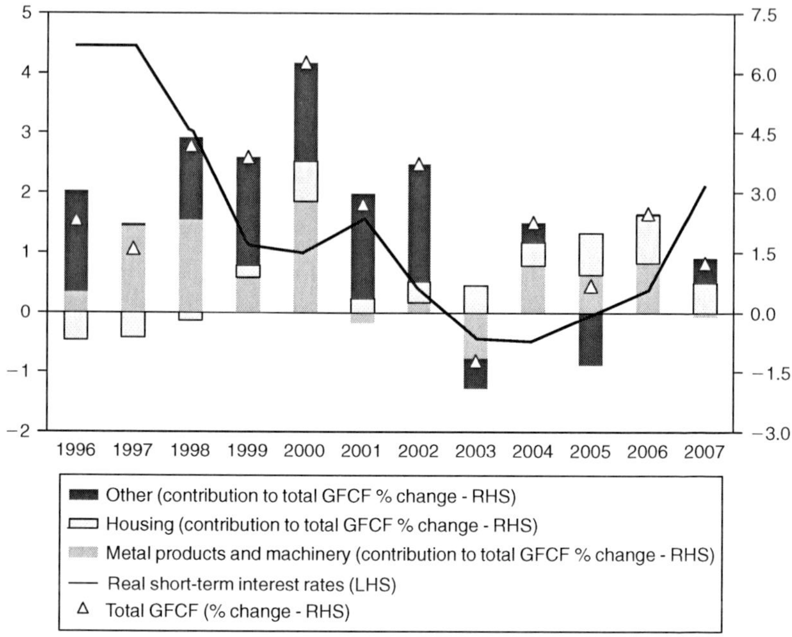

Figure 2.10 Italy – GFCF and real interest rates
Source: Commission services.

time-horizon rate fixing. Other factors also come into play to determine the demand for housing credit, including cultural attitudes. For example, population growth has played a very important role in Spain (Martinez-Mongay *et al.*, 2007).

As for investment by firms, it remained subdued during the first eight years of euro membership despite the historically low interest rates and the increase in indebtedness (Figure 2.9, Panel B), essentially reflecting the loss of competitiveness experienced in this period. In particular, after the boost linked to some fiscal incentives in 2002, investment in 'metal products and machinery' contracted sharply in 2003 and has remained muted since then (Figure 2.10). Subdued investment in Italy after the euro adoption also reflects a dismal growth of the corporate sector gross operating surplus, well below that recorded in the other large euro-area countries, especially Spain.[11]

To sum up, prospects of the elimination of the exchange rate risk premium and the price stability-oriented monetary policy at national level brought about a significant reduction in real interest rates in Italy during the 1990s, as in other euro-area countries with historically high and volatile inflation. This supported domestic demand, in particular private consumption, but subdued real disposable income growth largely offset these positive developments. In the subsequent euro-area years, a less marked reduction in real interest rates coincided with a still relatively weak growth of domestic demand, even though a shift in demand towards housing underpinned construction investment. All this suggests that the real interest rate channel has operated as expected in Italy, but that it was offset to a large extent by other factors operating at the same time. In particular, the negative TFP shock experienced in Italy has implied a slowdown in productivity and dismal output growth, with related poor (present and expected) disposable income growth. Through a loss of external competitiveness, it also resulted in subdued investment growth, in particular in the tradable sector. Additional factors that may have weakened the impact of the real interest rate channel are financial market imperfections and negative confidence effects as fiscal imbalances re-emerged.

2.3.3 Adjustment through the competitiveness channel

Italy's ability to compete in world markets

The evolution of the external position of the Italian economy was pinpointed in Section 2.2 as a distinguishing factor of the poor growth performance during the first eight euro-area years. In particular, it was observed that Italy's disappointing performance in exports, under the impact of globalisation, was mirrored by a subdued evolution of imports, also reflecting slow domestic demand. This helped contain the deterioration in the current account balance with the rest of the world, which went from a surplus of 1.9 per cent in 1998 to a deficit of 1.7 per cent of GDP in 2007, despite the sizeable worsening in terms of trade (Figure 2.11). By contrast, in France and especially Spain, the negative contribution of net exports to growth and the related marked current account deterioration have been primarily related to buoyant domestic demand.

While in the context of the analysis of macro-adjustment through the real interest rate channel the attention focused on domestic demand, the present section concentrates on Italy's negative export performance. The question addressed is how adjustment through the competitiveness channel worked in Italy after the loss of the exchange rate tool as national policy.

The most striking manifestation of Italy's disappointing export performance has been the steady loss of market shares that the country has experienced over the past decade. While a mature economy is not expected to consistently gain additional market share, in view of the

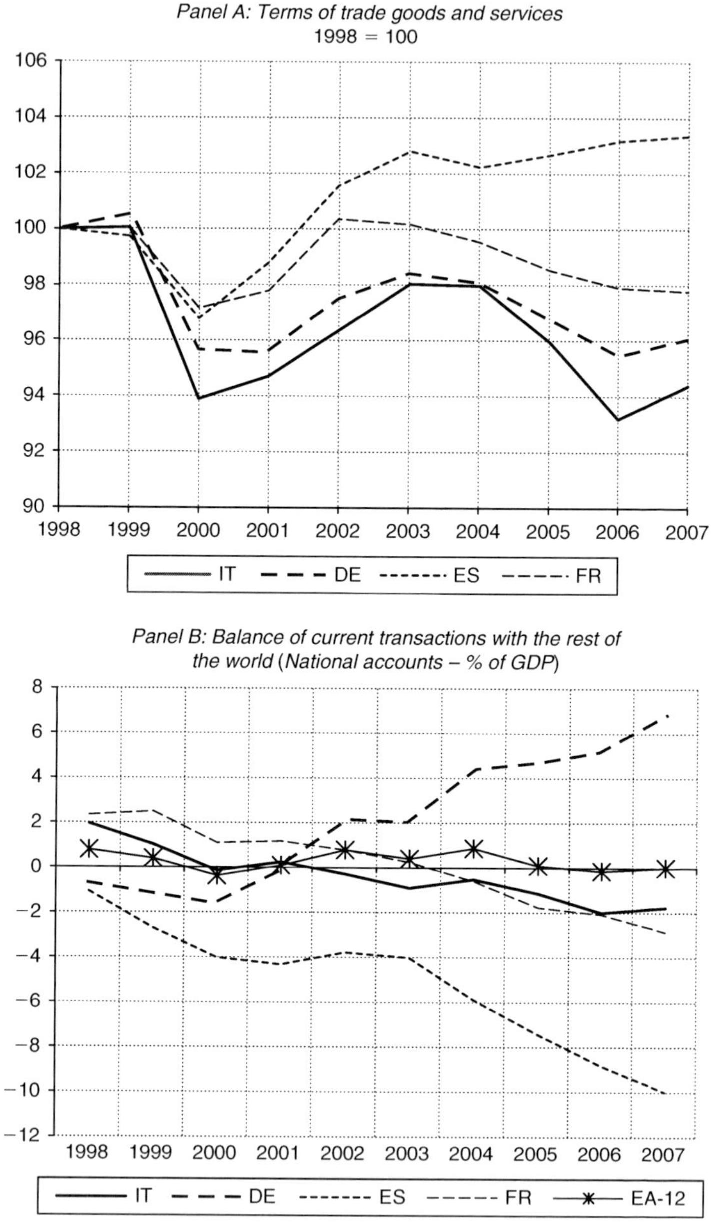

Figure 2.11 Terms of trade and current account balances
Source: Commission services.

advance of emerging economies, Italy's performance nevertheless compares unfavourably with other large euro-area countries. When measured in volume terms, Italy's loss of market shares for goods and services over 1999–2007 was close to 3 per cent per year on average, continuing a trend that had already started in 1996 as the lira appreciated in nominal terms from the low point attained early that year (Figure 2.12). This contrasts with the export performance of Germany, which, over the same period, recorded a gain of market shares of around 2 per cent per year, whereas France lost only 1.5 per cent per year. However, when measured at current prices, the contraction of market shares appears more contained and slightly less pronounced than that of France (Figure 2.12, Panel B), but still disappointing if compared with that of Germany and other euro-area countries. This is due to a dynamics of estimated export prices well above that of the other euro-area countries.

Chapter 3 of this book offers various explanations of the apparently anomalous price-setting behaviour of exporters, who, in spite of a dismal performance in volume terms, seem to keep increasing their prices more than competitors. Overall, three alternative reasons appear plausible: i) estimation errors; ii) qualitative upgrading, either as firms manage to improve their exported products or because the low-end segment of production is displaced; and iii) pricing strategies, whereby Italian firms protect profit margins while sacrificing volumes.

We will come back later to this issue, but the point here is that, however measured, there appears to be a specific problem in Italy concerning its ability to compete in foreign markets. Developments in foreign direct investment (FDI) provide a further worrying signal of this. Both the stock and the inflow of FDI from abroad have remained well behind that of most other euro-area countries. In 2005, the accumulated stock of inward FDI amounted to 13 per cent of GDP, only half or less the figure recorded in France, Germany and the rest of the euro area. Italy also underperforms in its capacity to invest abroad. Italy therefore appears to be lagging behind as a potential location choice and, at the same time, Italian firms appear to be laggards in the process that should transform them into 'global players'.

Cost competitiveness developments

Under the euro, changes in competitiveness *vis-à-vis* the other euro-area countries can be achieved through relative price or cost movements. We consider below the evolution of cost competitiveness as measured by the real effective exchange rate based on nominal unit labour costs (hereafter REER) against the other large euro-area countries. This measure

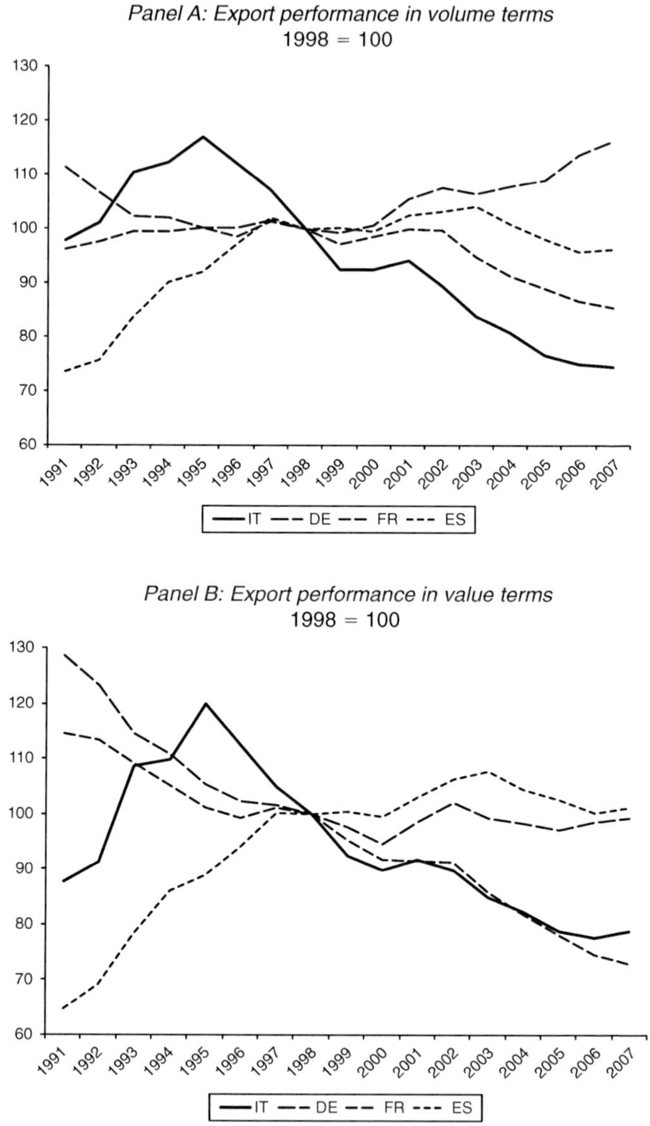

Figure 2.12 Comparison of export performance in volumes
Source: Commission services.

best highlights the issue of the alignment of wage and productivity developments.

To start with, Italy's still positive current account position at the time of the euro adoption suggests that the fixed exchange rate established for the changeover to the euro was not particularly punitive for Italy's competitiveness on the foreign markets.[12] The appreciation of the euro *vis-à-vis* the currencies of non-euro-area trade partners after 2000 explains only part of the deterioration in Italy's cost competitiveness during euro-area years (Panel A of Figure 2.13). This was of course common to the other euro-area countries, even though the slightly larger appreciation of the nominal effective exchange rate for Italy suggests that the country was somewhat more affected by the euro appreciation through the geographical composition of its foreign sales.

On top of the nominal appreciation, Italy's cost competitiveness suffered from an unfavourable development of unit labour costs, as witnessed by the relatively sharp and consistent appreciation of Italy's REER between 2000 and 2007 (Panel B).

It seems therefore that the competitiveness channel in Italy delivered what it was expected to deliver, that is, a worsening of the current account and of the contribution to growth of net exports as a result of deteriorating cost competitiveness. However, the unabated appreciation of the real exchange rate based on unit labour costs since the turn of the century suggests that the adjustment through this channel is not working smoothly and that something else must be holding it back.

Once again, it is argued that the stagnation in productivity growth in Italy since the end of the 1990s is the key factor that hampered adjustment through the real exchange rate, as was the case for the adjustment through the real interest rate. Such stagnation, which was widespread in both the tradable and non-tradable sectors, went largely beyond the wage moderation achieved through the incomes policy agreements with the social partners of the early 1990s, thereby pushing up unit labour costs. Table 2.1 below provides an illustration of this development in the manufacturing sector by comparing growth in productivity, wages (nominal compensation per employee) and unit labour costs in Italy, France and Germany.

The role of Italy's trade specialisation

Particularly for Italy, an analysis of competitiveness must take into account the fact that diminishing barriers to trade and global developments (i.e., globalisation) may have altered the mechanism of adjustment via the competitiveness channel.

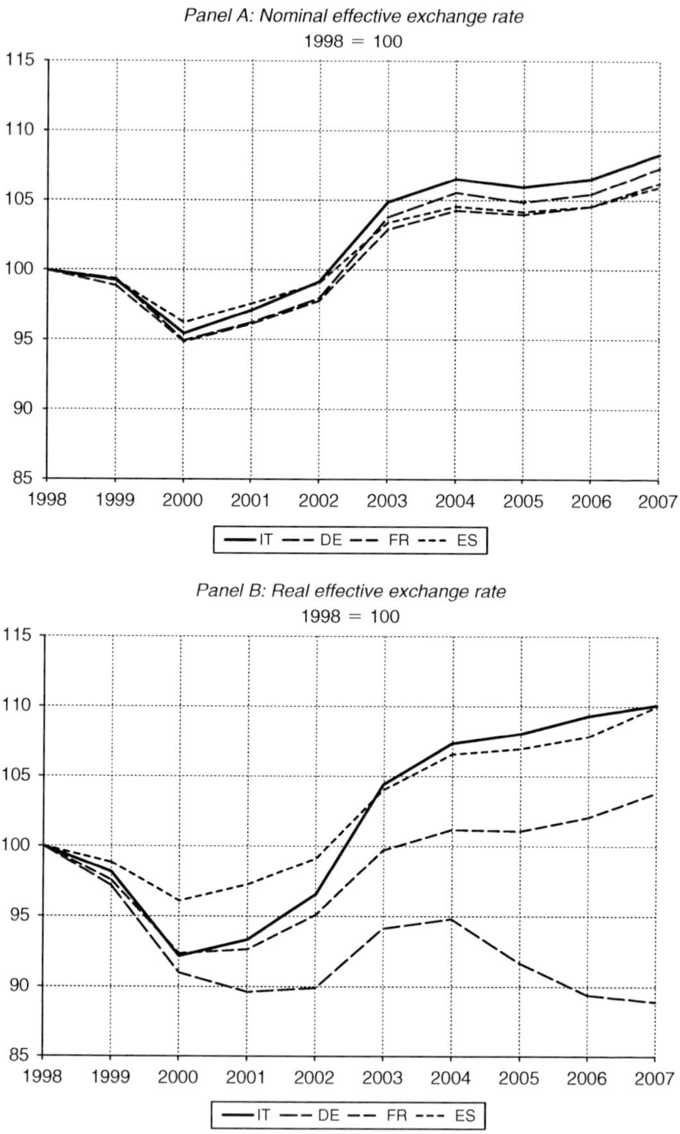

Figure 2.13 Nominal and real effective exchange rate

Note: Performance relative to the rest of 35 industrial countries; double export weights.

Source: Commission services.

Table 2.1 Unit labour losts and their determinants in manufacturing (percentage change – employment in full-time equivalent terms)

	1992–1998	1999	2000	2001	2002	2003	2004	2005	2006	2007	1999–2007
Labour productivity											
DE	3.5	2.4	6.6	1.8	0.4	3.8	5.8	3.3	7.2	4.9	4.0
FR	3.8	3.9	3.7	0.4	2.0	4.4	4.6	4.2	3.0	2.4	3.2
IT	2.7	0.7	4.6	0.2	−1.8	−2.8	1.7	0.7	0.1	−0.1	0.3
Nominal compensation per employee											
DE	5.2	2.3	4.8	2.4	1.9	2.6	2.6	0.7	4.3	1.9	2.6
FR	3.1	2.7	1.6	1.2	3.6	2.0	5.0	3.2	4.2	1.2	2.7
IT*	4.2	2.6	2.6	3.3	2.3	2.9	4.2	2.8	2.6	2.5	2.9
Unit labour costs											
DE	1.7	−0.1	−1.7	0.6	1.5	−1.2	−3.0	−2.5	−2.8	−2.9	−1.4
FR	−0.6	−1.2	−2.0	0.8	1.6	−2.3	0.3	−1.0	1.2	−1.1	−0.4
IT*	1.5	1.9	−2.0	3.1	4.2	5.9	2.5	2.1	2.5	2.6	2.5

* The 1992–8 average is affected by a reduction in social contribution partly compensated by a new regional indirect tax on economic activities (IRAP). Excluding this; the average annual increase would be around 0.5 pp higher.
Source: Commission services.

Chapter 1 already highlighted the role of Italy's trade specialisation in exposing the Italian economy to the impact of globalisation to a greater extent than in other euro-area countries. An analysis of exports by their technological content based on OECD trade data[13] shows little or no sign of change in Italy's trade specialisation. Italy appears to have actually strengthened its specialisation in some of the traditional sectors, while making no progress or even losing ground in the production of scale-intensive or science-based goods. By contrast, Germany and France seem to be moving towards high-skill production in reaction to fiercer competition on low-skilled labour-intensive goods. In this context, ISAE (2007a) argues that closer European integration may have left Italy, and in particular its Southern regions, more exposed than other partners in the area to the competitive shock of globalisation.

Nevertheless, the anomalously high export prices already evoked above seem to signal that some kind of restructuring, within sectors rather than across sectors, has indeed occurred in Italian industry and has taken the form of a qualitative upgrading of Italian exports (see Chapter 3). In this process, less efficient companies in the traditional industries have been forced to exit the market, with a consequent shift of these productions to higher quality segments more sheltered from competition by emerging economies. In contrast, competitive companies have maintained healthy profits thanks to a high quality output and specific targeted markets that have provided them with some price-setting power. This has implied an overall shrinking manufacturing sector, particularly in the most traditional industries, with its share in total value added declining from 22 per cent in 1998 to 18 per cent in 2006.[14] Developments in 2006 and 2007, indicating a stabilisation of market shares at current prices, may suggest 'a possibility of structural improvement such as quality upgrading' (Lissovolik, 2008). Although the recovery of Germany and strong demand from oil-producing countries certainly supported these developments, this could be a first sign that the ongoing restructuring in the tradable sector is bearing some fruit.

These structural changes, however, do not seem sufficient to warrant a full recovery of the country's competitiveness.

2.3.4 The interaction of the real interest rates channel and the competitiveness channel: what can we expect next?

The potential interaction of the real interest rate channel and the competitiveness channel can be visualised by looking at developments in the monetary conditions index (MCI),[15] shown in Figure 2.14. Between

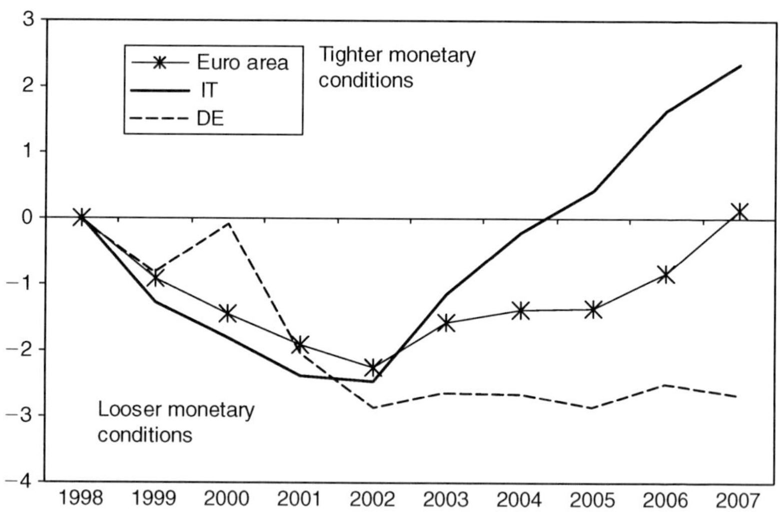

Figure 2.14 Monetary conditions index (MCI) in the euro area, Germany and Italy

Note: Weighted average of the percentage point change in the real short-term interest rate and the percentage change in the real effective exchange rate from a base period – Relative weights used: 6 to 1 for the euro area; 3 to 1 for Italy; and 4 to 1 for Germany.
Source: Commission services' calculations.

1998 and 2002, Italy experienced loosening monetary conditions, as a result of the depreciation of the REER up until 2000 and falling real interest rates throughout the entire period. Germany and the euro area as a whole experienced a broadly similar evolution of monetary conditions.

Since 2002, however, the stabilisation and subsequent increase in real interest rates, combined with an appreciating REER, have implied tighter monetary conditions for Italy. By contrast, monetary conditions have remained broadly stable in Germany, thanks to positive developments in the REER component. Also at euro-area level, the MCI points to tighter monetary conditions since 2002, but less so than in Italy (partly because of the estimated lower weight of the REER component).

Based on the observation of this indicator, prospects for the Italian economy in the medium term appear rather worrisome. As the positive EMU start-up shock of falling real interest rates is clearly vanishing, the Italian economy is left to cope with the (persistent) negative shocks it has so far failed to adjust to. This suggests that, in coming years, adjustment to adverse shocks for the Italian economy may be longer and more painful than in the rest of the euro area. In other words, while adjustment so far may not have been a big issue for Italy, thanks to the monetary convergence bonus, this risks no longer being the case.

2.4 Policy-based adjustment

There is significant scope for national policies to influence the adjustment process through the fiscal stance and, over the medium term, structural policies. Fiscal policy can play an important role in adjusting to macroeconomic shocks, whereas structural policy, aimed at enhancing the functioning of product, labour and financial markets, can improve the efficiency of adjustment by promoting wage and price flexibility. In addition, financial market integration can act as an adjustment mechanism to country-specific shocks by smoothing consumption over time and across countries through cross-border portfolio diversification. Experience with these types of policy-based adjustment is the focus of this section.

2.4.1 Fiscal policy

Sound public finances are a core objective of EMU. At the level of the euro area, a major focus has been on the need for sound fiscal positions as underpinning the ECB's primary objective of price stability. At the national level, the loss of national monetary independence means that national fiscal policies are the main tool by which governments can achieve macroeconomic stability in the event of asymmetric shocks. This requires, however, that the initial fiscal position is sufficiently sound. Fiscal consolidation is all the more important as the high Italian government debt and a rapidly ageing population exerting heavy pressure on public spending put the long-term sustainability of public finances at risk.

With a budget deficit still at double-digit levels at the beginning of the 1990s, meeting the Maastricht criteria on the fiscal front and maintaining fiscal soundness thereafter represented a major challenge for Italy. Yet, a considerable policy effort, supported by the reduction of the cost of servicing the debt originating from the sharp fall in interest rates, allowed Italy to bring the deficit down to 1.7 per cent of GDP in 1999 and put the debt ratio on a downward path. Starting from this, optimism prevailed that the debt ratio could continue shrinking rapidly thanks to a stable primary surplus of around 5 per cent of GDP and further savings from the steady decrease in interest rates. Unfortunately, these hopes did not materialise as lack of commitment towards fiscal consolidation resulted in rising primary expenditure and untimely tax cuts. By 2005, the primary surplus was almost fully eroded and the public debt ratio rose again. After the euro adoption, the savings from lower interest expenditure was therefore fully offset by the rise in primary expenditure and revenue reductions. With re-emerging fiscal imbalances, the positive confidence effects related to the euro adoption vanished soon. Even though the underlying situation of public finances improved over 2006–7, largely thanks to a new increase in the revenue ratio, fiscal consolidation continues to represent a key challenge for Italy as structural primary expenditure remains stubbornly high. Public debt remains above nominal GDP and the related interest expenditure absorbs an amount almost twice as high as in the rest of the euro area.

Overall, the fiscal policy stance did not act as a stabilisation tool for the Italian economy over 1992–2006. Taking account of the cyclical conditions of the period under observation, the run-up to the euro was characterised by an (inevitable) pro-cyclical restrictive fiscal policy stance. The fiscal stance turned markedly pro-cyclical and expansionary during the period of positive output gap 2000–2,[16] due to a combination of significant tax cuts and primary expenditure growth well above the rate of potential growth. Italy thus lost the opportunity to improve its underlying budgetary position as economic conditions were favourable. The Italian public finances continued to deteriorate in structural terms until 2003 (Figure 2.15). Thereafter, the need to bring the deficit ratio

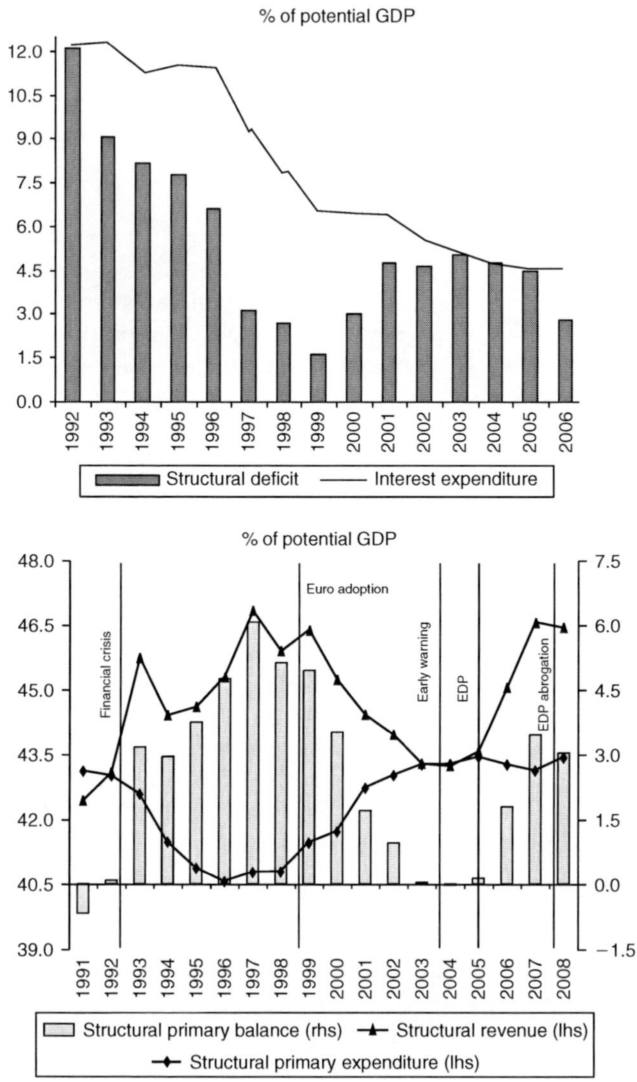

Figure 2.15 Italy – structural government deficit and its main determinants
Source: Commission services' calculations.

below the 3 per cent threshold triggered a new consolidation effort in a period of negative output gap.

With a tax burden that is already well above the euro-area average and perceived as very high in the political debate, curbing the growth of primary expenditure is the only way to ensure sound and sustainable public finances (see Chapter 4). Together with the savings in interest expenditure stemming from a resolute fiscal consolidation, this would also make additional resources available for more productive uses, in particular to enhance expenditure on knowledge acquisition, human capital and infrastructure, with a view to addressing the structural weaknesses of the economy.

Although the level of public expenditure in Italy is only slightly higher than in the rest of the euro area, the increase in its structural primary component since the euro adoption is not consistent with the need to rapidly reduce the very high public debt-to-GDP ratio, while avoiding a further increase in the tax burden. In particular, some items of public expenditure highlight the need for more effective mechanisms to control expenditure at local level, whereas others – namely public sector wages – exhibit trends that appear unrelated to the underlying economic conditions. Furthermore, the composition of public expenditure is biased towards a high cost of debt servicing and high pension spending, which takes its toll on more productive expenditure as well as other social spending. There is also evidence that the scope for improving the quality of services provided is large. In this context, curbing public expenditure growth while at the same time improving its quality can only be achieved by substantially improving the effectiveness and cost efficiency of public spending.

Against this background, the Italian public finances face three important challenges. First, it is crucial that they become sustainable in the long term, particularly in light of the heavy pressure stemming from a rapidly ageing population. Second, in an economic policy strategy aimed at addressing the structural weaknesses of the Italian economy and enhancing its efficiency, a wisely conducted fiscal policy can help reduce economic uncertainty, create more favourable conditions for investment and make room for enhanced expenditure on knowledge, human capital and infrastructure. Finally, in the context of EMU, public finances have an important role as a stabilisation tool. None of these challenges can be met without achieving first a resolute and durable fiscal consolidation. So, fiscal policy should remain restrictive until the achievement of a balanced budget.

2.4.2 The labour market

Employment growth, largely concentrated in the private, non-agricultural sector, has been the strong point of the Italian economy since the end of the 1990s. The employment rate gradually increased to more than 58 per cent of the working age population in 2006, up from 51 per cent in 1995, with significant progress for women. The unemployment rate fell below the euro-area average by 2003 and, in spite of negative cyclical conditions, continued declining to reach 6.1 per cent in 2007, from above 11 per cent in the mid-1990s. As also argued in Chapter 3, the wage moderation policies and the new flexibility afforded by the labour market reforms since the mid-1990s counted for a lot in these positive developments.

An incomes policy agreement that was signed by the social partners and the government in July 1993 introduced a two-tiered bargaining framework. The first tier is based on national labour contracts, the main purpose being to maintain the purchasing power of wages. The second tier is based on firm-level contracts, the main purpose of which was to distribute company-level productivity gains to workers. With the aim of curbing the inflation rate while protecting workers' purchasing power, the reform established that wage increases at the first, national level should no longer refer to past inflation but to the government's planned inflation rate. At the time of the renewal of the wage agreement, the gap between planned and actual domestic inflation would be taken into account.

It is widely recognised that the 1993 wage agreement effectively contributed to laying the basis for the structural reduction of inflation in Italy and its eventual entry into the euro area. Once in the euro area, wage growth was largely driven by the inflation targets set by the ECB at euro-area level, which *ex-post* resulted in lower than actual inflation. In particular, from 1999 until 2007, actual price growth has been around 2.2 per cent per year on average, which compares with an average planned inflation rate at around 1.5 to 1.6 per cent.

The effects of the incomes policy agreement are summarised in Figure 2.16. Growth in real earnings per employee for the total economy actually decreased in the period 1992–5 and grew by a modest 1 per cent on average in the period 1996–8. After the euro adoption, real wage growth remained broadly stable, with the major exception of wages in the public sector, which increased at a much faster pace.

In the period before euro adoption, real wages in Italy seriously lagged behind productivity (European Commission, 2008). As the single currency was created, however, Italy posted a sharp increase in real wages relative to productivity, but more as a result of a deceleration in productivity in this sector than of dynamic wages.[17] That is, the moderate real wage growth did not translate into a similarly favourable development in

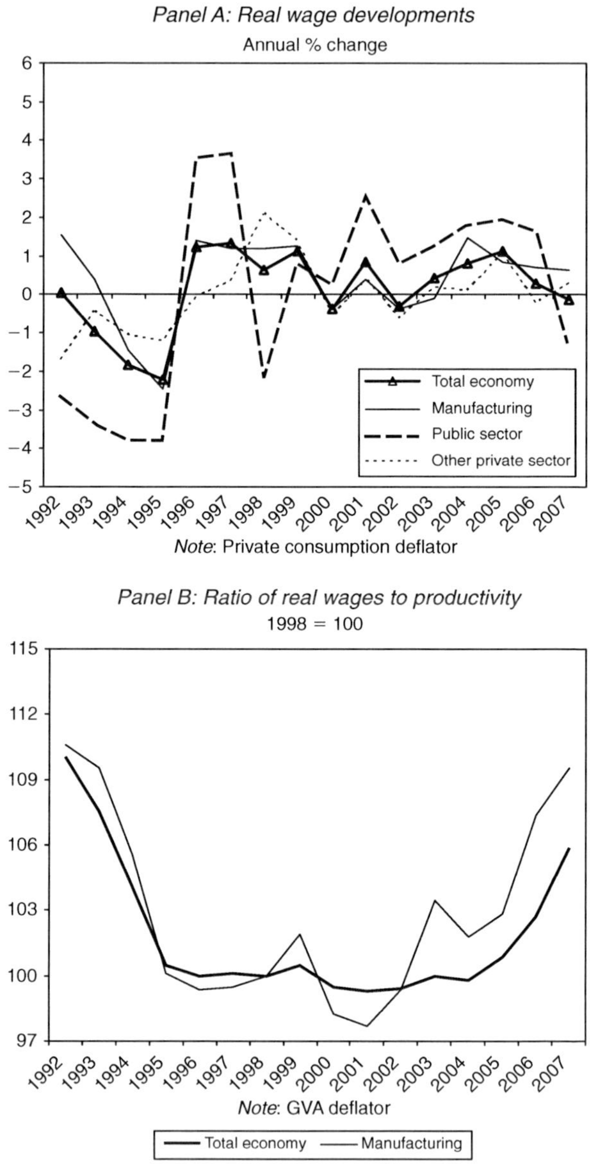

Figure 2.16 Italy – wage and productivity developments 1992–2007
Source: Commission services' calculations.

real unit labour costs because of the decline in labour productivity growth.

The nominal wage rigidity underlying this development is largely the reflection of an insufficient use of firm-level bargaining. The use of the second level of the two-tier system introduced by the 1993 agreement was insufficient and unbalanced in its diffusion by firm size, sector and geographical area. Bargaining at the firm level occurs mainly in the North and is more common in large, usually more unionised, firms. The two-tier system contributed to an increase in wage dispersion across sectors and between the North and South of Italy. Still, the widening of the wage spectrum has been insufficient to reflect the productivity differentials across regions and loosen regional imbalances. A change in the mix of national and firm-level contracts towards more decentralised bargaining may contribute to the reduction of the regional imbalances. It may also help reallocate resources towards high-growth sectors and activities.

The labour market reforms undertaken since 1997 have been along the lines of targeting flexibility of work contracts for new entrants, thus significantly reducing hiring and firing costs at the margin, while leaving the legislation on incumbent permanent employment unchanged. Although temporary contracts still provide a relatively small contribution to overall employment growth, this development considerably increased labour market segmentation, creating the risk of precariousness traps (see Boeri's comment in Chapter 3), and also because the Italian welfare system still does not provide generous support to unemployed people. The unemployment insurance system is characterised by a large number of schemes unevenly distributed across the different categories of workers as to eligibility conditions, replacement rates and duration of benefits, with little attention to 'making work pay' issues. The most generous schemes are confined to the minority of workers in large firms in the industrial sector. In this context, any measures aimed at rebalancing employment protection in the labour market should be part of a broader reform programme where an appropriate system of social shock absorbers and preventive policies is put in place, in a so-called 'flexicurity' approach.

2.4.3 Product market regulation and the business environment

In Italy, an overly regulated business environment and weak competitive pressures hamper adjustment by sheltering uncompetitive industries and firms. This weakens incentives to innovate and increase productivity. Product market competition intensified in the 1990s thanks to liberalisation of network industries and local services, public administration reform, extensive privatisation and active enforcement of competition legislation. Further steps to reduce barriers to entry, cut bureaucratic red tape, expand consumer choice and diminish rents in protected sectors were taken in 2006–7. In some sectors, namely telecommunications, prices have decelerated significantly. However, more incisive action is needed, given the scale of the challenge and the need to modernise Italy's industrial base. According to the OECD indicators of product market regulation, Italy remains one of the most strictly regulated countries among OECD countries, despite having made considerable progress.[18] In particular, the service sector appears to lack competitive pressure to resist cost increases and to encourage managerial and technological innovation. Accordingly, Italy records very high mark-ups (price-cost margins) particularly in the non-manufacturing sectors (Høj *et al.*, 2007). Entry barriers remain substantial in the professional services and the retail distribution sectors, despite various regulatory reforms over the years. A consequence of protected high-cost services is that input costs for the Italian tradable sector are relatively high and rise faster than those in major trading partners.

Administrative burdens and red tape associated with running a business are still considered to be major problems by firms. A particular problem seems to be the inefficiency of the judicial system, particularly in the area of civil justice and labour trials (Commissione Tecnica per la Finanza Pubblica, 2007a). For instance, the average length of a trial for non-execution of contracts is around four times as that in France and Germany. This factor plays a key role in the underdevelopment of capital markets, by inducing higher interest rates and lower availability of credit. As such, it can partly explain the scarce level of incoming FDI. It also has a sure impact on the birth, growth and survival rate of firms since it acts as an entry barrier and discourages investment; as such, it helps explain, at least in part, the prevalence of small enterprises in Italy. The inefficiency of the judicial system, particularly its slowness, also contributes to a *de facto* high degree of strictness of employment protection for permanent workers. Labour trials (first degree) have an average duration of two years in Italy. This compares with one year in France and six months in Germany.

The international competitiveness of the Italian industry is also affected by its structure and governance (OECD, 2005). The enterprise sector is still characterised by a prevalence of small firms, suggesting the existence of disincentives or obstacles for small firms to grow. Although small firms have traditionally been a source of dynamism, their limited resources appear to hamper their ability to invest in R&D and human capital. Furthermore, Italy's relatively low attractiveness as locational choice for FDI is probably due to the same factors that hamper domestic businesses: red tape, product and labour market rigidities, an inefficient public administration and infrastructural gaps.

2.4.4 Research and development (R&D) and education

Italy is notoriously lagging behind other developed countries in the fields of R&D and education. This is particularly unfortunate as both factors have been shown to be among the most significant determinants of differences in productivity growth. The latest figures, referring to 2005, show that Italy spent around 1.1 per cent of GDP on R&D activities, only half the EU-15 average. As mentioned above, low R&D may simply be symptomatic of the small size of Italian firms, but it also reflects an adverse industry composition, geared towards low R&D.

The comparison with other advanced economies is even less heartening as far education is concerned (see Chapter 1). Italy, especially the South, performs below the EU average, sometimes significantly below, in terms of educational attainment, quality of education, early school leaving and participation in training. Compared with other euro-area countries, an above-average proportion of the Italian population has only lower-secondary education, particularly among older workers (OECD, 2007a). Even though Italy spends comparatively high amounts per student up to upper secondary education, the results of the OECD Programme for International Student Assessment (PISA) show that 15-year-olds have attainments well below the average, in particular in mathematical and problem-solving skills. A high proportion of young people is neither in education nor in the labour force, suggesting a difficult school-to-work transition. As for tertiary education, a relatively small proportion completes it and the years spent in obtaining a qualification at this level are greater than average, raising the opportunity cost of tertiary education.

Yet, it is not that appropriate incentives to human capital investment are lacking at the individual level. In Italy, individuals who do not complete upper secondary education face considerable and increasing penalties in the labour market, in terms of unemployment, difficult transitions from school to work and earnings. By contrast, the labour-market benefits of tertiary education continue to be high, as people with tertiary qualifications command significantly higher salaries than those with only secondary education. Part of the problem may be related to the specialisation of Italian industries in low-tech sectors and the small size of Italian firms, which may hamper the demand for high-skill workers and reduce R&D capabilities. There is also an issue of efficiency of public spending and the choice to spend significant resources on a large pool of poorly paid teachers is not obvious (OECD, 2007a). At tertiary level, academic appointments lack transparency, there are considerable barriers to entry for young professors, promotion is not always linked to performance and resources devoted to research are significantly lower than in other advanced economies.

2.4.5 The financial sector

An efficient financial sector can facilitate cross-border integration, promote financial development and thereby enhance not only economic performance but also increase the adjustment capacity of euro-area economies. In particular, international portfolio diversification can reduce the effects of country-specific shocks.

In the 1990s, the Italian banking system carried out a rapid and far-reaching transformation: privatisations and wide productivity differentials between banks led to a process of mergers and restructurings that is still underway. With the reduction in the number of banks, their average size and the overall concentration of the industry increased, but so did competition. Recent developments in the Italian banking sector have been positive (OECD, 2007b). Financial soundness indicators have generally improved, and credit growth has remained robust. Under the new Saving Law, responsibility for regulating anticompetitive behaviour has been transferred to the Antitrust Authority, and the coordination between different supervisory authorities has been intensified. The Bank of Italy's Statute has been modified to increase transparency and accountability and to improve the overall governance of the bank. The Bank of Italy is promoting important regulatory reforms that favour replacing detailed rules with supervisory principles and self-regulatory mechanisms. Signs of greater contestability in the system, including by cross-border players, are encouraging (20 per cent of total assets are now in the hands of foreign institutions). Other reforms that have been adopted in recent years and should produce benefits soon are: the reform of company law allowing, *inter alia*, the adoption of new, innovative governance structures, the reform of bankruptcy law that should lead to a significant reduction of the duration of procedures, improving flexibility and recovery rates. The July 2006 and January 2007 decree laws (Bersani decree I and II) introduced new measures to enhance competition and serve consumer interests in the banking and insurance industry.

Overall, it can be said that there has been a marked improvement in this area in Italy. Yet there are still challenges because the financial sector still relies heavily on bank intermediation. In particular, non-banking financing sources such as venture capital, crucial to the growth of new firms, are underdeveloped.

Banking services are characterised by higher average prices of basic services, higher staff costs and lower efficiency than the EU average. In 2007, the Italian Competition Authority released the results of a sectoral investigation concluding that fees on bank accounts are the most expensive among major EU countries. An inquiry by the European Commission (2007b) on retail banking also found that banks in Italy reported among the highest levels of fees for both managing and closing accounts. Prices show enormous variability (customers pay up to 10 times more for the same service) and net interest margins have been slightly above the EU average.

Capital markets are developing rapidly, but remain undersized. A range of key indicators are below the euro-area average, some considerably so: the number of listed companies and the ratio of their total capitalisation to GDP; the proportion of private equity investment dedicated to venture capital operations and start-ups; the capacity of small firms with innovative projects to raise funds on the capital markets; and the role of institutional investors, as pension funds. This situation is due to various factors, namely: bankruptcy and debt recovery procedures remain lengthy and the enforcement of corporate governance provisions has shortcomings. A history of high tax evasion may compound these problems.

2.5 Conclusions and the way ahead

After the adoption of the single currency, the Italian economy continued to underperform the euro-area average in terms of real GDP growth. Structural weaknesses feeding into low productivity growth and high public indebtedness still represent major challenges for the Italian economy.

The analysis in this chapter argues that the major problem that the Italian economy encountered in the past decade was the pronounced and protracted slowdown in productivity, which was widespread in most sectors of the economy. The inability by the Italian economy to adjust smoothly and efficiently through the market-based adjustment channels that are available in the context of a monetary union is primarily due to this factor. In particular, as the unfavourable productivity developments were not, or could not be, translated into an adjustment in labour costs, the country has lost external competitiveness at a steady pace since the mid-1990s. In other words, even in a context of overall wage moderation, cost pressures in Italy mounted relative to the euro-area average because of a more marked decline in productivity growth. The productivity slowdown has deep-seated structural roots, which the loss of monetary independence simply brought forcibly to light. However, its impact on both domestic demand and external competitiveness was mitigated by the higher labour accumulation and the monetary convergence bonus from which Italy benefited to a greater extent than other euro-area countries. Looking ahead, prospects for the Italian economy appear particularly challenging, as further support from significant decreases in real interest rates can no longer be expected. In order to ensure that the market channels of adjustment unfold in a smoother and timelier manner, Italy has no choice other than to use structural reforms to improve the functioning of labour, product and services markets, including the continued fostering of a more dynamic financial sector, so as to boost competition. In doing so, any possible complementarities and synergies between the various policy approaches should be used to maximum effect. Structural reforms would provide firms, particularly those in the non-tradable sector, with the incentives to operate efficiently, invest in innovative technologies and undertake organisational change. More rapid changes in price and wage competitiveness would also be desirable, especially where the wage response to firm- or sector-specific shocks is concerned. That is, a bargaining structure that is closer to the level where price and investment decisions are taken would contribute to restoring competitiveness. A permanent consolidation of public finances is a prerequisite in this strategy. It would make room for the effective operation of the automatic stabilisers in the event of adverse economic shocks. It would also create more favourable conditions for private and foreign investment and room for enhanced expenditure on research and development, human capital and infrastructure.

The run-up to the euro was characterised by significant steps towards reforming the labour market, liberalising protected sectors, privatising state-owned companies and removing the excessive regulatory burden. The political economy argument that helped push these initiatives through was the prospect of euro-area entry, which was expected to be conducive to a more stable economy. However, by the time of the euro adoption, the reform process was far from complete. Since then, the drive for reform has slowed down, except perhaps in the financial sector and despite some recent steps towards the liberalisation of some services and products sectors. A factor that may have allayed the urgency of structural reform is the EMU start-up shock that reduced risk premia. A persistent problem is one of implementation of economic reforms. Given the tradition of fragmented coalition governments and the difficulty of finding social consensus, the political economy for structural reform and healthy public finances must rely on raising public awareness of the related benefits.

In this context, the Lisbon strategy seeks to accelerate structural reform through greater policy coordination, open advocacy of reform benefits and, to some extent, peer pressure on the member states. Italian policymakers should use this opportunity to carry the reform process forward.

Notes

1. The growth performance of the 'Mezzogiorno' has been substantially below that of the other Objective 1 regions in the 15 'old' member states of the EU: GDP per capita grew on average by 2.8 per cent per year, as against 4.5 per cent in Objective 1 regions, over the decade 1995–2004, and by only 0.4 per cent (3.8 per cent in Objective 1 regions) between 2000 and 2004. This development is largely – but not exclusively – due to the growth slowdown of the overall Italian economy. Indeed, taking account only of the differences between per capita GDP growth at regional and national levels, growth in the Southern regions has been 0.4 per cent on average per year in the period 1995–2000 and 0 per cent in the period 2000–2004, as against 1 per cent and 0.5 per cent, respectively, in the other Objective 1 regions of EU–15 (SVIMEZ, 2007).
2. European Commission (1999).
3. This result is confirmed in Daveri and Jona-Lasinio (2005), using a different measure of quality-adjusted labour input, which assumes a direct relationship between skills and occupations and ranks occupations by their skill intensity.
4. In 1999–2006, the standard deviation of output gap differentials relative to the euro area for Italy was lower than for most of the other euro-area countries.
5. The analysis of the real interest rate channel is a complicated subject. In this context, the relevance of real interest rates based on past inflation experience rather than on expected inflation and the time horizon of inter-temporal consumption and investment decisions by households and firms are also important. For a discussion of these issues, see European Commission (2006).
6. The introduction of euro notes and coins in 2002 also entailed a jump in perceived inflation, based on which perceived *ex-ante* real interest rates could have resulted lower than measured *ex-post* real interest rates.
7. In particular, concerning the latter factor, non-Keynesian effects may have indeed helped to lessen the direct negative effects on demand stemming from fiscal retrenchment in the 1990s. However, as fiscal adjustment was achieved mainly through lower interest spending, higher taxes and lower investment expenditure, such effects may have been relatively small (European Commission, 1999; Larch, 2004).

8. The saving rate, i.e., gross savings in percentage of gross disposable income, of the households and NPISH sector fell from around 27 per cent at the beginning of the 1990s to a trough of 14.2 per cent in 2000.
9. This latter effect was also confirmed in the model-based analysis in European Commission (2006), which used a new Keynesian dynamic stochastic general equilibrium (DSGE) model.
10. Bassanetti and Zollino (2007) point to a marginal propensity to consume out of housing net worth in the range of 1.5 to 2 cents compared with 4 to 6 cents for non-housing.
11. In Italy, the gross operating surplus in nominal terms increased on average by around 3 per cent per year between 1999 and 2006 as against more than 4 per cent in Germany, 3.5 per cent in France and 7.5 per cent in Spain.
12. Econometric estimates (IMF, 2007c; Alberola *et al.*, 1999) point to equilibrium, if not slight undervaluation, of Italy's REER at the time of euro adoption.
13. The pattern and degree of specialisation of exports is measured here by the Balassa index, defined as the ratio of a country's share in global exports of a given sector and the country's share in global exports of the economy as a whole. The technological content of exports was obtained based on a taxonomy developed by the OECD that regroups ISIC sectors into high, medium-high, medium-low, and low manufactures on the basis of the ratio of R&D expenditure in value added, following an OECD taxonomy.
14. According to registry data from the Chambers of Commerce, between 2001 and 2006 the overall balance in the number of registrations and deletions of manufacturing firms was negative by more than 50,000. The reduction was more accentuated in the Centre/North and in traditional sectors (in particular, textile and clothing firms and leather products and the footwear sector).
15. The MCI is an index number calculated from a linear combination of the short-run interest rate and the exchange rate. As a rule, the weights reflect the relative effects of the respective MCI component on aggregate demand. The weights are subject to estimation uncertainty, which may imply large confidence intervals for the parameters. In addition, different models can result in quite different MCI weights. Moreover, the appropriate relative weights may vary over time, while the parameters used in the calculations of the MCI are normally held constant.
16. This is an *ex-post* assessment. At the time, due to expectations of high economic growth, real-time cyclical conditions were estimated to be broadly neutral despite robust real GDP growth over 1999–2001.
17. In the same euro-area period, real gross fixed capital formation in manufacturing contracted on average by around 0.5 percentage points per year.
18. See the OECD Product Market Regulation Database (www.oecd.org/eco/pmr).

Comment on Chapter 2

Vittorio Grilli
Ministry of Economy and Finance, Rome

Italy's adjustment to monetary union and a better understanding of the country's many structural challenges were among Riccardo Faini's key research interests. This additional contribution by Bardone and Reitano goes to the core of the problem.

The run-up to the euro and its adoption do not appear to have had a homogeneous impact on the economies of member countries. In general, smaller euro-area countries have enjoyed relatively strong growth. This favourable outcome could be partly related to some catching-up effects (such as in Spain and Ireland) or to higher benefits from enhanced economic integration for countries more open to external trade (such as in the Netherlands). Growth performance of larger euro-area countries has been less satisfactory. French GDP is now around 35 per cent above that at the beginning of the 1990s. During the same period, in the US GDP has increased by 62.5 per cent, in the UK by almost 55 per cent. Growth in Germany and in Italy has been even more disappointing. In these two countries, GDP is now only around 27.5 and 25 per cent higher than at the beginning of the past decade. The chapter by Bardone and Reitano is an interesting review of the possible reasons for Italy's relatively weak performance during the past 15 years and any possible impact of the adoption of the single currency. In line with previous work by the European Commission, they identify a real interest rate and a competitiveness channel to explain countries' performance.

Italy has benefited from the real interest rate channel, especially through Ricardian-equivalence-like effects. Since 1995, when Italy's commitment to nominal and financial convergence became clearer, real interest rates started to decline. The decline had two effects: a) it lowered financing costs for companies and households; b) it contributed to the consolidation of Italy's public finances. Lower interest rates and an increase in the primary surplus made it possible to enhance public savings. The private sector perception that this improvement was structural became also stronger. As a result, private savings declined thus contributing to higher growth. In the second half of the 1990s, average growth in Italy was just below 2 per cent compared to an average of around 1.25 per cent in the first half of the same decade. However, when convergence was achieved, Italy's real interest rates approximately stabilised at the euro area average and, thus, their positive impact on growth waned. Other countries enjoyed stronger growth because of a more dynamic external sector, either as they could fully exploit the benefits of stronger integration or thanks to enhanced competitiveness.

By contrast, Italy's competitiveness has continued to deteriorate, exporting firms have suffered and resources have been shifted from tradable to non-tradable sectors. Italy's effective exchange rate has appreciated by almost 35 per cent in real terms since the beginning of the decade, whereas that of France is up by only 3 per cent and that of Germany has actually depreciated by 2 per cent. Italy's export market share in world trade has decreased by almost 1 percentage point over the past ten years, that of Germany has remained stable, that of the Netherlands has increased by around 0.75 percentage points and it is now higher than Italy's. The share of the value added of industry excluding construction over the total has shrunk to around 21.5 per cent in 2006 compared with 25 per cent in the middle of the 1990s.

Price competitiveness deteriorated partly because downward rigidities have hampered wage adjustments in line with productivity developments and partly because barriers to international trade have been progressively lifted. Since the mid-1990s, total factor productivity has stagnated in Italy while labour productivity has increased by 0.5 percentage points only as capital has been growing slightly more than labour. Thus, wage moderation since the early 1990s was not enough to balance the deterioration in price competitiveness. At the same time, non-wage costs have decreased significantly for companies and this could explain why labour demand remained strong during the past decade.

Moreover, during this period the role of emerging countries has increased in world markets. In the mid-1990s the Uruguay Round was completed. It eliminated trade barriers and reduced subsidies in many sectors. In 1995, the World Trade Organization was created and at the end of 2001 China was admitted. China became a global player: in 2006, its world export market share was more than 8 per cent compared with 3.25 per cent a decade earlier.

While the impact of these new actors has been felt everywhere in the industrialised world, Italy's trade specialisation made the country's economy more exposed to international competition. For the most part, production was based on traditional, 'mature', low-skilled products (textiles, shoes, furniture, etc.). Thus, companies exporting lower-quality products increasingly had to face direct competition from emerging countries with similar competitive advantages.

Have product specialisation and trade pattern become more favourable over the past few years? To some extent the answer is positive. First, Italy's traditional strength in machine tools has been maintained if not reinforced in the past decade. Demand for Italy's investment goods is strong not only in 'mature' markets such as Germany but also in booming ones such as China. Furthermore, there has been an ongoing shift towards higher-quality consumer products where Italy has a comparative advantage (textiles, for instance). Indeed, since the beginning of this decade, Italy's export market share in value terms has declined much less than in quantity terms. This might reflect quality improvements of Italian exports and increasing specialisation towards higher-quality products. For example, Italy's unit values have been rising more than Chinese ones for goods exported to countries like France and Germany (Istituto per il Commercio Estero, 2007). Moreover, a number of indicators suggest that over time quality difference between Italy's products and those of emerging markets has risen (Lanza and Quintieri, 2007).

A process of 'creative destruction' has also been at play. Smaller, less efficient, companies producing lower-quality products have been priced out of the market by competition from emerging countries. Small companies unable to grow or to exploit network benefits have suffered and many have closed down (Unioncamere and Istituto Tagliacarne, 2007). At the same time, more of the lower-skill production by larger companies has been outsourced elsewhere. The end result is a more competitive industry with surviving companies aiming at product innovation, thus maintaining stronger market power and the ability to charge higher prices for their products.

Of course, it is too early to conclude that the worst for Italy is over. First, more time, data and evidence are needed to reach more solid conclusions on the changing and supposedly upgraded specialisation model of Italian companies. Second, competition from emerging markets could 'upgrade' as well very soon. While traditional sectors could well remain the backbone of the Italian economy for a long time, Italy cannot postpone for long those changes needed to become a more attractive place for investment and human capital. This means improving its educational system, infrastructure, regulation and the public administration, and especially the security and judicial systems. It also means speeding up the consolidation of public finances to make room for lower taxes. The window of opportunity for these changes is constantly narrowing as emerging markets are getting closer to the top.

Daniel Gros
Centre for European Policy Studies (CEPS)

This is a wide-ranging chapter which touches on the major reasons why the Italian economy has so far 'underperformed the euro-area average in terms of real GDP growth'. It is difficult to disagree with the judgment of the authors that 'the Italian economy has so far failed to adjust smoothly and efficiently through the adjustment channels that are available in the context of a monetary union'. It might thus be useful to ask oneself why the country has failed to adjust.

One key indicator of the problems of the Italian economy is the loss of competitiveness Italy has experienced since the start of EMU. This issue has been extensively discussed among experts, but it has never aroused much debate at the political level or the attention of the broader public. The loss of competitiveness is apparently not considered a key issue for the country. This is in sharp contrast with the situation in Germany, where the issue of competitiveness has dominated policy-making and public debate for almost a decade. What is behind this fundamental difference in attitude? One explanation might be history: Germany has a much stronger industrial base and this is not the first time the country has had to live with a hard currency by lowering costs.

However, there might be another, deeper, reason why the social and political system of Italy has been, and probably will continue to be, slow to adjust to external challenges. The basic reason is simply that the Italian economy is much less open than that of Germany (and of most other EU member countries). The figure below illustrates this by comparing the degree of openness of the three large euro-area economies. The degree of openness is measured here by the average of the share of exports and imports (goods plus services) in GDP. This measure is designed to show the extent to which a country's economy is affected by international

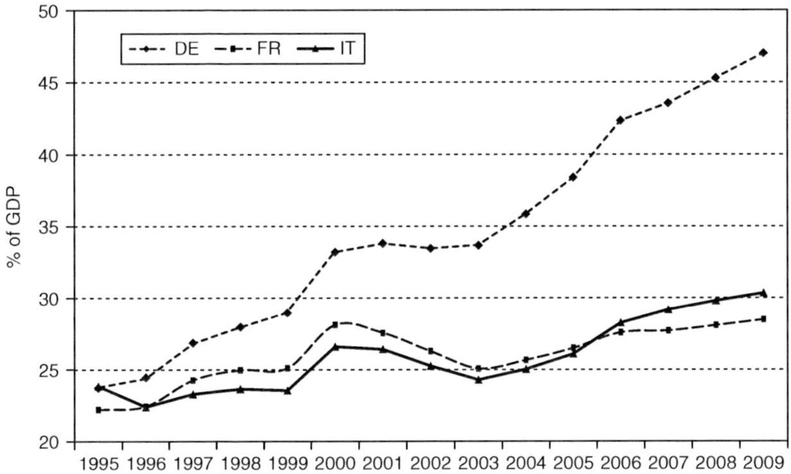

Figure 2.17 Average of exports and imports
Source: AMECO databank, European Commission.

trade (whether it has an external surplus or deficit does not matter in this context). The figures clearly shows the gulf that has opened between Germany and Italy (and to some extent also France) over the last decade.

The euro and globalisation seem to have led only to a minor increase in the openness of Italy whereas Germany's degree of openness has almost doubled. As there is no indication that this trend will reverse soon, it is likely that the difference in the drivers of economic policy will persist and even increase. Germany's policy is likely to become even more outward looking, primarily based on the idea that it is important to preserve the competitiveness of the country, whereas in Italy this consideration is less pervasive since the economy remains much less open to trade.

The large gap appears surprising in light of the similar starting position: in 1995, when preparations for EMU were seriously under way and China was not yet an actor in the global trading system, Italy and Germany started from a very similar position, with trade accounting for about 25 per cent of GDP. However, their evolution since then has been totally different. Italy's openness has barely moved, whereas that of Germany has soared to over 40 per cent.[1]

This suggests that one of the difficulties for Italy to adjust to the EMU is that its economy is less open, so that it is more difficult to find a constituency that supports the necessary adjustments. Both employers' federations and trade unions realise much more easily in Germany than in Italy that excessive wages threaten jobs because in Italy the link between jobs and a competitive price level is not so direct and important.

A low level of trade integration is not the only indicator of Italy's relative lack of openness: another, well known, indicator is that foreign direct investment (FDI) is much smaller in Italy than in either France or Germany. The stock of FDI amounts to only 14 per cent of GDP in Italy, compared to 28 per cent in Germany (and over 50 per cent in France).

Does it matter that Italy is so closed? It does, because reforms are always politically costly and tend to be undertaken only when there are strong outside pressures to change. The low productivity growth emphasised by Bardone and Reitano can only be overcome through reforms that confront entrenched interest groups. It seems that in Italy the pressure from international trade is still not strong enough to achieve this. There is thus a real risk that the gap between Italy and its major trading partners in Europe will continue widening.

Note

1. This is partly a return to a historical pattern: Germany had traditionally been significantly more open to international commerce than Italy, but this difference disappeared after unification when Germany concentrated on its internal problems.

3

Two Italian Puzzles: Are Productivity Growth and Competitiveness Really so Depressed?*

Lorenzo Codogno
Ministry of Economy and Finance, Rome

Abstract

This chapter focuses on two apparent puzzles for the Italian economy: i) How can an extremely poor performance in productivity growth be compatible with strong employment growth?; and ii) How can a sharp decline in competitiveness come along with higher export prices and a general situation for exporters that looks far from desperate? Some possible explanations to these puzzles are presented in this chapter. Special factors such as regularisation of immigrant workers and the entry of low-skilled workers into the labour market may have contributed to depressing measured productivity and overstating the loss in competitiveness. Against the backdrop of Italy's structural problems, this chapter asks whether the Italian economy can adjust and grow. Medium-term prospects for the Italian economy remain challenging: for instance, growth in total factor productivity is still disappointingly low and competitiveness keeps deteriorating. However, there have been encouraging signs of improvement, notably the labour market has performed well over the past few years and in response to pressures from fierce foreign

* This chapter is based on the presentation made on 2 March 2007 in Brussels at the seminar 'Can Italy Adjust and Grow?' organised by the European Commission in memory of Riccardo Faini. I am especially grateful to Francesco Nucci, Flavio Padrini and Roberto Torrini for useful comments. Views expressed in this chapter do not necessarily reflect those of the Ministry of the Economy and Finance. E-mail address: lorenzo.codogno@tesoro.it

competition some adjustment appears to have taken place in the exposed sectors.

3.1 Introduction

Italy's per-capita GDP (in purchasing power standards) has lost ground over the years. Since the early 1990s, the gap has widened by 26 percentage points versus the US and 11 percentage points versus France (Figure 3.1). Such worsening has been significant since 2000. Italy's per-capita GDP is now about 10 per cent below that of the European Union 15 (EU–15).

Many economists and international organisations have attributed Italy's poor per-capita GDP growth to a number of structural impediments. These are at the root of the well-documented modest growth in productivity and the erosion in external competitiveness. Some pundits have even gone as far as suggesting that these developments may eventually undermine the solidity of monetary union and/or force Italy out of the single currency area.[1]

Commonly available indicators appear to suggest not only that problems related to productivity and competitiveness have played a role, but also that they are sizeable. Yet, despite the decline in per-capita GDP, Italy's export and overall economic performance does not appear to show

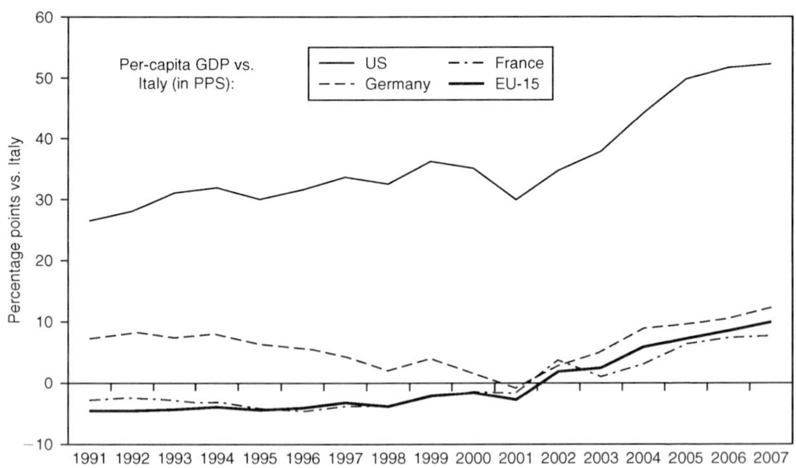

Figure 3.1 Italy's per capita GDP compared to other countries (in PPS)
Source: EU Commission, AMECO, own calculations.

the signs of the structural distress that these indicators would justify, thus raising some apparent puzzles about the Italian economy that the analysis in the present chapter sets out to unravel.

These puzzles are: i) how can an extremely poor performance in productivity growth be accompanied by strong employment growth?; and ii) how can the Italian economy reconcile a sharp decline in competitiveness with higher export prices and a general situation for exporters that looks far from desperate?

3.2 Low productivity growth and strong employment gains

Since the mid-1990s, Italy has achieved an impressive reduction in unemployment and a surge in employment, probably as a result of piecemeal reforms of the labour market. Unemployment has declined from levels above 11 per cent in the second half of the 1990s to a seasonally adjusted 6.5 per cent in the first quarter of 2008 after having reached 6.1 per cent in the first part of 2007. The employment rate of the working-age population increased from levels close to 52 per cent in the mid-1990s to around 58.3 per cent in the first quarter of 2008. Since the mid-1990s, and especially early in the current decade, a strong labour market performance has been accompanied by weak real GDP growth. A robust contribution of labour utilisation to GDP growth has been more than offset by a reduction in the contribution from labour productivity, resulting in weak overall GDP growth (in Figure 3.2 overleaf, labour productivity is given by the sum of total factor productivity and capital deepening).

By comparison, the US economy combined strong employment performance with acceleration in labour productivity during the same period. Also Italy combined employment growth with robust productivity gains in the 1980s. Then, following the 1992–3 currency crisis, employment collapsed and productivity jumped. Since the mid-1990s the situation has changed and weak productivity growth has been accompanied by persisting gains in employment (Figures 3.3, 3.4, 3.5 and 3.6). It was only in 2006 and for the first time since 1995 that employment growth was accompanied by an increase in labour productivity in the industrial sector.

In terms of levels, labour productivity used to be higher in Italy relative to the EU–15 and the US in the early 1990s. However, over the past few years growth in productivity has been modest, even negative in some years, and as a result the level of labour productivity is now low compared

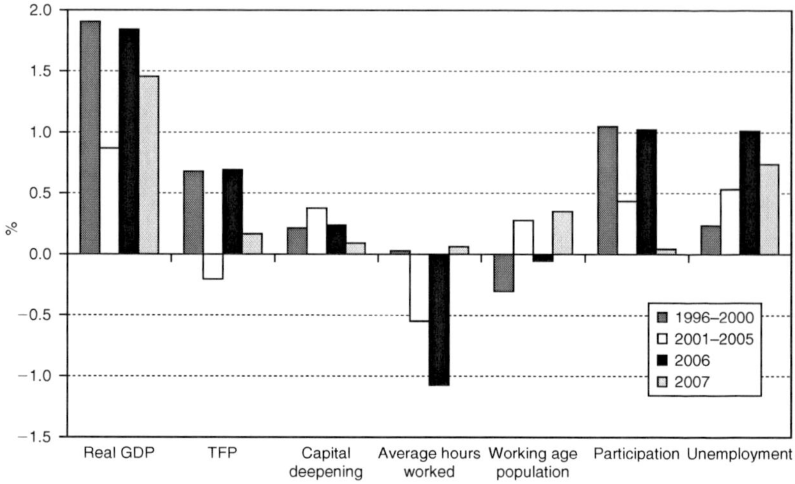

Figure 3.2 Growth accounting: annual growth rates and contributions to growth
Source: ISTAT, own calculations.

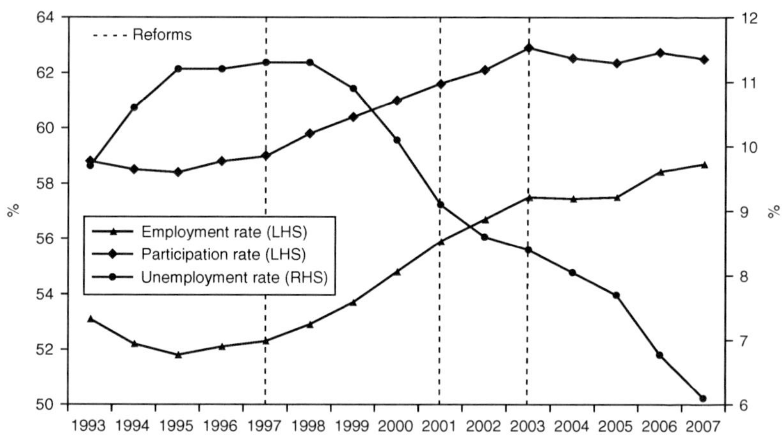

Figure 3.3 Labour market performance in Italy over the past 15 years
Source: ISTAT.

to that prevailing in the early 1990s, 1 per cent below the EU–15 average and almost 31 per cent below that for the US.[2]

There was a weak negative correlation between employment and labour productivity growth between the early 1980s and mid-1990s,

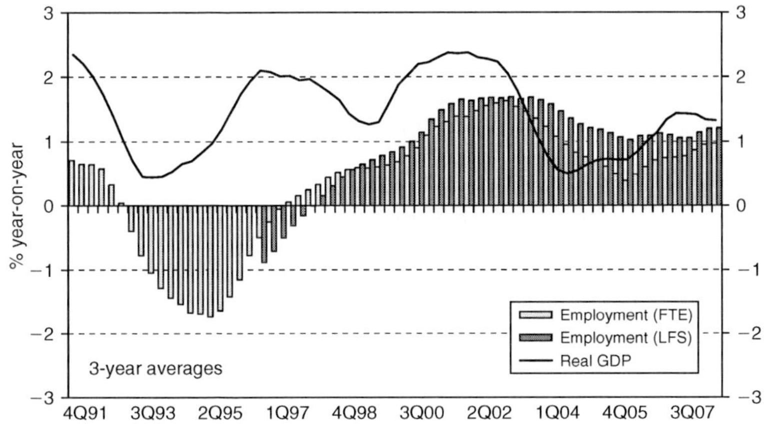

Figure 3.4 Real GDP versus employment growth
Source: ISTAT.
Note: FTE = full-time-equivalent workers. LFS = Labour Force Survey.

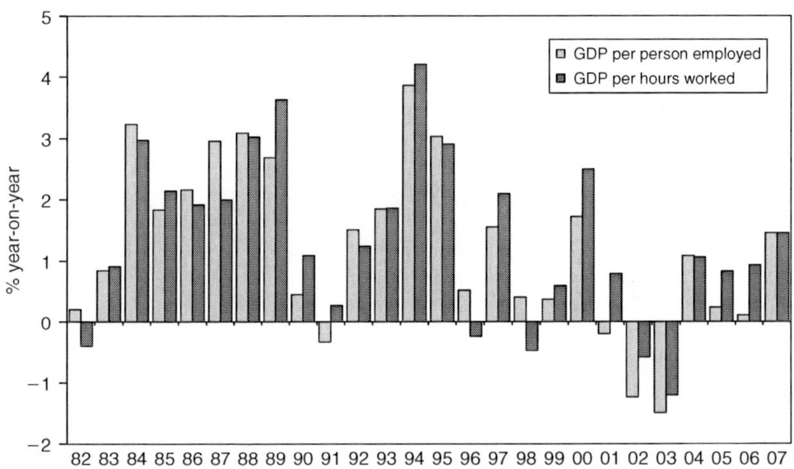

Figure 3.5 Labour productivity: a declining trend since the early 1990s
Source: ISTAT.

which has become significantly stronger since 1997 (Figures 3.7 and 3.8). Such a relationship should not be considered unusual, and indeed empirical evidence suggests that it has often been the case in many countries in the past. Yet, what is striking in Italy is the magnitude of the phenomenon and its relatively long duration.

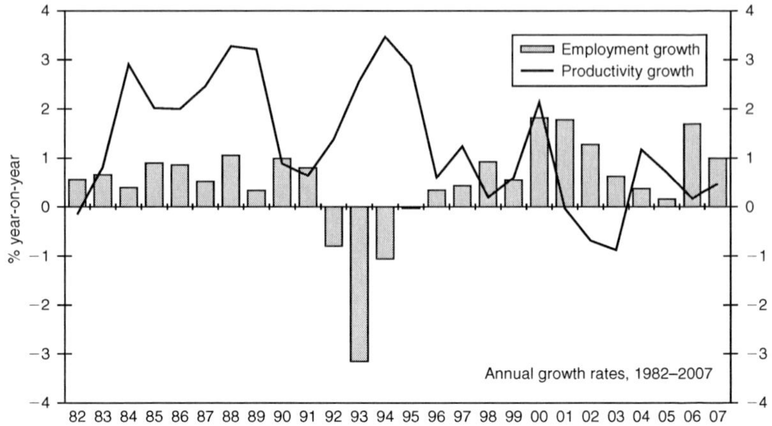

Figure 3.6 Employment versus productivity growth: the odd couple
Source: ISTAT and own calculations based on FTE workers.

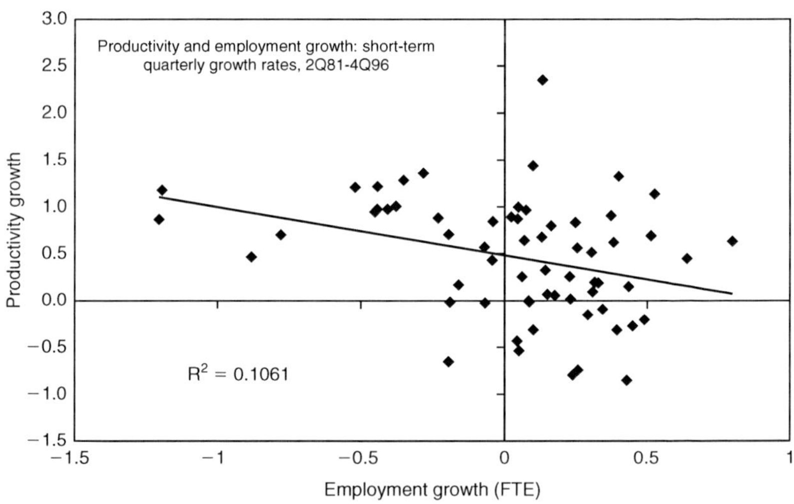

Figure 3.7 Productivity growth versus employment gains from 1981 to 1996
Source: ISTAT and own calculations based on FTE workers.

There are many possible explanations for this increasingly strong correlation: i) changes in technological progress; ii) cyclical fluctuations; iii) capital-labour substitution; iv) effects of migration; v) distortions in labour market statistics; and vi) a shift from industry to services.

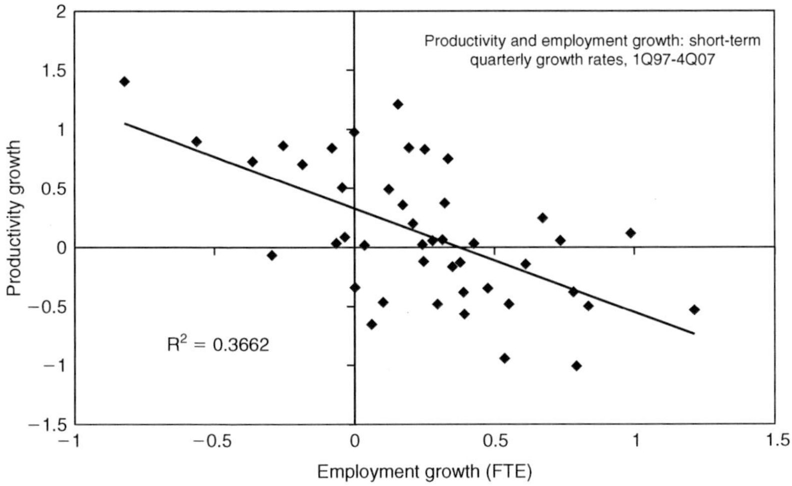

Figure 3.8 Productivity growth versus employment gains since 1997
Source: ISTAT and own calculations based on FTE workers.

3.2.1 Technological innovation

A decline in the pace of technological innovation in the economy could be at the root of the odd combination.

In economic growth theory, technological progress is neutral with respect to employment over the long run as it raises the productivity of both labour and capital (if we assume a Cobb-Douglas production function with elasticity of substitution between labour and capital equal to 1). The increase in labour productivity leads to a rise in real wages, with a broadly neutral impact on overall employment. Higher wages and an increase in the productivity of capital induce more investment in physical capital by companies. This eventually leads to a balanced growth path led by technological progress, with labour productivity, real wages and the capital intensity of production growing at the same rate. Technological progress reflects the overall efficiency with which factors of production are combined and is depicted by total factor productivity.[3] Once full employment is reached, employment would be expected to grow at the same pace as population in the long run. Equally, a decline in the pace of growth of technological progress should negatively affect productivity of labour and capital and be neutral for employment.

Although the question of whether technological advance is totally exogenous is still an open one, policy actions could contribute to influence total factor productivity. Given the declining trend in total factor productivity recorded in Italy over the past few years, it looks like policy measures have by and large failed to stimulate technological progress and enhance the trajectory of the balanced rate of productivity growth and the growth potential of the economy. By stimulating investments in the broader sense (physical capital, education and training, research and development) and by defining appropriate 'framework conditions' for businesses to operate and take full advantage of such investments, policy action can influence total factor productivity and, therefore, labour productivity. Some empirical work seems to support the view of weaker technological progress in recent years despite capital accumulation, as for example Bassanetti *et al.* (2004). Others point to the lack of innovation (Daveri, 2006). Beaudry and Collard (2002) show that a trade-off between productivity and employment growth may temporarily emerge when countries undergo a major endogenous technological change, which however is a factor that does not appear to have played a substantial role in the Italian case. Galí (1999) documented that positive technology shocks lead to a decline in labour input and tend to generate a short-term negative correlation between that variable and productivity, mainly due to rigidities in prices. This theory found support in the literature but appears to explain only short-term dynamics.

All in all, a decline in the pace of technological progress may partly explain the recorded trends in productivity (while being neutral for employment), although it can hardly be regarded as the most important factor in explaining Italy's performance.

3.2.2 Cyclical fluctuations

In the short run productivity growth can vary inversely with employment, for instance due to labour hoarding during recession or below-par economic activity or conversely when capital intensity cannot keep up with the growth of labour input during expansions. To some extent this may have played a role in Italy, especially at the beginning of the current decade. Still, labour hoarding seems to be more useful in explaining the cyclical behaviour of productivity rather than the divergent trend in productivity and employment growth, especially over such a long period of time.

3.2.3 Capital-labour substitution

In the medium term, labour productivity and employment can also deviate from the balanced growth path due to capital-labour substitution. If

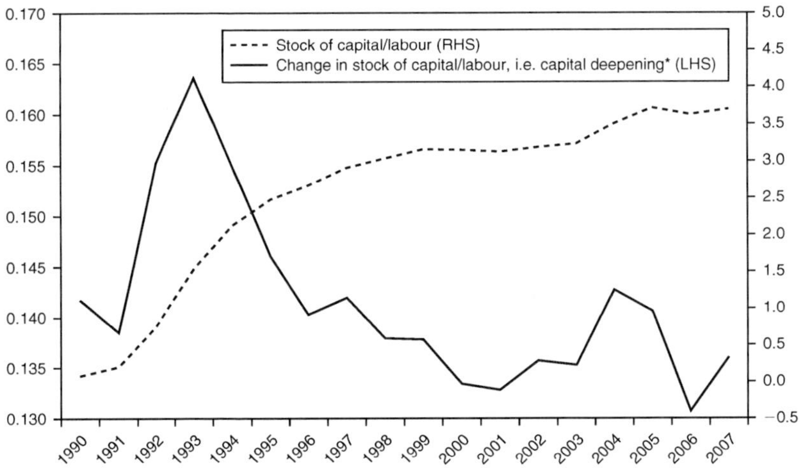

Figure 3.9 Labour versus capital utilisation
Source: ISTAT and own calculations.

employment grows faster than the amount of capital, labour productivity growth would temporarily be below the balanced rate. This should be regarded as a temporary phenomenon and not a trade-off. In fact, a higher employment rate implies an increase in per-capita GDP and no negative long-term implications for productivity growth in the *existing* workforce. However, the entry of less productive 'marginal workers' temporarily depresses labour productivity.

The effectiveness of labour market reforms implemented in Italy could have determined a capital-labour substitution, even if the lower interest rates that have prevailed since the run-up to monetary union should have reduced the user cost of capital. Since the early 1990s there has been a slowdown in the growth rate of the ratio of the stock of capital to labour, i.e., capital deepening, possibly as a result of less capital-intensive technologies and activities and the expansion of the services sector where labour input is prevalent (Figure 3.9). This evidence is consistent with capital-labour substitution. Labour could have become cheaper relative to capital and more flexible as a factor of production. While not changing the long-term path for growth, this shift may have explained the somewhat odd behaviour of productivity and employment.

At first glance, the empirical evidence does not appear to support the hypothesis of cheaper labour. Available measures of nominal unit labour costs[4] suggest that Italy has become less competitive compared to

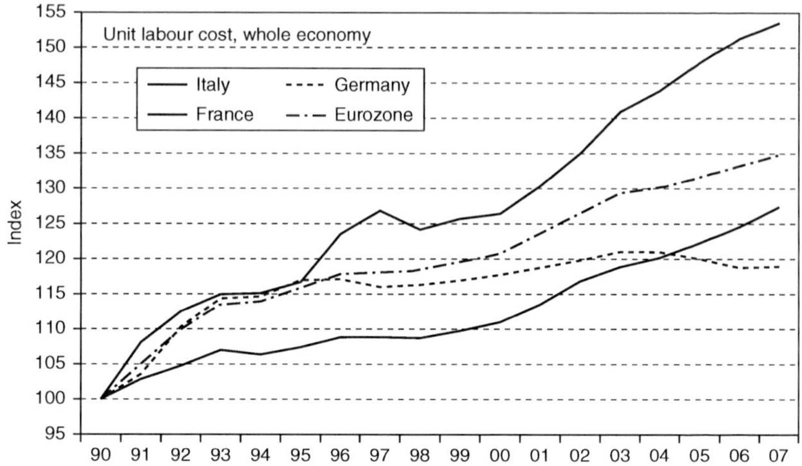

Figure 3.10 Nominal unit labour costs, whole economy
Source: EU Commission, AMECO and own calculations.

other major European countries over the past few years (Figure 3.10). This mainly reflects inflation differentials, especially after monetary union, and a relatively disappointing performance in labour productivity growth, while real compensation per employee has not diverged significantly from that of other major European countries. In 1999–2006, growth in real compensation per employee was on average 0.4 per cent in Italy versus 1.0 per cent in France, 1.0 per cent in Germany, –0.7 per cent in Spain and 0.6 per cent in the euro area. Growth in nominal unit labour cost was instead 2.6 per cent in Italy, 2.9 per cent in France, 1.9 per cent in Germany, 3.1 per cent in Spain and 2.6 per cent in the euro area over the same period.[5] Therefore, the first impression would run counter to the idea of cheaper labour as a factor of production relative to other countries.

The share of wages on value added does not provide support to the idea of cheaper labour either. This share has declined since the late 1970s (Figure 3.11) and it was low by international standards at the beginning of the 1990s (Bassanetti *et al.,* 2006). Since the beginning of the current decade, however, there has been a sharp pickup, partly due to poor cyclical conditions (the share of wages on value added tends to follow a cyclical pattern and rise during downturns), partly to a rebound driven by manufacturing from historically low levels and partly

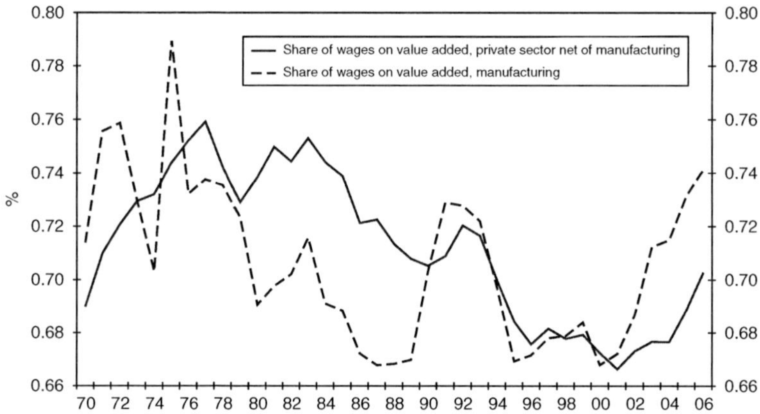

Figure 3.11 Wages versus unit labour costs: high despite moderation
Source: Bank of Italy series based on ISTAT data. Data are at factor cost net of real estate rentals and adjusted for self-employed by attributing to self-employed the average cost of the relevant sectors. The private sector is calculated net of the public administration, health care and education sectors.

to continuing strong growth in employment. Also, a still rigid and protected labour market for insiders and the two-layer bargaining system not allowing downward wage flexibility have prevented a more pronounced moderation in compensation growth which would have put it more in line with the poor productivity developments that have prevailed since the beginning of the decade.

However, it is the cost of the *marginal* worker that counts for the hiring decisions by companies and this cost has declined significantly in Italy over the past few years, notwithstanding relatively high *average* cost. In fact, labour market reforms in Italy have only been partial and they have generated a dual market, opening a gap in earnings and employment flexibility between insider workers and new labour market entrants. Insider workers' jobs are protected and their wages are downwardly rigid due to the wage negotiation system and the trade unions' objective function, while greater flexibility in working arrangements has been allowed for new entrants. In addition, policy has been oriented at reducing youth unemployment, thus allowing further reduction in the cost of hiring young workers (for example, through cuts in social security contributions and tax credits). Both hiring conditions (increased use of temporary contracts) and wages (downward flexibility) have made for a fall in the relative price of labour at the margin and thus a substitution of capital for labour, benefiting employment.

This story is well documented in Brandolini *et al.* (2007). The trigger for reforms was the withdrawal of the Italian lira from the EMS on 17 September 1992. The severe financial crisis made for a steep downturn in economic activity (GDP growth was –0.9 per cent in 1993), with a loss of more than 860,000 jobs (3.3 per cent) in six quarters (1,080,000 units from 1991 to 1995). It was the most dramatic employment crisis since the Second World War. This called for emergency policy measures on the budget side but also set the stage for the all-important incomes policy agreement of 23 July 1993.[6] The agreement included the abolition of the wage indexation mechanism (*scala mobile*) and introduced a two-tier bargaining system, with industry-wide national contracts devoted to protect purchasing power and company-level contracts devoted to performance-related pay rises. These changes were instrumental in abating inflation and, by introducing a framework of cooperation among social partners, set the stage for a major change in the Italian labour market. Since the early 1990s, strong labour demand in the business sector has sustained net job creation in the face of weaker output growth. Brandolini *et al.* (2007) show that greater reliance on fixed-term contracts contributed significantly to restrain growth in labour cost.[7] They conclude that available evidence supports the idea of a shift in the relative price of labour versus capital compared to the previous expansion.[8]

Rosolia and Torrini (2007) find evidence that entry conditions in the labour market deteriorated since the early 1990s, after substantial improvement between the mid-1970s and the late 1980s. They document a decline of about 12 per cent in real weekly wages of male workers who entered the labour market at age 21–22 between 1992 and 2004. The decline is 4 per cent for entry at age 25–26.[9] They also find that the age/earning profile experienced during the working life of cohorts that entered the labour market after 1992 is broadly unchanged over time, i.e., younger cohorts do not experience any catching up. Therefore, the entry loss entails a persistent loss with respect to previous cohorts. The wage gap between old and young workers went from 20 per cent in the late 1980s to 35 per cent in the early 2000s. The behaviour of economy-wide wages have not matched the weakness experienced in entry wages, thus contributing to the development of a two-tier market over time and a 'generation gap'. These findings do not include new working arrangements of jobs as independent contractors, with less favourable conditions than the standard dependent employment contracts, which have become increasingly important in recent years. Their inclusion would probably further widen the gap, especially considering that pension benefits accrued by these workers have been far less generous. Rosolia and Torrini (2007) exclude potential explanations offered by economic theory related to market forces, such as relative supply developments, technological change and the selection of less productive young workers in the labour market, leaving only changes in institutional arrangements as a possible explanation. The evidence is compelling for a structural break at the beginning of the 1990s that does not appear to be matched by similar developments in other European countries. Boeri and Garibaldi (2007) find a sizeable negative effect of temporary workers on changes in productivity at the firm level by using a panel of 1,300 firms between 1995 and 2000.

Lack of flexibility also has a cost attached to it. It is well-known that temporary contracts have been used as a device to bypass the rigid regulation of individual dismissal. In the early 1990s temporary contracts took off. Their share on total employment went from 6 per cent in 1993 to 13.2 per cent in 2007. Cipollone and Guelfi (2006) estimated the value that employers attach to flexibility. The results show that firms value the possibility of increasing by 1 per cent short-term workers as equivalent to a reduction in the range of 1.3–2.8 per cent in labour cost of open-ended workers. By extending these estimates to the whole economy, they conclude that for employers the almost 10 percentage-point increase in the share of fixed-term contracts among new hires recorded between 1995 and 2003 is equivalent to a 10.4–22.4 per cent wage-cost reduction. Given the elasticity of employment to wages, enhanced flexibility of the Italian labour market accounts for anything between 37 per cent and 80 per cent of employment growth in the private sector. These rough estimates suggest that the increased flexibility had a sizeable effect on overall labour costs, thereby contributing to change relative prices of labour versus capital.

Hence, the headline increase in average unit labour costs for the economy hides a substantial decline in labour costs at the margin, which helps to explain the apparent puzzle of poor productivity growth combined with substantial employment gains.

3.2.4 The impact of migration

In addition to the above labour demand effects, labour market reforms combined with a substantial influx of migrant workers and produced a labour supply shock. As economic theory would suggest, this has long-term effects on employment levels and no effect on productivity (if constant returns to scale are assumed; the effect would be negative if the marginal worker is assumed to be less productive as previously mentioned). Bank of Italy estimates[10] indicate a positive correlation between foreign presence and employment and an even stronger correlation for the participation rate. It looks as if the presence of foreigners, and especially foreign women, even enabled Italian women to better reconcile work with family responsibilities, thereby increasing participation in the labour market.

In the period 2002–4 a significant influx of immigrants was officially recorded. The influx increased from 151,932 in 2001 to 411,970 in 2002, 380,737 in 2003, 266,829 in 2005 and 237,614 in 2006.[11] The total number of foreigners residing in Italy was 2,938,922 as of 1 January 2007 and, according to the latest labour force survey, the number of foreigners in employment was 1,519,000 in the first quarter of 2008. In 2007, foreign residents accounted for more than 65 per cent (154,000 units) of additional employment. The employment rate of working-age foreigners is 81 per cent for men and 50.5 per cent of women, significantly higher than that for the native population and this is only partly explained by demographics. Resident foreigners made up 6.4 per cent of total employment recorded in 2007, with peaks of more than 10 per cent in the hotel and restaurant sector and in construction, and more than a quarter of women employed in services to households and other social services. These data show that the phenomenon is sizeable. Thus, by having long-term positive effects on employment levels, the labour-supply shock is believed to have indirectly contributed to the widening gap between employment and productivity growth.

3.2.5 Distortions in labour market statistics

The large influx of immigrant workers and regularisation of both foreign illegal workers already in Italy and national illegal workers may have caused statistical distortions. The Italian Statistical Office (ISTAT) estimates the unobserved components of GDP and employment, including the output of undeclared workers. This is done according to the rules established within the European System of Accounts (ESA) 1995 and by using a variety of statistical sources and techniques. The estimates of total value added by the statistical office are obtained by multiplying labour units by per-capita value-added. Therefore, if undeclared workers are properly estimated by the statistical office, the level and dynamics of employment, output and productivity in national accounts should not be affected. For instance, regularisation of illegal immigrants should mostly result in reclassification of labour inputs from undeclared to declared,[12] leaving relevant national account aggregates

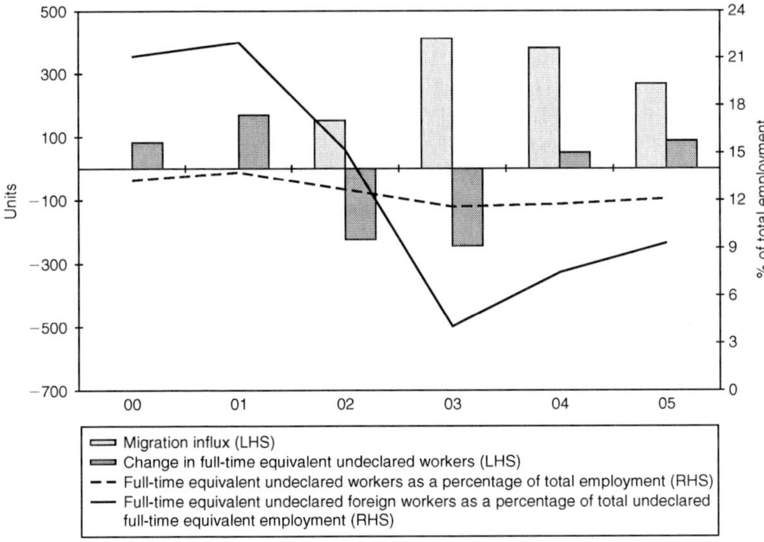

Figure 3.12 Migration influx versus changes in full-time equivalent employment
Source: ISTAT and Bank of Italy.

unchanged. However, if the number of undeclared workers is underestimated, the level of employment and output on the supply side would go under-recorded, although productivity measures would remain largely unaffected.

There is evidence suggesting that the number of undeclared workers indeed went under-recorded in the past. The Immigration Law introduced in 2002[13] did not aim at increasing the influx of immigrant workers, but rather at regularising those already in Italy. Thus, a large part of regularisation is believed to have mostly changed the status of workers from undeclared to declared rather than registered new immigrant entrants (no data is available to distinguish between genuine influx and regularisation). Yet, in 2002 the number of regularisation requests was about 700,000, more than the estimate of illegal foreign workers made in the previous year (about 500,000).

The irregularity rate (ratio between full-time equivalent undeclared workers over total) fell in 2002 and 2003, and then recovered slightly thereafter. In 2005 (the latest available data) total illegal workers still accounted for around 12.1 per cent of full-time equivalent employment. This share declined by 1.1 percentage points both in 2002 and 2003, the most important years for regularisation (Figure 3.12). What is striking, however, is that the percentage of undeclared foreign workers over total undeclared workers plunged during the same period from an estimated 22 per cent in 2001 to meagre 4 per cent in 2003, probably as a result of the change in legislation that made illegal immigrants regular in November 2002. However, undeclared foreign workers dropped to only 0.5 per cent of total full-time equivalent employment in 2003. This may arouse the suspicion that undeclared foreign workers in the national accounts may have not been properly estimated.

Under-recording may also be at play for native workers. Undeclared workers may have gone under-recorded in national accounts in the past and the new fixed-term contractual arrangements may have succeeded in allowing some undeclared workers to be declared. It is no coincidence that the estimated irregularity rate started to stabilise in 1998, the year that followed the introduction of the so-called 'Treu package', which gave a boost to temporary work contractual arrangements. Then it started to decline in 2001. In sum, if indeed the undeclared workforce was under-recorded in the past, the rise in employment since the mid-1990s would not be entirely genuine as it would partly be a shift from undeclared work outside official estimates to declared work.

Still, even assuming that undeclared work was underestimated would not explain the observed divergence between employment and productivity growth. Observing the behaviour of productivity in those sectors where the presence of undeclared workers is believed to be higher (notably hotels and restaurants, agriculture and fisheries and construction) seems to suggest that some distortions may be at play on the productivity side as well. Figure 3.13 shows an unusual collapse in total factor productivity growth around the start of the current decade in two of the sectors where the percentage of undeclared workers over total is believed to be higher: agriculture and fisheries and hotels and restaurants. Growth in total factor productivity went deeply negative in both cases. The trend is less clear in the construction industry, where it is also believed there is a high presence of undeclared workers.

3.2.6 The shift from industry to services

Another possible explanation for poor productivity in the economy is the secular shift from industry to services. In 1995, the share of value-added on GDP of industry excluding construction was 24.2 per cent. By 2007 this share had declined to 21.5 per cent. Over the past 10 years, net employment gains have mostly occurred in the non-capital-intensive service sectors and some of these sectors were characterised by relatively low productivity growth and levels. Of course many services

Figure 3.13 Contribution of total factor productivity to value-added growth
Source: ISTAT and own calculations.

are high-productivity activities, as for instance financial services in many countries. Others are far less productive. An example is the distribution sector, where employment growth has combined with strict land regulation and other forms of regulation that have limited consolidation in the sector and growth of large retail outlets, depressing gains in productivity.

Looking at available evidence, however, recomposition by sectors does not appear at the root of lower productivity in the past 10 years. Daveri and Jona-Lasinio (2005), for instance, found little evidence of this. Moreover, in the same period the manufacturing sector, which is supposed to be a high-productivity-growth sector, has performed poorly, somewhat at odds with the performance in the 1970s and 1980s and with that of other countries. As explained in the next section, some statistical problems with the deflator of exports may at least partly justify this odd performance, given that manufacturing is the most export-oriented sector in the economy. At any rate, the productivity slowdown in the private sector has to some extent been led by manufacturing. Therefore, although in theory recomposition in favour of services would entail a drop in productivity growth and a one-off negative level effect, this has not happened in Italy because of the poor productivity showing of manufacturing.

Summing up, of the above-mentioned possible reasons explaining the productivity/employment behaviour that has prevailed since the early 1990s, the most important ones are probably capital-labour substitution, regularisation of immigrant workers and low-skilled low-productivity workers entering the labour market. Some of the above considerations seem to suggest that the combination of strong employment gains and poor productivity growth may be transitory, although it has already lasted for many years.

3.3 Italy's competitiveness and export price rises

Since the mid-1990s, the Italian economy has combined a sharp decline in competitiveness with high export prices. Italy used to have a market share in world trade second only to Germany within the EU–15. In 1995, Italy's market share in world trade was 5.0 per cent in volume terms. The share declined to 3.8 per cent in 2000 and to 3.5 per cent in 2006. Italy now ranks below Germany, France and the UK on this metric[14] (see Figure 3.14 for an index of performance). Even within the EU–15, Italy's share of trade has steadily declined. During the same period, unit labour costs have increased markedly (see also Figure 3.15).[15] Yet, Italy's average unit values of exports (a proxy for export prices) have continued to increase over the years, leading to another puzzle (Figure 3.16).

The Italian Statistical Office (ISTAT) does not release export prices. It publishes export unit values (i.e., export values divided by quantities), which combine changes in both prices and the product mix.[16] Export unit values have increased significantly over the years and especially

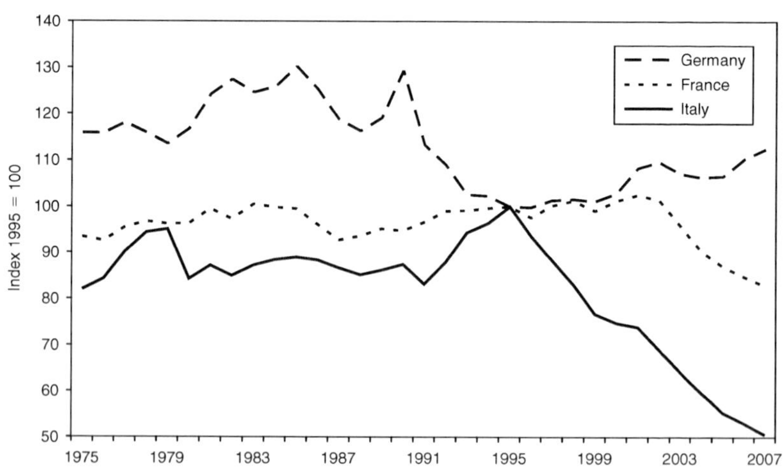

Figure 3.14 Index of export performance relative to market
Source: OECD and own calculations.

recently. Between 2005 and the fourth quarter of 2007 they increased at an average annualised rate of 4.9 per cent (Figure 3.17). The evidence is also supported by qualitative sectoral data on prices by export markets which show that since 2002 Italian exporters, especially those in

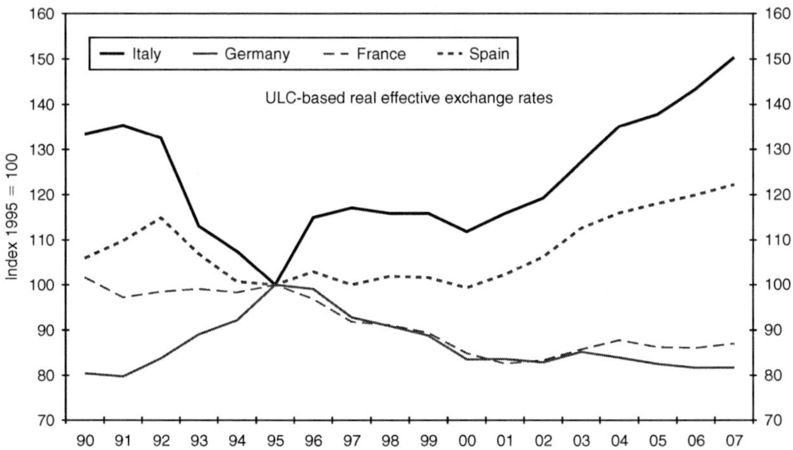

Figure 3.15 The unit labour cost gap has widened
Source: IMF and own calculations.

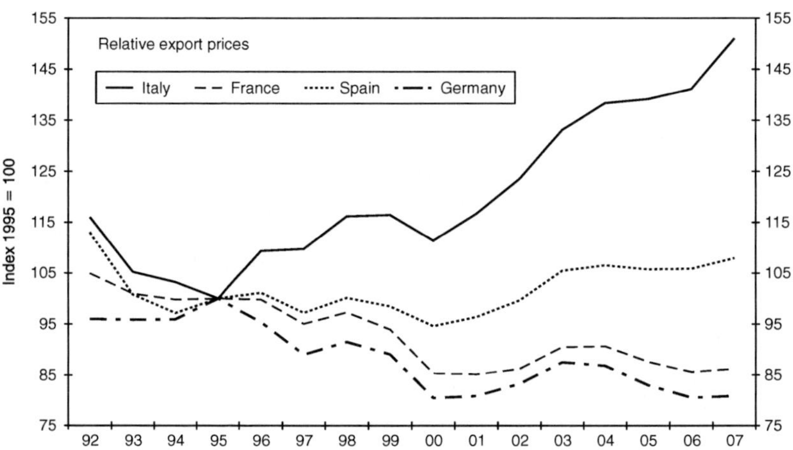

Figure 3.16 Italian exporters have been able to increase prices
Source: OECD and own calculations.

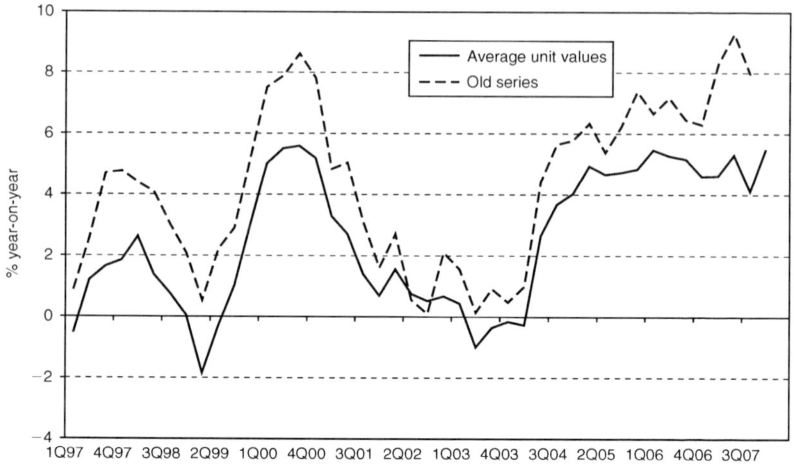

Figure 3.17 Strong rises in average unit values
Source: ISTAT.

traditional sectors, have increased export prices more than domestic prices in the face of an appreciation of the euro exchange rate and increased competitive pressure (Basile *et al.*, 2007).

The trends in market shares and export unit values raise a few questions. Are Italian exporters trying to protect profit margins at the expense of market shares? Or is there a significant quality upgrading of export products combined with increased pricing power? Is there any other possible explanation?

The economic debate on the Italian competitiveness problem has mainly focused on structural issues such as Italy's unfavourable market specialisation, biased towards low technological production, hence exposing exporters to competition from low-cost producers, and the size of Italian firms (mainly small to medium), which prevent firms from fully exploiting economies of scale in an increasingly global market.[17] A few contributions have also tried to address the apparent puzzle of export prices.

Possible explanations of this apparent puzzle are: i) companies protecting profit margins; ii) a shift in product mix/specialisation; iii) off-shoring of low-quality production/market exit and upgrading of product quality; iv) increased pricing power or, more generally, market power; and v) measurement errors.

3.3.1 Companies protecting profit margins

One may suspect that the broad-based export recovery recorded since 2006, particularly when exports are measured in values, is simply cyclical, and that exporters have preferred to increase prices rather than recover market shares. However, rises in export prices above those of other competitor countries have been recorded for many years. After several years of consistent and prolonged growth in export prices it seems difficult to assume a deliberate and suicidal attempt by Italian companies to try and protect profit margins at the expense of market shares, although this hypothesis has initially been aired by international institutions and economic commentators. Protecting profit margins is usually a short-term strategy that cannot be sustained over the long run. Thus, this is not believed to be a valid explanation.

3.3.2 A shift in product mix/specialisation

According to the OECD,[18] the correlation between Italy's sectoral specialisation (by using the RSCA, the Revealed Symmetric Comparative Advantage index) and that of the dynamic Asian economies is a significantly positive one and the highest among industrialised OECD countries, implying that there is a strong competition. This correlation has also increased over the years.

Despite this strong competition, there has been no significant shift in Italy's product specialisation. The Balassa index shows that there has been a small decline in traditional *Made in Italy* sectors since 2000. Overall, the shift has been limited. The value of the specialisation index in traditional sectors remains extremely high (as in Spain). These sectors are exposed to competition by newly developed countries. The Balassa index also shows: i) a still high specialisation in low-technology manufactures, which has been declining only slowly since 2000; ii) a mild increase in specialisation in medium-low technology manufactures, which is now significantly higher than in France and Germany and in line with Spain, where specialisation is declining; iii) a mild increase in specialisation in medium-high technology manufactures, which remains the lowest compared to Germany, France and Spain; iv) a low and declining specialisation in high-technology manufacturing, which remains well below that of Germany and France (Spain has caught up with Italy), while all European countries are below the G7 average.

It could be argued that the OECD classification by technological content is not truly representative of the sophistication in production. In fact, a low-technology product which has a high content of design, branding and highly complex production processes, as is often the case for Italian productions, may no longer be considered as low technology. Yet, by this metric the shift in product specialisation has been small for Italy, and certainly unable to explain the rise in export unit values.

3.3.3 Offshoring of low-quality production/market exit and upgrading of product quality

Under the pressure of newly industrialised countries, Italian exporters could have restructured production by relocating low-quality production to low-cost countries. Moreover, the competition faced by low-cost producers could have forced some companies to exit the market. Both phenomena would have resulted in a recomposition of the export mix towards the high-end of the quality and price scale, justifying the increases in the export deflator recorded over the past few years.

A deliberate strategy to upgrade the quality of domestically produced goods might also partly explain this phenomenon. While some domestic firms producing at the lower end of the quality scale may have had to close down in the face of fierce competition from emerging countries, others are believed to have increased the quality of products in terms of marketing, design content, complexity and the like and also relocated low-quality production abroad. This would have allowed them to increase prices.

Empirical evidence seems to support this view. Lamieri and Lanza (2006) find that two out of three Italian companies have upgraded the quality of their products as a reaction to the introduction of the euro (40 per cent of companies show a full-scale upgrading on all range of products). Of the remaining third, some were already at the higher end of the quality scale (silk and leather, for instance) and already have a quasi-monopolistic pricing power on niche products. Other sectors seem to have been unable to adjust in the same way (ceramics and wool). Borin and Lamieri (2007) present several methodologies to estimate quality upgrading and propose a model that shows that greater quality of exports results in lower price elasticity of demand.

3.3.4 Increased pricing power or more generally market power

Closely linked to the previous point, although of a different nature, is the possible increase in pricing power of exporters. Lanza and Quintieri (2007) show a significant reduction in price elasticity of market shares between 1995–9 and 2000–5 in traditional *Made in Italy* sectors, such as wine, vegetable oil, ceramic and glass products, furnishing, and mechanical products. For instance, the Italian olive oil price is about 140 per cent higher than the European average and export unit values have continued to rise (+40 per cent in 1998–2005). Yet, Italy's market share has remained largely unchanged. Another example is furnishing. The sector is retaining a competitive edge by increasing the complexity of production. The higher the complexity of production, the greater the ability to include functional and aesthetic features, so as to sell at higher prices. Not all sectors show reduced sensitivity to relative prices (jewellery, for instance). Nevertheless companies appear to enjoy higher pricing power in several sectors and especially in traditional *Made in Italy* sectors. De Nardis and Pensa (2004) use the concept of relative mark-up as an indicator of market power by exploiting the relationship with the elasticity of the residual demand curve. They show that Italian exporters have been able to practice mark-ups over marginal costs in most destination markets despite intense competition from low-cost producers, thereby showing increased market power.

Another potential explanation is an increased ability to 'price to market'. By using survey data between the first quarter of 1999 and the second quarter of 2005, Basile *et al.* (2007a) say that 'impulse-response analysis shows non-negligible reactions of export-domestic price margins to unanticipated changes in cost competitiveness and in foreign and domestic demand levels. [...] For the period 1999–2001 a typical pricing-to-market behaviour emerges, while over the most recent years favourable foreign demand conditions have allowed firms to increase their export-domestic price margins in the face of a strong deterioration of their cost competitiveness'.

3.3.5 Measurement errors

Pushed up by low productivity growth, unit labour costs have been higher in Italy than in other major euro-area economies, although marginal labour costs have declined. Price competitiveness measures, such as real effective exchange rates based on average unit labour costs, have deteriorated sharply.[19] However, if the deterioration in labour productivity is overstated, as was previously suggested, that of unit labour costs would similarly be overstated as would competitiveness losses measured on the basis of unit labour costs.

There are other potential measurement errors in export unit values. Given that export unit values are not fully indicative of underlying export prices, comparing unit values to other measures of export prices could give an estimate of the bias. According to Bugamelli (2007), who used survey data of the Bank of Italy and adjusted for quality of products, in the last decade (1996–2005) export unit values have overestimated export price increases by 2 percentage points on average every year. This would imply underestimation of volumes, and thus real GDP growth, as original export data are in value terms.[20]

To sum up, it appears that several factors may help unravel the apparent puzzle of rising export prices while exporters are facing competitiveness problems. Price competitiveness problems may also be overstated by simply looking at *average* labour costs for manufacturing or for the whole economy. Deep restructuring in Italian industry over the past few years may have put surviving exporters in a substantially better position than in the past, thereby allowing them to move upscale in terms of product quality and thus increase prices.

Still, Italy scores pretty low on numerous pillars of the World Economic Forum indices. Although the subjective nature of these indices suggests that they may not be the best gauge of competitiveness, overall they signal that the problem is broader. 'Framework conditions' are still not favourable and the factors that are critical to driving productivity and competitiveness need to be improved.

3.4 Italy's reform process

Against the backdrop of Italy's structural problems, can the Italian economy adjust and grow?

Growth accounting and structural indicators can provide some clues to Italy's structural problems. The gap of per-capita GDP versus the EU–15 average in 2004–6 (6.5 percentage points) is almost entirely explained by a negative total factor productivity differential, which cannot entirely be explained by the above-mentioned distortions. Italy has a level of labour hourly productivity at only 89 per cent of the EU–15 average. Labour productivity is driven down by low labour quality (possibly partly explained by Italy's low-tech productive specialisation) matched by poor performance in the education and lifelong learning policy indicators.

Italy lags far beyond in terms of labour participation, mainly because of low participation by older people (55–64), youth and – to a lesser extent – women. Moreover, the reduction of youth participation since the early 1990s (which has speeded up since 2002–3) does not combine with much improved educational performance (as measured by the level of educational attainment). Recent immigration developments are likely to mitigate the participation problem in the future. Nevertheless, worrying demographic trends make improving labour participation all the more important.

Structural indicators show that wage bargaining and wage setting policies and making-work-pay policies have seen a relative deterioration *vis-à-vis* the EU–15, calling for a revision of the current labour-relations framework. Wage dispersion is low across regions and combines with a high level of regional dispersion in unemployment, suggesting that wage differences and/or labour mobility across regions is rather low compared to the rest of Europe.

As for the policy setting deemed to affect productivity performance, Italy has problems with level indicators of efficient financial markets and access to finance, barriers to entrepreneurship and business environment, openness to trade and investment, and R&D innovation and ICT. In the field of competition, the average mark-up at industry level is higher than in the rest of Europe (although there is no problem in network industries). Market integration measures such as trade and investment indicators underline an insufficient degree of openness. Indicators signal low openness to trade and investment, especially for the cost and time to trade across borders and the level of protection given to investors. Problems are also indicated in the business environment, especially in terms of administrative burdens for companies and low efficiency of public administration. Doing business still appears relatively difficult in Italy, especially in terms of paying taxes, dealing with licences, enforcing contracts and the time to close a business. Italy shows a relatively high level of regulation in the access to credit and a high cost of bank services.

Substantial progress has been made in many areas over the past few years, but a lot more needs to be done to address the above-mentioned problems. Speeding up the reform process is essential for boosting Italy's potential growth and competitiveness. By removing impediments to a full and efficient use of resources, reforms increase sustainable growth with higher levels of employment. Besides ensuring long-term fiscal sustainability, as discussed in Chapter 4, the priority goals of Italy's reform process could be summarised as follows: i) enhance competition and simplify regulation, through actions to reduce entry barriers and liberalise services; ii) promote research and innovation; iii) increase participation in the labour market, make the labour market more flexible, and encourage investment in human capital; iv) upgrade tangible and intangible infrastructure; and v) reconcile environmental protection with technological progress.

High regulation and low competition in the non-tradable sector (especially the cost of financial services) are at the root of poor productivity gains. Important reform steps have already been taken by improving the functioning of markets and extending competition to previously protected sectors. As part of the drive to enhance competition, government initiatives have improved the functioning of markets and extended the area of free choice. Reforms have been introduced, aimed at lifting restrictions on market access (such as restrictions on supply, eligibility for doing business, minimum distance, and antitrust caps at local level), lifting restrictions on business (such as range of products offered, minimum prices and ban on advertising, discounted products, constraints on the portability of bank accounts and company type), reorganising the electricity and gas markets (increasing competition through unbundling of distribution and selling of electricity, and organisational unbundling of transmission and distribution system operators in the gas sector), ensuring energy supply at competitive costs by setting minimum targets of fuel-mix diversification, increasing the security of gas supplies by encouraging investments in new infrastructures, promoting policies to sustain renewable sources by increasing energy efficiency, and, finally, measures to reduce red tape (strengthening the 'one-stop shop' for business activities and cutting administrative requirements). Enhanced competition would keep a lid on inflation and in turn benefit competitiveness. Higher inflation in Italy than in other countries was one of the key reasons for deteriorating competitiveness in the past.

More effort is needed to strengthen innovation in the economy. For this reason, a research and development target equal to 2.5 per cent of GDP by 2010 has been set by the government (two-thirds from the private sector), which is below the European target (3 per cent) but still extremely ambitious given that research and development spending is very low (1.1 per cent in 2005). Weak investment in R&D may reflect the specialisation of Italian firms in traditional sectors as well as the prevalence of small family businesses, whose innovation and investment in R&D appears to go under-recorded. However, R&D spending appears low even after controlling for industry structure. Innovation is also closely linked to foreign direct investment. Openness to foreign direct investment is increasing, but remains low compared to other countries. The small number of foreign multinational enterprises may have constrained technological transfers and spillovers of best practice to domestic firms. Furthermore, outsourcing and offshoring has led to geographical fragmentation of value-added chains, threatening the Italian industrial district model (*distretti*). However, this should also have allowed Italian firms to cut costs in low-value-added areas through redirecting resources to what they do best and facilitating the diffusion of productivity-enhancing technology. Yet, investment in communication technology, which is more closely associated with total factor productivity enhancements, remains one of the lowest in the OECD.

Within the budget constraints and without losing sight of the need to cut taxation, additional resources need to be found to increase infrastructure spending and in particular: improving general production efficiency and business competitiveness through better logistics, upgrading the existing networks in order to integrate Italy within the European transport system, encouraging innovative projects in the transport sector, and reducing the infrastructure gap between Central/Northern and Southern Italy.

Despite major labour market reforms in the past, the functioning of the labour market is far from optimal. A lot more needs to be done, notably: further reforms to encourage young people and women to join the workforce through active employment policies (in addition to immigration policies); introduction of re-employment incentives to postpone retirement; promotion of social policies providing more services and assistance (including family-support policies and childcare provision); and decreasing the size of the shadow economy and reducing regional disparities.

A key challenge for the Italian economy is to increase labour market participation. Over the long run, employment is affected mainly by the functioning of the labour market as well as broad influences on labour supply such as growth in the working-age population and labour participation. While there is limited scope to influence the former, the scope for a larger contribution to GDP growth from the latter and in general from labour market functioning is substantial. In Italy, levels of participation are low in the formal economy and below those of most industrialised countries. This is particularly true of women and older workers and there are huge regional gaps, which represent a sizeable source of untapped growth potential. More employment-friendly arrangements should provide stronger incentives to participate in the labour market, including tax incentives, and a better market functioning should contribute to a better match of supply and demand and a more efficient allocation of labour.

Moreover, a significant reduction in the divide between labour market insiders and outsiders is badly needed. Incomes policies in the 1990s and early in the current decade have been crucial to the improvement in terms of macroeconomic stability and labour market functioning. However, these highly successful developments have come at the cost of an increasing duality in the labour market. These developments have also exposed the inadequacy of Italy's safety nets and low unemployment benefits. Shock absorbers in the labour market are insufficient and fragmented. Benefits are generally lower than in the rest of Europe and mainly limited to industry. Globalisation and the far-reaching restructuring process in Italian businesses call for smoother transition from unemployment to employment and require a more efficient mechanism to match labour demand with supply as well as unemployment benefits based on proper incentives. The current divide between insiders and outsiders looks unsustainable for the future, calling for a significant enhancement of safety nets on the one hand and a substantial reduction in job protection for insiders on the other.

Italy needs to invest more in human capital, as educational achievements are weak by international standards, and improve the matching of labour with capital, thus contributing to the improvement in total factor productivity. The issue of increasing the accumulation of human capital in addition to physical capital needs to be forcefully addressed to enhance growth potential over the long term.

Finally, another key challenge is modernising the public administration, also through e-government programmes, to improve the framework conditions for the reform process to take place efficiently. This is especially important given the large size of the public sector in the economy and the potentially large productivity gains that could be achieved, with positive spillovers into the rest of the economy.

3.5 Concluding remarks

Without downplaying the structural issues at stake, this chapter presents evidence suggesting that the short- to medium-term outlook for the Italian economy may be less bleak than some indicators depict. The decline in productivity growth, partly as a result of labour market changes, may have concealed a genuine structural improvement that is now gradually emerging. Under the pressure of globalisation, healthy restructuring in the sector most exposed to competition has been encouraged through a process of 'creative destruction'. Despite poor demographic trends, reforms in the labour and, more recently, product markets should help enhance potential growth over time.

As indicated in the final section of this chapter, a number of important reforms and policy measures have already been introduced to respond to Italy's economic challenges. It could be argued that some of these reforms still have to fully produce their impact on the economy, and thus part of the explanation for the poor performance may lay with adjustment lags. This optimistic interpretation considers the recent period as a necessary and temporary adjustment that entails economic growth below full potential. However, there is plenty of evidence suggesting that Italy is lagging behind on a number of structural counts and thus still faces daunting challenges. A lot more needs to be done.

Notes

1. See for instance Gros (2006) 'Will EMU survive 2010?' and Connolly (2005) 'Europe's Italy Problem'.
2. Eurostat, structural statistics, Labour productivity per person employed, GDP in purchasing power standards (PPS) per person employed.
3. The concept of total factor productivity does not exactly coincide with that of technological change for many reasons. The most important is that total factor productivity is a 'measure of our ignorance' (Abramovitz, 1956) as it is calculated as a residual. It captures only 'costless' improvements in the way labour and capital resources are transformed into real GDP. Technological change that results from research and development spending would not be captured by total factor productivity as research and development is generally included in labour and capital factors of production. A second reason is that changes in the organisation of production, for instance, would also contribute to total factor productivity without being regarded as technological progress.
4. Labour costs include wages paid to employees as well as non-wage labour costs, i.e., social security contributions paid by employees and employers.
5. Source: European Commission.
6. The 1993 agreement was preceded by a provisional three-party agreement in July 1992, which abolished the indexation mechanism of wages and introduced a short-term wage freeze, and by Law 223 in 1991, which eased legislation for collective dismissals.
7. The hourly post-tax earnings of temporary workers working year-round fell short of those of other workers by 19 per cent, after controlling for individual characteristics in 2000. Since then, the gap has widened further.
8. These conclusions are reinforced by a secular recomposition of demand towards labour-intensive services.
9. This compares with a 33 per cent gain for aggregate average yearly real wages per standard labour unit in the private sector (National Accounts) between 1976 and 1992.
10. See Banca d'Italia (2007).
11. Source: ISTAT (2007), Foreign population resident in Italy, October. Resident immigrants are recorded in official statistics once they enter the National Register (*anagrafe*). Almost all immigrants with a regular permit are recorded in the National Register, although with some time lag.
12. This is argued in various publications by the Statistical Office and in Rosolia (2007). The shift from undeclared to declared could also be noticed in the different trend of total employment in national accounts (where undeclared

are included) and the Labour Force Survey (where only legally resident households are surveyed).

13. Law 189 Article 33 dated 30 July 2002 and 222 of 9 October 2002.
14. Based on UN Comtrade and European Commission data.
15. Measures of competitiveness based on producer or consumer prices show a different picture. These measures may be perceived as more reliable indicator given that labour input represents, on average, only a small part of total costs as exporting firms generally purchase raw and intermediate goods and services as a sizeable component of their cost base.
16. Only very recently (11 June 2008), ISTAT published a series of producer prices of industrial products sold in foreign markets for the years 2002–8.
17. Italy's smaller average size of firms compared to other major economies limits the ability to penetrate foreign markets, and especially the most dynamic emerging Asian markets for several reasons: i) fixed costs to access foreign markets (Bugamelli, Cipollone and Infante, 2000; Bugamelli and Infante, 2003); ii) lower propensity to innovate (Basile, 2000); iii) sizeable initial sunk costs make it more difficult for firms to enhance productivity by product and process innovation (Lotti and Schivardi, 2005). Moreover, the small size bias of Italian industry does not appear to be related to the sectoral specialisation of Italian firms (Pagano and Schivardi, 2003).
18. OECD (2007d) *OECD Economic Survey: United Kingdom.*
19. If measured by unit labour costs in manufacturing, deterioration is less dramatic (wages have increased more in the public sector and in sectors less exposed to international competition, notably in services).
20. The deflator of imports has been rising strongly, possibly having been overestimated as well. Still, the larger weight of exports over imports does not make for a full offset on the contribution by net export to GDP growth. Moreover, Moëc (2007) noted that this underestimation on the demand side would match a similar underestimation on the supply side as growth in the deflator of value-added in manufacturing appears overstated as well. Similar considerations were made by Chaney (2007).

Comment on Chapter 3

Tito Boeri
Università Bocconi, Milan

Riccardo Faini's contributions to research have shed light on several economic puzzles in Italy. I still remember the first academic seminar I attended in Italy after coming back from the OECD. He presented a paper – published a year later in the *European Economic Review* (Faini *et al.*, 1997) – in which he convincingly explained how a rich Northern Italy with its shortage of workers and a poor Southern Italy with its shortage of jobs were able to coexist for so long even though there was very little internal migration. Moreover, I am sure that, if Riccardo Faini were still with us today, he would also be able to help us understand the two economic anomalies pointed out in this insightful chapter by Lorenzo Codogno. These two new Italian puzzles are indeed also at the centre of Faini's research interests, shared between trade theory and labour economics. The first puzzle has to do with the remarkable performance of the Italian labour market over the last decade and the dismal performance of labour productivity. The second puzzle has to do with Italy's export performance: why was it not poor in a period which saw unit labour costs increase significantly in Italy in comparison to its major trading partners?

Codogno produces a large number of interesting statistics documenting these puzzles. It is difficult to argue with these facts. It is likewise difficult to argue with the measurement issues pointed out by Codogno. My only comment in this respect is that measurement problems typically go in both directions. We may underestimate or overestimate something and the direction of the bias is unpredictable. I also do not want to enter a sort of philosophical debate about whether we should be optimistic or pessimistic about the future of the Italian economy. It is a matter of taste. Fortunately none of us is so influential as to affect the mood of

Italian consumers and the business climate, hence we are not generating self-fulfilling prophecies.

I see my role here as confined to putting the evidence produced by Codogno in a (somewhat) broader perspective. Economic history books are overcrowded with Italian anomalies and my (secret) hope is to convince the readers that we may be dealing with puzzles that do not necessarily speak Italian, let alone of the fact that they are truly puzzles.

From jobless growth to growthless job creation

Let me begin then with the first puzzle, which I would call 'growthless job creation' as opposed to the 'jobless growth' of the early 1990s vividly documented by the OECD. As I was at the OECD at the time of the OECD *Jobs Study* in 1994, I am tempted to recall how Europe (and not only Italy!) was perceived at the time.

> The labour market has become particularly worrying in Europe . . . slow employment growth has always been a feature of the EFTA and EC regions . . . there are indications that employment has been unusually weak vis-à-vis output growth . . . In the EC employment growth has been generally sluggish . . . (OECD, 1994)

The OECD *Jobs Study* basically was pointing the finger at the low employment content of growth in Europe, suggesting that the employment to output elasticity should have been similar to that prevailing in the US. Since then there has been a considerable change in the responsiveness of employment to output in Europe (and not only in Italy!).

Figure 3.18 displays average yearly growth rates in the employment rate (vertical axis) and GDP (horizontal axis) in the EU–15 in the period 1996-2005. The employment rate is taken to control for demographics, notably the large migration inflows which occurred throughout the region in the last decade and which significantly affected total employment levels, notably in Spain and Italy. The diagonal line is the US apparent employment to output elasticity (the ratio of employment growth rates to GDP growth rates) at the time of the 1994 OECD *Jobs Study*. As the above citations recall, the latter was significantly higher than in high-unemployment, sclerotic, European countries. The Figure shows that matters changed quite dramatically after then. The Olive Belt countries, in particular, display a responsiveness of employment to output growth which is considerably higher than that of the US, which we were envying in the mid-1990s.

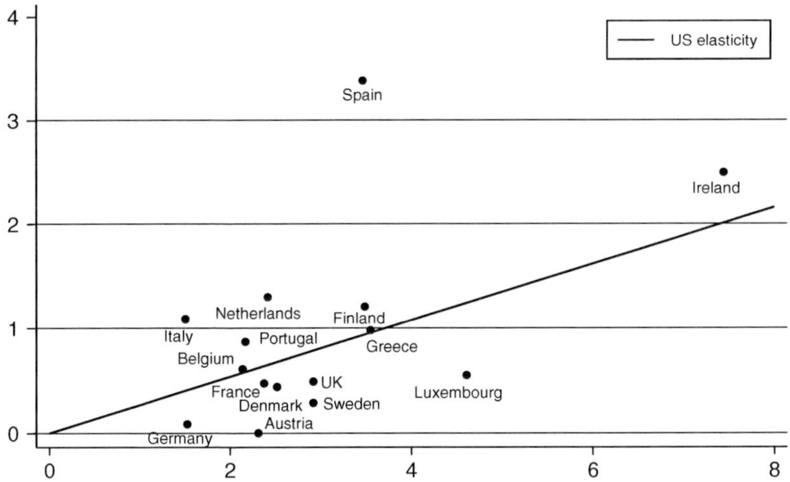

Figure 3.18 Employment (vertical axis) and output (horizontal axis) average yearly growth rates in the EU–15

A possible explanation for this fact lies in dual-track reform strategies. As discussed by Boeri and Garibaldi (2007), the apparent employment-to-output elasticity increased after reforms that introduced two-tier systems of employment protection with an increasing number of flexible temporary contracts coexisting with rigid permanent contracts. The fact of the matter is that the dualism between highly flexible temporary contracts and rigid permanent contracts induces asymmetric adjustment of firms to shocks: in good times, employment increases more than in the past; in bad times downward employment adjustment is still constrained by rigid contracts. This increases average employment in firms per given output, reducing labour productivity.

Temporary contracts (including fixed-term contracts, according to the definition provided by Eurostat) indeed contributed disproportionately to the growth of employment in these countries. Net variations in the stock of temporary workers were large both in absolute terms and relative to the stock of employees at the beginning of the period. In Spain, in particular, 3.3 million jobs were created in the so-called *contractos temporales* after the inception of this programme, contributing to a net growth of almost 30 per cent in the stock of employees. In Italy, fixed-term contracts accounted for about 850,000 new jobs and nine hires out of ten for persons aged less than 35 are in these temporary contracts.

These reforms are creating two-tier regimes that have been successful in increasing employment rates in Europe. But this honeymoon is likely to be over soon as firms no longer have the incentives to build up a 'buffer stock' of flexible contracts to accommodate output fluctuations. Moreover, dual labour markets segregate many workers in jobs offering little incentives for human capital investment and that are highly exposed to labour market risk.

Another factor which could have explained the diverging dynamics of employment and labour productivity is immigration. Migrant workers do not carry with them capital stock, which means that the influx of immigrants into jobs entails a decline in capital use per worker. Moreover, first-generation migrants are typically employed in low-skill, gap-filling activities, and have few opportunities for training and upgrading. The dualism between temporary workers and permanent workers tends to segregate them in low-productivity jobs.

Thus, my reading of the first puzzle is that European job creation in the last decade occurred at the cost of low-productivity growth. Jobs were created for persons with little or no work experience, segregated in secondary labour markets with little training on the job. This trade-off between employment and productivity growth is ultimately due to the fact that we are still in the middle of the river in reforming labour markets and largely unprepared for managing migration. The problem does not concern only Italy; it concerns Europe as a whole. Some solutions, notably those concerning migration, should be found at the European level.

Declining competitiveness, but not exports

I have less to say on the second puzzle, perhaps because I am much less poliedric than Riccardo Faini. In order to understand the paradox of rapidly declining competitiveness without a collapse of Italian exports, we should perhaps go to a more micro level. It is a matter of an increasing heterogeneity among Italian firms, somewhat concealed by aggregate statistics capturing unit labour costs for an aggregate of firms that includes many non-exporters. As noted recently by Baldwin *et al.* (2007), there is evidence of successful firms also in industries facing tough competition from cheap-labour countries, as well as in high-tech sectors. These successful exporters are relatively large, endowed with skilled human capital, use more advanced technologies and invest heavily in ITC. Moreover, they export a large share of their output to several and distant markets and are involved in other international activities such as FDI or foreign production agreements. Such strategies involve bearing high fixed costs and undertaking large risks.

These firms can benefit from the geographical unbundling of economic activities (Grossman and Rossi-Hansberg, 2006) made possible by the gradual reduction of the cost of trading goods, moving people and sharing ideas. This new dimension of globalisation has, on the one hand, exaggerated the underlying weaknesses of Italy, but, on the other hand, has made it possible for some successful firms to penetrate very large and rapidly expanding markets.

We are bound to experience more and more of this heterogeneity in Italy. If policy-makers want to avoid a trade-off between employment and productivity growth, they must favour more reallocation of capital and workers across firms. Bargaining structures artificially compressing wage structures, subsidies to ailing industries and obstacles to labour mobility will simply make it more difficult to increase employment and productivity at the same time, that is, to promote total factor productivity growth. Promoting reallocation does not mean deciding which type of reallocation should take place. Governments should also abstain from deciding what the strategic advantages of Italy are. Nobody knows them. They are increasingly unpredictable. The borders between advantages and disadvantages are within sectors more than across sectors.

Sergio De Nardis
Istituto di Studi e Analisi Economica (ISAE), Rome

A country with problems, not in decline

The puzzles mentioned in the title of the chapter by Lorenzo Codogno regard the long-lasting co-existence in the Italian economy of apparently contrasting phenomena: i) dismal productivity performance accompanied by brilliant employment growth; and ii) dismal (volume) market share performance accompanied by high and increasing export unit values (relative to competitors). While several pundits have long overlooked these facts, at most considering them as a confirmation that Italy is the real sick man of Europe (after all, they give rise to statistics showing labour inefficiency and loss of price competitiveness), the author takes a different view. He points out that their most likely explanations go precisely in the opposite direction: they suggest that the Italian situation is not as gloomy as available indicators seem to signal and, consequently, that the competitiveness of the country may have been understated. Needless to say, recognition that Italy is not an economy in decline does not imply an underrating of the many-sided structural problems that restrain growth (also inducing social inequities) and ask for reforms; these are thoroughly discussed in the final section of the chapter.

I basically subscribe to this view and in my comments I will try to argue how those puzzles conceal more than a clue about the features of the macro and micro adjustment of the Italian economy.

Regime shifts in the labour market

In Codogno's analysis, capital/labour substitution together with some other factors (regularisation and hiring of low-skilled workers) plays an important part in explaining productivity/employment behaviour. The author also underlines that movements in relative factor input demand have been affected by labour market reforms, particularly those that contributed to increase flexibility at the margin. Let me elaborate on this and discuss, on the grounds of some work made at ISAE, the nature and implications of such changes.

I tend to think that labour market reforms produced modifications in agents' behaviour on both the supply and the demand sides of the labour market. Indeed, it is inappropriate to speak of supply and demand in an uncompetitive environment, so that the responsiveness of real per-capita compensation to labour market imbalances is better described by a wage-setting equation. Estimates of such a relationship for Italy, conducted by ISAE, show that the elasticity of per-capita real wage to unemployment underwent a structural shift in the mid-1990s: according to the point estimates before and after the break, such elasticity rose by a factor of 2.[1] This move went in the direction of a drastic reduction of labour market structural imbalances, favouring a shift of the Italian economy from a regime of high-equilibrium to one of low-equilibrium unemployment. A piece of evidence suggesting that, from a macroeconomic perspective (that is, disregarding the important inequities inherent to these kinds of reforms, with flexibility weighing only on one segment of the active population), policy changes delivered a better functioning of the labour market is the fact that the NAIRU fell.

But this was just one effect. As noted by Codogno, labour market reforms may have also determined some capital-labour substitution. However, surprisingly enough, unit labour requirements rose beyond what would have been justified by movements of factor (average) prices.

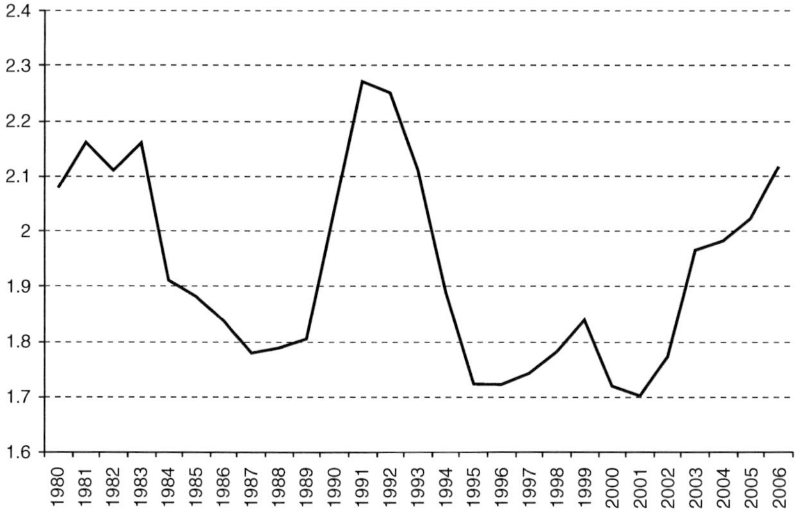

Figure 3.19 Ratio between total wages and total profits in Italian manufacturing

This phenomenon can be better highlighted with reference to the industrial sector. Figure 3.19 shows that, after a marked downward correction in the first half of the 1990s, the ratio between wages and profits in manufacturing increased again, particularly during the current decade. This movement can be attributed to some more vigorous labour demand relative to capital (that is, slower capital deepening), but not only to that. Figure 3.20, showing changes in factor quantity and factor price ratios, reveals that something else has been at work: while there were co-movements between changes in relative factor prices and relative factor quantities up to the mid-1990s (that is, capital deepening accelerated as the wage/profit ratio rose), this positive relationship breaks up thereafter. Since 1995, and particularly during the years after 2000, increases of the wage rate relative to profit have been accompanied by decelerations of capital deepening (that is, an acceleration of the demand for labour relative to capital).

Econometric estimates using a CES (Constant Elasticity of Substitution) production function framework seem to confirm what descriptive statistics already indicate: in the mid-nineties, the elasticity of the unit labour requirement (employment per unit of output) to real product wage (per-capita labour cost deflated by output price) decreased.[2] Since

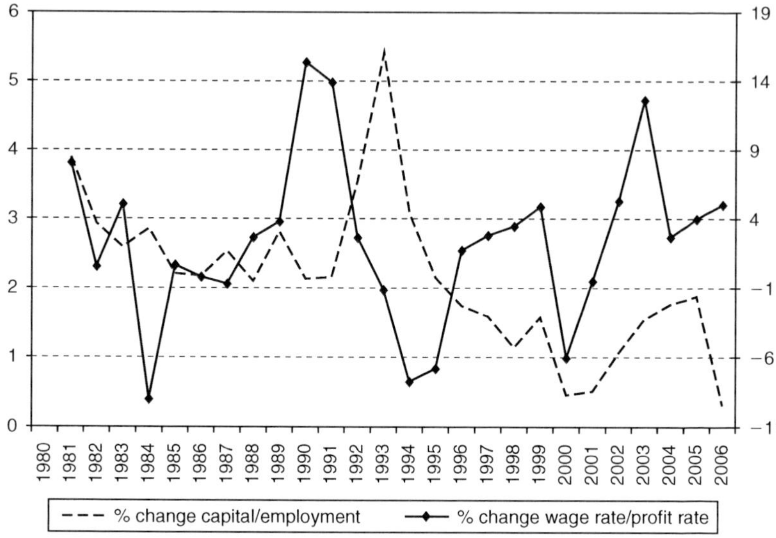

Figure 3.20 Wage rate/profit rate (rx) and capital stock/employment in Italian manufacturing (y-o-y % change)

this estimated elasticity is related, in a CES framework, to the elasticity of substitution between labour and capital, the shift would point to a downsizing, after the structural break, of such a (non-observable) measure of substitution between factors. This is a move that, if interpreted literally, would signal a modification in the form of the isoquant (becoming more convex), rather than a movement along it (induced by relative factor price).

It is admittedly difficult to envisage a modification in the shape of the isoquant (corresponding to a change in the set of available technologies): other factors may have been at work. In this chapter Codogno argues that what is relevant for hiring decisions is not the headline average cost, but the cost of the marginal worker, which has become lower due to the presence of more flexible work arrangements affecting new hires. My slightly different position is that explicit factor costs (measured by national accounts) do not say all about input costs. The apparent discontinuity in the relationship between explicit relative factor prices and relative factor demands in the Italian manufacturing sector was likely affected by the reduction of the implicit (statistically non-observable), non-monetary labour costs, that mainly concerned new hires. This encouraged firms' labour demand to an extent otherwise not conceivable solely on the grounds of the evolution of explicit factor costs.[3]

A corollary to this is what Codogno notes: a portion of the measured productivity slowdown (and the ensuing competitiveness loss) in Italian manufacturing is not genuine technological deterioration; it is rather a by-product of changes that involved production techniques, following labour market reforms. As such, part of Italy's poor productivity performance could be transitory. But transitory for how long? It will persist until unemployment reaches the new lower equilibrium level.

Interference with macroeconomic adjustment

Consequences of labour market changes do not stop here. Both modifications affecting the labour market – wages more sensitive to unemployment and higher labour requirement per unit of output – interfered with Italy's alleged inefficient macroeconomic adjustment in the first few years following the adoption of the euro. In a monetary union, in the absence of nominal exchange rates as policy instruments, adjustment to competitiveness shocks is assigned to the price/wage channel:[4] in the case of Italy, this would have implied a reduction of prices and wages to correct the emerging competitiveness loss *vis-à-vis* the euro-area partners. But how could wages be more moderate than they have been given that the unemployment rate decreased and wage responsiveness to labour market imbalances increased? To make this point clearer, let me resort to some back-of-the-envelope computations that should be taken just for their qualitative flavour. Between 2000 and 2006, against stagnant labour productivity, real product wages increased by 3.6 per cent, while unit labour cost rose by 19.5 per cent. Had nominal per capita wages during this period stayed in line with productivity, unit labour costs and equilibrium output prices would have stood constant at their 2000 level and the real product wage would have been, in 2006, lower by 3.1 percentage points. Could this outcome have been 'possible'? The answer is: maybe yes, but only with a significantly higher unemployment rate. Table 3.1 indicates that if the labour content of GDP growth (admittedly a very raw proxy of labour demand per unit of output) had remained at its pre-2000 level (0.5 instead of 1), the unemployment rate would have been 37 per cent higher than it actually was in 2006 (9.3 per cent versus 6.8 per cent). Using as wage elasticity an estimated pre-structural break value of –0.1, the real consumption wage and real product wage would have remained about stable (as unit labour cost).

Table 3.1 Italy in 2006: history and fiction (without changes in the labour market)

	History A	Fiction* B	% Difference B/A
Employment (index number 2000 = 100)	106.0	103.2	−2.6
Unemployment rate (Level in %)	6.8	9.3	36.8
Real consumption wage (index number 2000 = 100)	103.4	100.2	−3.1
Real product wage (index number 2000 = 100)	103.6	100.4	−3.1
Unit labour cost (index number 2000 = 100)	119.5	100.0	−16.3

*Fiction is obtained supposing an elasticity of employment to GDP of 0.5 (instead of 1), an elasticity of real consumption wage to unemployment of −0.1 (which is given by the estimate of the pre-break elasticity obtained in Costantini and de Nardis, 2007) and a ratio between consumer and producer equal to history.

Clearly, this is just a mechanical exercise with too many implicit assumptions, but it helps to throw light on the fact that the downward rigidity of Italy's labour costs (or, in other words, the mis-functioning of the price/wage channel of adjustment) did not materialise in a slack labour market. Quite the contrary: thanks to structural changes in the labour market, demand for labour (per unit of output) was vigorous and the signal of a weak economic cycle and the competitiveness loss did not fully transmit to that market.

Firms' behaviour and specialisation: time to change the view?

Let me add a few considerations on the second puzzle considered by Codogno, the one of rising export unit values even in the presence of competitiveness losses. The recent positive performance in value terms in international markets of Italian firms signals that some kind of spontaneous adjustment at firm level has taken place, along the lines suggested in this chapter (that is, quality upgrading and increased market power on the side of successful exporters). In my view, this observation could provide a useful occasion to consider the possibility of re-thinking the approach that is traditionally followed when discussing specialisation. Let me put it this way: isn't it time to dismiss an old view of specialisation (that juxtaposes 'good' versus 'bad' sectors) so often applied to the Italian case? I think that the recent Italian experience suggests several indications in this direction, which I summarise in the points below:

- Increasing competitive pressures, particularly from low-cost countries, trigger movements of resources not only across sectors, but also (and predominantly) within sectors, forcing quality upgrading and shifts toward more capital-intensive and less price-sensitive activities. Resource reallocations within the same industry seem typical of traditional productions located in advanced countries, where branding, design and technology are important competitive factors. The story of the apparent lock-in experienced over the years by the Italian specialisation model, despite fierce competition from emerging economies, is there to show us the relevance of this pattern of adjustment.
- Closely related to the former point is the fact that being specialised in the 'good' sectors (high-tech, high-value-added, high-demand sectors) seems less important, in terms of aggregate productivity, than being able to adjust and being mobile (exit/entry) at firm level. In other words, you may be good at producing microchips or potato chips, but what is really important for productivity is that the best products and firms are selected by competition, whatever the sector.
- Since inter-firm reallocations (within industry) are the relevant drive for improving efficiency, international competition is crucial: it forces the exit of the least efficient firms and leads to the survival and expansion of the more productive ones. In this perspective, the distinction in the Italian debate between 'active' quality upgrading (export unit values rise because firms actively improve their products) and 'passive' quality upgrading (export unit values rise because the low-end segment is displaced) does not make much sense: 'passive' upgrading is precisely what is needed for raising aggregate productivity.
- There is obviously room for 'active' adjustment too. As competition forces reallocation of firms within industries, by the same token it can induce product reallocation within firms: product switching (the abandonment of less efficient lines of production and development and expansion of better products) may provide an appreciable contribution to adjustment. Evidence coming from ISAE surveys shows that the successful exporters were those who were able to carry out investment in product, as well as process, innovation, suggesting that

this form of adjustment was actually at work in the recent Italian experience.[5]

An economy asking for reforms

In my comment I addressed the two main themes of the chapter by Lorenzo Codogno, arguing why I agree with the author's view that the misinterpretation of some key indicators led analysts and commentators to an overly gloomy assessment of the Italian economy. Obviously, this does not imply that Italy is a no-problem economy. Quite the opposite. The final section of this chapter gives an exhaustive account of the several structural issues that ask for urgent and comprehensive reforms. My argument is that there has been a spontaneous adjustment process by firms. It was dictated by international competition and took place under the constraints of the existing institutional environment. This process, however, was relevent to only about 20–25 per cent of the economy. Improvements to the rest of the economy are now the task of the policy-maker, and this is clearly the most demanding part of the effort.

Notes

1. From −0.1 to −0.2, see Costantini and de Nardis (2007) and ISAE (2007a).
2. A reduction by a factor of 4, according to the point estimates presented in de Nardis (2007).
3. On the importance of non-monetary labour costs in affecting Italian firms' behaviour see Brandolini *et al.* (2007) and, for a quantification of implicit costs, Cipollone and Guelfi (2006).
4. See Chapter 2 and European Commission (2007).
5. See de Nardis and Pappalardo (2007).

4
Ensuring a Sustainable Fiscal Consolidation

*Daniele Franco and Pietro Rizza**
Banca d'Italia – Economic Research Department

4.1 Introduction

For about 25 years, from the mid-1960s to the early 1990s, Italy ran unsustainable fiscal policies. High deficits, stemming from persistent primary imbalances, fuelled inflation and caused an accumulation of public debt (up to 121.5 per cent of GDP in 1994). From the mid-1980s debt stabilisation became the main target of Italian fiscal policy. Fiscal consolidation gained momentum in the early nineties, when primary deficits were replaced by sizeable primary surpluses. The debt-to-GDP ratio moved to a downward path. Pension liabilities were substantially reduced. By the end of the 1990s, the overall deficit declined from double-digit levels to well below the 3 per cent limit set by the Maastricht Treaty. In 1999 Italy joined the Economic and Monetary Union (EMU).

In the following years the primary surplus gradually contracted. Notwithstanding large one-off measures, the deficit repeatedly breached the 3 per cent limit. The debt ratio increased in 2005 and 2006. The marked slowdown in economic growth contributed to the worsening of the public finances. Driven by revenue growth, there was a new improvement in 2006 and 2007. A balanced budget is targeted for the year 2011.

This chapter argues that Italy's fiscal consolidation effort has been largely successful but it is not over yet. The worsening of the fiscal situation in the first years of the new century highlights the risks of

*The views expressed in this chapter are those of the authors and do not commit Banca d'Italia. The authors would like to thank Maura Francese, Raffaela Giordano, Maria Rosaria Marino, Sandro Momigliano, Renzo Pin, Alessandra Staderini, Pietro Tommasino and Stefania Zotteri for their useful comments.

complacency and points to the difficulty of slowing down expenditure growth. The length of the consolidation process reflects the size of the imbalances, the unsatisfactory macroeconomic developments, but also the difficulties in improving fiscal institutions.

The challenges facing Italian fiscal policy in the coming years are very similar to those of most other developed countries, such as coping with the ageing of the population and the impact of globalisation. But there are also country-specific challenges, such as those stemming from the high debt ratio, the size of the irregular economy, the unbalanced structure of social protection and the sizeable income differences within the country.

Section 4.2 briefly describes budgetary developments up to the mid-1980s. Section 4.3 considers the phase of consolidation from the mid-1980s to 1997. Section 4.4 covers the period 1998–2007, characterised by new fiscal imbalances followed by an improvement in the public finances. Section 4.5 outlines the medium-term prospects. Sections 4.6 to 4.8 examine, respectively, the issue of fiscal indicators, budgetary procedures and fiscal decentralisation. Sections 4.9 to 4.10 consider the pension system and the long-term budgetary prospects. Section 4.11 highlights the priorities in the fiscal policy agenda and offers some sonclusions.

4.2 A long fiscal crisis

Since its unification in 1861, Italy has been a high-debt country.[1] After unification the debt ratio gradually increased from 40 to 120 per cent of GDP at the end of the 19th century. Fiscal restraint and high economic growth allowed a sharp reduction of the ratio before the First World War. The ratio increased again to an even higher level during the war. Inflation and fiscal restraint brought about a new reduction during the 1920s and 1930s. The debt ratio rose again during the Second World War but was soon brought down by inflation to the lowest level since unification. The debt ratio was below the 60 per cent Maastricht threshold for only about 40 years.

While recourse to deficit finance has long been part of the Italian fiscal policy menu, what makes the last episode of debt accumulation special is the fact that it took place in peacetime and in a period of relatively strong economic growth.[2] The fiscal crisis was long and severe. The country ran primary deficits from 1965 to 1990. It had deficits in the range of 10 per cent of GDP from 1975 to 1994. Public debt rose from 40 per cent in 1970 to 121.5 per cent in 1994 (Figure 4.1). Over the same

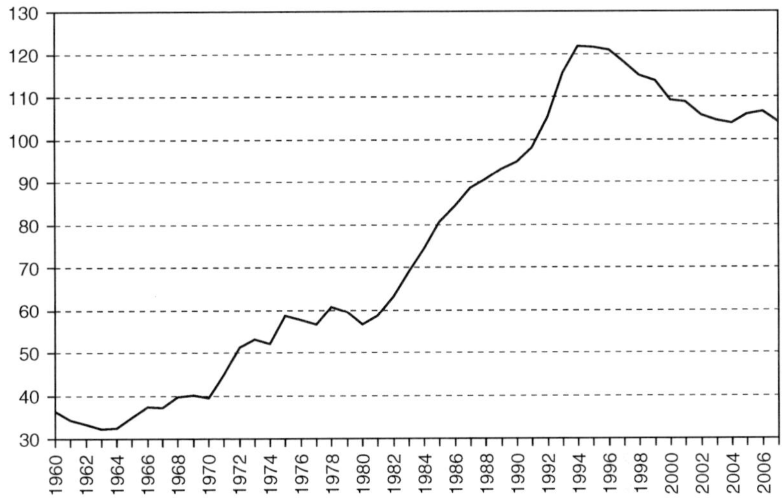

Figure 4.1 General government debt to GDP ratio
Source: based on Banca d'Italia data.

period, future pension liabilities gradually increased to about four times GDP (Beltrametti, 1996). Loose fiscal policy and rapid population ageing set public finances on an unsustainable path, with large generational imbalances and prospective deficits.[3]

The roots of Italian budgetary troubles can be traced back to the mid-1960s, when sizeable primary deficits were first recorded. Between 1964 and 1979 government expenditure increased from 30 per cent to 42 per cent of GDP, at a similar pace to that recorded in other European countries. The growth of expenditure was not matched by a similarly sized growth of revenue: over the same period the ratio of revenues to GDP increased only from 29 to 32 per cent (Figure 4.2). As a result, the primary deficit progressively increased, peaking at 8 per cent of GDP in 1975, and it fluctuated around 4 per cent of GDP in the late 1970s and early 1980s. However, up to the early 1980s, the increase in the debt-to-GDP ratio was offset by high inflation and negative real interest rates.

Revenues increased considerably in the first half of the 1980s (to 39 per cent of GDP in 1985), but further expenditure growth (to 51 per cent of GDP in 1985) prevented the reduction of the deficit. Italy's expenditure-to-GDP ratio, which had long been below the EU average, rose above it in 1983. While fiscal consolidation prevailed elsewhere in Europe, Italian imbalances increased even further. In the 1980s, with

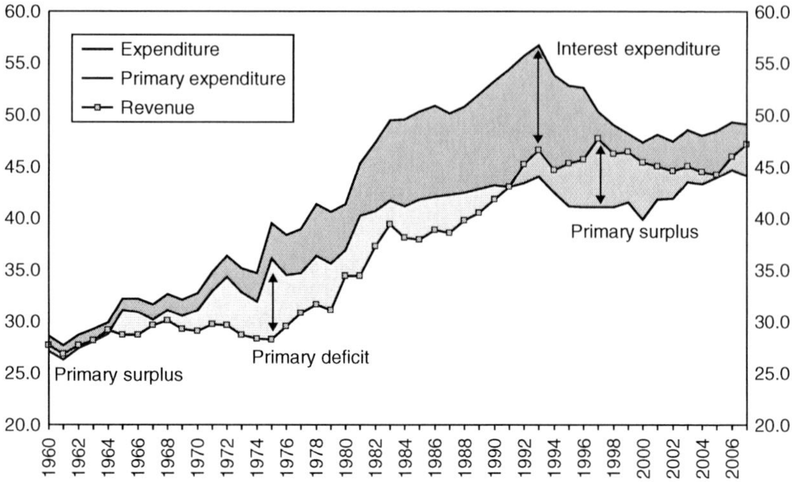

Figure 4.2 Public expenditure, revenues and budget balance
Source: Based on ISTAT. Data for 2007 are a government forecast from the update to DPEF for the years 2008–11.

the shift in monetary policy (which reduced the role of the Bank of Italy in the funding of the deficit), the opening of financial markets and the world-wide rise in real interest rates, the cost of public borrowing rose sharply and debt accumulation hastened its pace.[4] In 1984 the average interest rate on public debt became higher than the GDP deflator; in 1989 it rose above the nominal GDP growth rate (Figure 4.3).[5] In those years the unsustainable state of the public finances became widely recognised and fiscal consolidation was made the main objective of budgetary policies.

The large deficits in the middle of the 1980s were not the outcome of an exogenous shock or a temporary fiscal slippage but the result of two decades in which interest expenditure as well as part of primary expenditure were financed by additional borrowing. Together with persistent inflation, Italian fiscal imbalances reflected a number of political decisions and events, economic and institutional factors, and weak budgetary procedures (Reviglio, 1977; Romani, 1980). The very concept of meeting expenditure needs with revenues was lost (Steve, 1978; Salvati, 1984). Budgetary targets were systematically missed. Rules for local government finances were frequently breached. There was a persistent incapacity to modify the pension system, which promised unsustainable benefits and gradually crowded out other social benefits. As late as

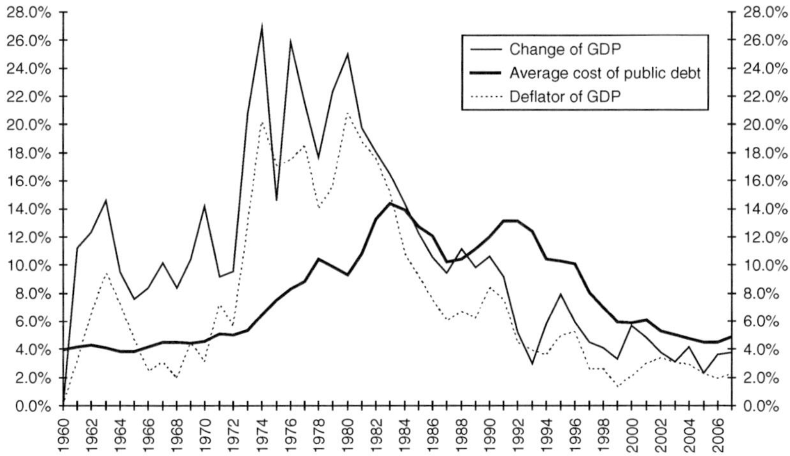

Figure 4.3 GDP growth rate, cost of debt and GDP deflator

1990, legislation was introduced to further increase pension expenditure. Overall, the Italian deficit appears to have been more entrenched than in most European countries.[6]

4.3 A painful consolidation process

Against this background, from the mid-1980s debt stabilisation became the main target of Italian fiscal policy (Amato, 1990). Initially, in spite of the favourable macroeconomic conditions, results were limited. Progress on the primary balance was offset by increasing interest expenditure (Sartor, 1998). Italy lost the last chance of implementing a gradual fiscal adjustment. It also missed the opportunity to stabilise the debt-to-GDP ratio without necessarily creating high primary surpluses.

In 1992 an exchange rate crisis triggered policy actions.[7] There was a broad consensus on the need to avoid the economic, social and political costs of debt default. The budget for 1993 represented a turning point in Italian fiscal policy. In order to curb the expected deficit, expenditure cuts and revenue increases amounting to nearly 6 per cent of GDP were implemented. Structural measures were also adopted to attenuate the expansionary trends in the major expenditure items. The pension system was eventually reformed after the long inconclusive debate of the 1980s. The organisation and the financial structure of the national health service was reshaped with a view to decentralising decisions and responsibilities. Local authorities' powers of taxation were broadened. The rules governing public employment were also reformed and an independent body was set up to conduct bargaining.

Fiscal consolidation gained momentum.[8] Primary deficits were replaced by sizeable primary surpluses. The debt-to-GDP ratio peaked in 1994 and declined thereafter. New measures were taken in 1997 to ensure Italy's participation in EMU (Ministero del Tesoro, 1998).[9] The overall deficit declined from double-digit levels to below the 3 per cent limit established in 1992 with the Maastricht Treaty. There was also a dramatic improvement in the inter-generational imbalances.[10] These remarkable and generally unexpected results were obtained in a relatively unfavourable macroeconomic context.[11]

The decline in the cost of servicing the debt, ascribable to the increasing confidence in the success of the consolidation effort and to the reduction of the inflation rate, significantly contributed to the outcome. Italy's participation in EMU consolidated these results by further reducing the risk premium on Italian bonds.

The consolidation process was very costly. Two to three fiscal packages were introduced every year. Corrective measures with temporary effects were frequently used. Altogether corrective measures amounted to 11 percentage points of GDP in 1990–2 and 17 points of GDP in 1993–7 (Balassone *et al.*, 2002). The focus on deficit reduction left little space for issues related to stabilisation policies. Allocative and distributive targets were also frequently forfeited. The adjustment relied on significant increases in tax revenues and a sharp reduction in capital expenditure. In 1997 the tax-to-GDP ratio was 2.5 percentage points higher in Italy than in the other 14 members of the EU. Capital spending as a percentage of GDP was about one-third lower than in the early 1990s.

The ratio of primary current outlays to GDP did not change significantly in the years 1996–2001. However, in evaluating the composition of the adjustment, an element to recognise is that the fast-rising expenditure trend of the previous decade was halted thanks to reforms of the pension system and to reductions in the resources transferred to local governments. Public employment was reduced by about 5 per cent. Pension liabilities were cut by about a third. Primary spending remained below the EU average.

Notwithstanding the success of the adjustment, its characteristics may have been unsuited to minimising its costs. The heavy reliance on tax increases and capital-spending reduction may have hampered the growth performance of the economy. The recurrent corrective measures may have negatively affected expectations of households and firms. Emergency action frequently prevailed over long-term solutions. This applied particularly to the pension system, where reforms were incremental, and to local government finance, where the rationing of transfers was preferred to the design of permanent budgetary rules. The drastic compression of health-care expenditure was obtained essentially by means of cash limits, while leaving structural problems largely unresolved. In the tax domain, the pressure to sustain revenue levels conflicted with the need to reconsider allocative targets in a context of increasing economic integration. Structural reforms have finally been set up in recent years. However, their design has not followed a linear path and subsequent changes have at times pulled the system in opposite directions (Balassone and Franco, 1995). These factors may explain why, in spite of the large reduction in interest rates, the success of the consolidation effort has not lead to a significant acceleration in growth.[12]

Summing up, the consolidation was highly successful, but it had to be continued. This required, among other things, further structural reforms, better institutions and procedures, and a strong determination to keep the debt on a downward trend.[13]

4.4 1998–2007: new imbalances

After the birth of EMU, the goals of Italian budgetary policy gradually changed, partly reflecting the problematic legacy of the previous consolidation process. A balanced budget remained a target for the medium term, in line with the Stability and Growth Pact (SGP). However, the reduction of the fiscal burden and the implementation of policies to support growth became priorities in the action of the governments (Balassone *et al.*, 2002; Bernardi, 2000). Reforms were introduced to simplify the tax system, reduce distortions in productive and financial decisions and gradually reduce the tax burden (Staderini, 2001). Reforms were also passed concerning the financing of the health-care sector and policies to sustain growth in the South; new budgetary rules were introduced for local governments (Giannini and Guerra, 2000; Onofri, 2001; Rossi, 2002). A restructuring of social programmes was widely debated, with spending to be shifted from pensions to unemployment and welfare benefits, but little progress was achieved (Commissione per l'analisi delle compatibilità macroeconomiche della spesa sociale, 1997; Rossi, 1997).

The Finance Bills for the years 1998, 1999 and 2000 did not aim for a further, large reduction of the deficit. The extent of the correction was usually small. In spite of the relatively favourable economic context,[14] the primary surplus progressively deteriorated, partly as a result of the tax cuts implemented in September 2000 following higher than expected revenues for that year. Only the reduction of interest expenditure allowed net borrowing to continue declining.

For the first time since its introduction in 1978, the Finance Bill for the year 2001 explicitly increased net borrowing with respect to its trend expected value (by about 1 per cent of GDP). Based on the assumption that higher than expected revenues in 2000 were permanent, the government tried to boost economic growth by reducing taxes on households and firms. On the expenditure side, new additional resources were made available for social protection and health. The outcome was a new increase in fiscal imbalances. In 2001 the borrowing requirement (net of privatisation receipts) reached 4.9 per cent of GDP, up from 2.9 per cent in 1997.

In the period 2002–5, against a background of marked slowdown of economic growth,[15] budgetary policy again had to restrain the progressive deterioration of budget balances and was again based on restrictive measures. Finance Bills were often supplemented by additional corrective measures in the course of the year. Substantial recourse was again made to temporary measures.[16] This period was also marked by measures to sustain growth and by reforms concerning, among other, taxation, public and private pension provisions and the management of the State's assets (Brunetta, 2003; OECD, 2003; 2005).

Overall, the primary balance, at 6.6 per cent of GDP in 1997, shrunk to virtually nil in 2005. In the initial years, the deterioration was offset by the reduction in interest payments (Figure 4.4). Moreover, because of statistical problems (see Section 4.6), the extent of the worsening in the primary balance did not emerge immediately. Only in 2005 did the European Council identify the presence of an excessive deficit and ask the Italian government to redress the situation by 2007 at the latest. Excluding privatisation receipts and other one-off measures, the general government borrowing requirement averaged around 6 per cent of GDP over the period 2003–5. In 2005 the ratio of debt to GDP began to increase again, rising to 105.8 per cent. Without the measures to reduce capital assets and restructure liabilities, the upward trend would have resumed in 2001.

The widening public deficit reflected, especially in 2002–5, the gap between the rapid growth in primary current expenditure and the modest growth in GDP. Between 1998 and 2006, while GDP grew at an average annual rate of 1.4 per cent, primary current expenditure rose at a rate of 2.1 per cent in real terms. In Germany – which, like Italy, had a low rate of economic growth (1.4 per cent) – in the same period primary current expenditure grew by 0.2 per cent per year. In the rest of the euro area,

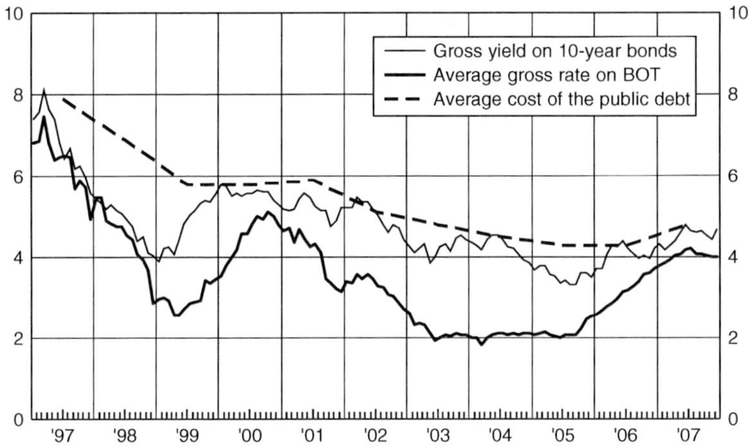

Figure 4.4 The cost of public debt

current primary expenditure grew in line with GDP, by 2.8 per cent per year (Table 4.1).

The growth of current primary public expenditure was about the same under the two coalitions in power in 1998–2001 and 2002–6.[17] The impact on the budget balance was different because of the marked slowdown in GDP growth: 2.2 per cent per year in 1998–2001, 0.7 per cent per year in 2002–6.

Important differences emerge from looking at different levels of government. The rate of growth of current primary expenditure of central government declined sharply from 1992 and was even negative between 1993 and 2001; in 2002–6 it increased again faster than GDP growth. Local governments, which are responsible for health-care expenditure, curbed the growth of public spending during the years 1993–7; after 1998 their spending grew faster than GDP. The expenditure of social security institutions grew at a rate of over 4.5 per cent in real terms up until 1997; afterwards, when the effects of the pension reforms of the 1990s began to come through, the growth rate halved. However, it remained well above the growth rate of GDP.

While the unadjusted primary balance declined through the whole period 1998–2005, the deterioration of the structural primary balance was concentrated in the years 1998–2003, amounting to 6 per cent of GDP (Marino *et al.*, 2008).[18] The structural balance remained broadly stable in 2004–5 and improved significantly in the following two years (around 3 per cent of GDP; Figure 4.5). The structural deterioration in

Table 4.1 Real growth rates of primary current expenditure and GDP

ITALY						INTERNATIONAL COMPARISON		
	General Government	Central Government	Local Government	Social Security bodies	GDP	PERIOD 1998–2006		
1970–1985	6.1				3.2	Country	Current primary expenditure	GDP
1986–1992	4.6	4.0	4.7	4.6	2.6			
1993–1997	0.7	−3.9	0.5	4.8	1.3			
1998–2001	2.2	−0.4	4.2	2.4	2.2	Italy	2.1	1.4
2002–2006	2.0	1.4	3.2	2.2	0.7	Germany	0.2	1.4
						Other 10 euro area*	2.8	2.9

(*) Excluding Slovenia
Sources: for Italy, ISTAT. For International comparisons AMECO November 2007.

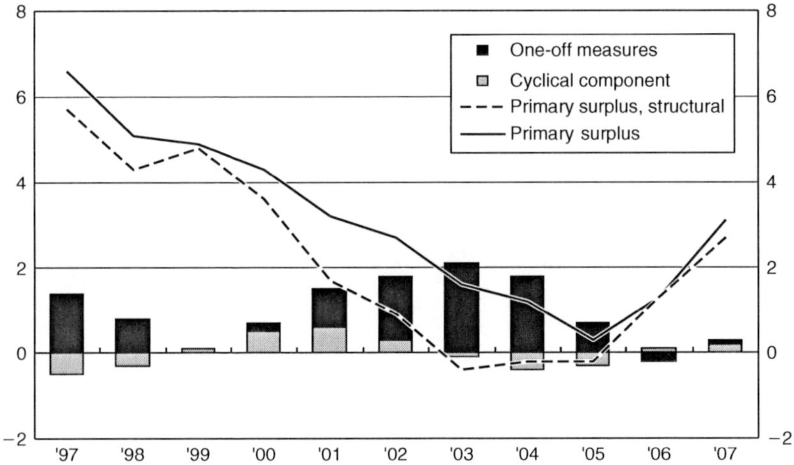

Figure 4.5 Primary balance and temporary factors
Source: Marino *et al.* (2007).

the initial six years can be largely attributed to government measures, which permanently reduced revenue by 3.5 per cent of GDP. The increase in primary spending (2.8 per cent of GDP) was concentrated in capital and health expenditure.

The worsening of the structural primary balance contrasted with the targets set annually in the Economic and Financial Planning Document (*Documento di programmazione economico-finanziaria*, DPEF), which aimed to keep (or gradually restore) the primary surplus to 5 per cent of GDP, a level the Italian government had pledged to maintain in the medium term when Italy joined EMU (Figure 4.6). The results for expenditure are the mirror image of the fiscal consolidation of the early 1990s, which was marked by large cuts in health expenditure and public investment (Franco, 2005). As for revenue, the outcomes are broadly in line with the objective, indicated in the various DPEF since 1997, to reduce the fiscal burden. Again, as in the case of expenditure, this result is rooted in the nature of the fiscal consolidation implemented in the early 1990s (the tax ratio had risen by 4 percentage points between 1991 and 1997). This may provide some support for the findings of the recent strand of empirical research linking the probability of success of fiscal consolidations to their composition.

The improvement of the structural balance in 2004–7 was mainly driven by the increase in revenue. This reflected cyclical developments as

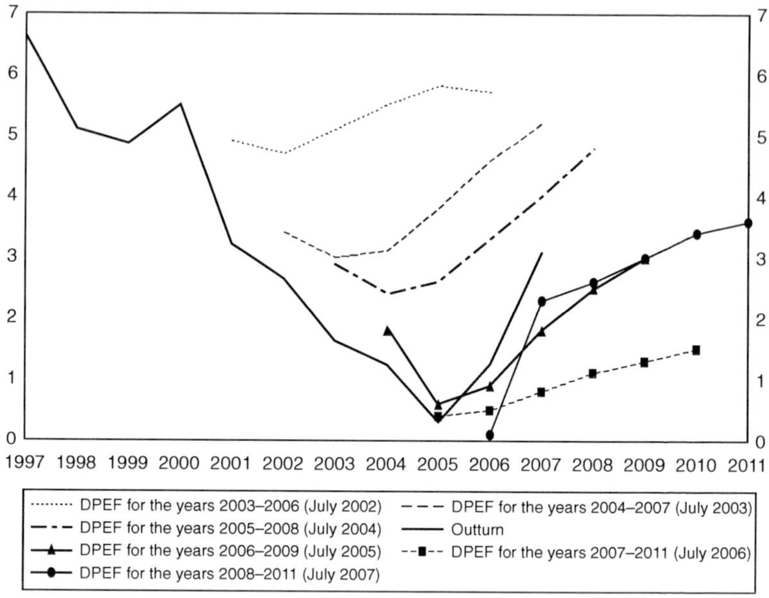

Figure 4.6 Primary surplus: objectives and outturn

well as policy measures (including measures aimed at curbing tax evasion and erosion) and structural developments (Locarno and Staderini, 2008). The latter include the greater role of large-scale retailing, which reduces the scope for evading VAT, and the shift in the composition of household spending towards goods subject to the standard VAT rate of 20 per cent and offering less scope for evasion given the structure of supply.

The ratio of primary expenditure to GDP remained virtually constant, reflecting a sizeable reduction in public investment. It would thus appear that the recent adjustment presents some of the weaknesses highlighted in the consolidation of the early nineties. Additionally, the ratio of primary current expenditure to GDP is at a post-Second World War peak, while the revenue-to-GDP ratio is very close to the 1997 peak (Figure 4.7).

A major feature of Italian fiscal policy in the EMU period is the use of temporary measures, mainly aimed at complying with the European fiscal rules (Reviglio, 2006a). After 1997, consistently with the commitment to reach a budgetary position in balance or in surplus in the medium term, temporary measures should have been progressively replaced by more structural measures. However, from 2001 onwards extensive use was again made of temporary measures. In the period

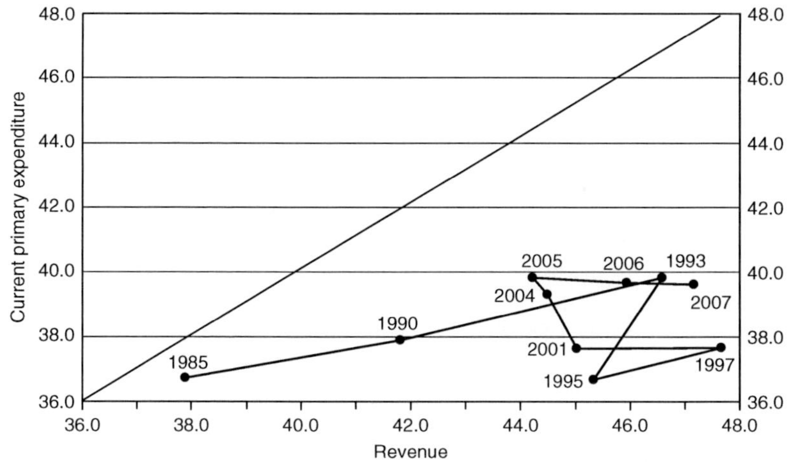

Figure 4.7 Revenue and current primary expenditure: selected years

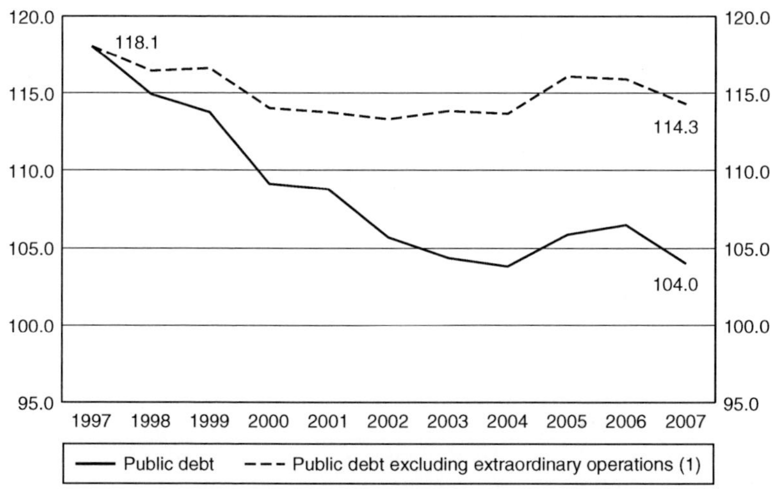

Figure 4.8 General government debt and the effect of extraordinary operations
Note: Extraordinary operations include debt restructuring and sales of financial assets and real estate.

1997–2007 they averaged about 1 per cent of GDP. The main temporary measures were sales of real estate, tax amnesties and legislation anticipating tax revenues.[19] Apart from contributing to delaying structural adjustment, recourse to temporary measures may have introduced some distortions in the economy.[20] Momigliano and Rizza (2007) suggest that policy-makers used temporary measures to buy time in an unfavourable economic context. The temporary measures reached a maximum level in 2003, while the negative peak of the cycle was reached in 2005. Marino *et al.* (2008) attribute the wrong timing of this strategy to the unexpected persistence of the downturn that begun in 2001. Italian policy-makers – as well as virtually all forecasters – expected a rapid recovery, whereas the low growth lasted for five years.

Extraordinary operations of debt restructuring and sales of assets also had a major effect on the evolution of the general government debt. Excluding the effect of such operations, public debt would have declined by around 3.5 percentage points since 1997, compared with an actual decline of 14 per cent (Figure 4.8).

4.5 The medium-term outlook

Since the late 1990s the achievement of a balanced budget has been the medium-term target of all Italian governments, consistent with the requirements of the SGP. A balanced budget is essential also for purely national reasons, if the debt is to be reduced significantly. Debt reduction would reduce the exposure of the budget to interest rate fluctuations and make available adequate resources with which to defray the costs associated with the ageing of the population. In 2007 the government set 2011 as the year in which to achieve this goal via a further increase in the primary surplus (about 1.5 per cent of GDP over the period 2008–11 (Ministero dell'Economia e delle Finanze, 2007a). The target was confirmed in the June 2008 DPEF (Ministero dell'Ecocomia e delle Finanze, 2008).

As the government has repeatedly recognised, the crucial challenge of Italy's public finances consists in simultaneously bringing down the debt ratio and reducing the fiscal burden on the economy. To achieve these objectives it is necessary to curb primary current expenditure, which over the last ten years has grown at an average real rate of between 2 and 2.5 per cent per year.

While in recent years the mismatch between the rate of growth of current spending and the rate of growth of potential GDP (which has been estimated at about 1.5 per cent) has been offset in turn by the decline in interest spending, the recourse to temporary measures, cuts to capital spending and revenue growth, none of these options can be relied upon in the coming years.

By the year 2006 the interest bill had completed its declining path: the gap between the average cost of public debt, which is affected by past issues of high-yield bonds, and the cost of newly issued bonds, which mirrors EMU rates, has been closed. In the future, interest expenditure reduction will only come from a reduction in the size of the debt.

Recourse to temporary measures is limited by EU-level commitments and by the lack of sizeable margins for further operations.[21]

Between 1992 and 2007, public investment expenditure averaged 2.4 per cent of GDP in Italy, compared with 2.6 per cent in the rest of the euro area. There is a wide gap between the endowment of infrastructure in Italy and that in the other main European countries (Kamps, 2004; ANCE, 2005). In fact, Italy's poor endowment of infrastructure is one of the reasons for its falling below the other main industrial countries in international rankings of competitiveness. Between 2003 and 2007, public investment declined from 2.7 to 2.4 per cent of GDP (net of sales of public assets). A further cut would not be advisable.

Taxes and social security contributions rose from 40.6 per cent of GDP in 2005 to 43.3 per cent in 2007, which is close to the peaks recorded in 1997 and almost 2 percentage points above the euro-area average (Table 4.2). The gap is wider in terms of the amounts effectively paid by the taxpayers who fulfil their obligations, owing to the large size of the underground economy in Italy.

In 2007 the Italian statutory tax rate applicable to corporate income was higher than in any other country except Germany. Between 2000 and 2007 the euro-area average corporate income tax rate fell by 10.2 percentage points, to 26.4 per cent; in Italy it fell by 4 points, to 37.25 per cent (including IRAP, the regional tax on productive activities).[22] The statutory tax rates on labour income are also among the highest by international standards. In 2006, excluding IRAP, the fiscal component was 45.9 per cent of labour costs, against a euro-area average of 43.1 per cent. The tax wedge in Italy was smaller than in France (49.2 per cent) and Germany (52.2 per cent), but much higher than in Spain (38.9 per cent) and the United Kingdom (34.1 per cent). During the 1990s average personal income tax rates increased significantly, partly as a consequence of fiscal drag (Figure 4.9). At 20 per cent, the ordinary VAT rate in Italy is slightly higher than the euro-area average and the rates in France and Germany. It is much higher than the rates in Spain and the United Kingdom.

A further increase in the level of taxation would widen distortions in the economy and hamper the competitiveness of Italian companies. It would also counter the pressures towards lower tax rates stemming from the integration of the European single market and the process of globalisation.

In the end, the government's ability to restrain the growth of current primary expenditure will be crucial for balancing the budget and

Table 4.2 Fiscal burden and statutory rates of the main taxes[1]

	ITALY		FRANCE		GERMANY		SPAIN		EURO AREA		UK	
	2007	Var. 2000–07	2007	Var. 2000–07	2007	Var. 2000–07	2007	Var. 2000–07	2007	Var. 2000–07	2007	Var. 2000–07
Fiscal burden (2)	43.3	1.7	45.2	−0.4	40.4	−2.3	38.1	3.3	41.5	−0.5	37.4	−0.1
Source: ISTAT												
Statutory tax rates on labour income (3)												
Tax wedge as % of labour cost	45.9	−0.5	49.2	−40.4	52.2	−1.8	38.9	0.3	43.1	−0.5	34.1	1.5
Tax wedge as % of gross earnings												
borne by employer	*32.1*	*−2.0*	*42.0*	*0.8*	*19.7*	*−0.8*	*30.2*	*−0.4*	*24.9*	*−0.9*	*10.8*	*1.5*
borne by worker	*28.5*	*0.3*	*27.8*	*−1.0*	*42.8*	*−1.7*	*20.4*	*0.6*	*29.3*	*−0.4*	*27.0*	*1.2*
of which: personal taxation	*19.0*	*0.0*	*14.1*	*1.3*	*22.0*	*−2.0*	*14.1*	*0.7*	*16.3*	*−0.2*	*17.7*	*0.3*
Implicit tax rates on labour income (4)												
as % of gross earnings	43.1	−0.2	42.1	0.1	38.7	−2.0	30.1	2.0	36.7 (5)	−0.9	25.5	0.1
Statutory tax rates on capital income (6)												
Corporate income tax	37.3	−4.0	34.4	−2.3	38.3	−13.3	32.5	−2.5	26.4	−10.2	30.0	0.0
Statutory tax rates on consumption (7)												
Ordinary VAT rate	20.0	0.0	19.6	−1.0	19.0	3.0	16.0	0.0	19.4	0.7	17.5	0.0

(1) Changes are calculated as the difference between the rates in 2000 and 2007, except for the implicit tax rates on labour income, for which they are the difference between 2000 and 2005.
(2) Sources: for Italy, ISTAT; for the other countries and the Euro area, European Commission, *Spring Forecasts*, April 2008.
(3) Source: OECD, 2007, *Taxing Wages 2006–2007*. The figures refer to the average industrial worker, unmarried and without children.
(4) Source: Eurostat, 2007, *Taxation Trends in the European Union*.
(5) The Euro area average is calculated excluding Portugal, for which the figure for 2005 is not indicated.
(6) Source: European Commission, 2006, *Structures of the Taxation Systems in the European Union: 1995–2004* . The implicit rates on labour income refer to 2004.

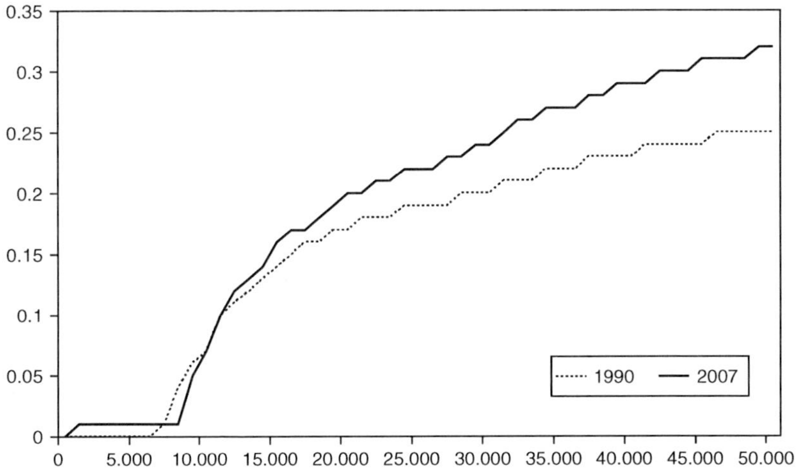

Figure 4.9 Personal income tax: average tax rates for a single employee, including regional and local rates

providing resources for tax cuts and capital spending increases as further rises in taxes or cuts in capital expenditures would be inadvisable.

In the macroeconomic scenario envisaged in the September 2007 update of the DPEF, in order to achieve the target of a budget balance in 2011 without increasing taxes or cutting back investment from the levels planned for 2008, the ratio of primary current expenditure to GDP needs to fall by more than 2 percentage points in the three years 2009–11; expenditure would have to decrease slightly in real terms. If the revenue-to-GDP ratio is to be reduced to the 2005 level (44.4 per cent), the ratio of primary current expenditure to GDP would have to fall by more than 4 percentage points in 2009–11, with expenditure contracting in real terms by more than 2 per cent per year.

The size of the necessary adjustment calls for an extensive correction based on structural reforms and involving local authorities. It is necessary to 'spend better' by improving the effectiveness and efficiency of public-sector operations. The Green Paper prepared in 2007 by the Advisory Committee for the Public Finances (Commissione Tecnica per la Finanza Pubblica, 2007a) reveals ample scope for achieving savings in all the main expenditure items by reorganising departments, reviewing priorities, assigning duties more precisely and establishing clear criteria for the evaluation of results. The revision of the classification of the State

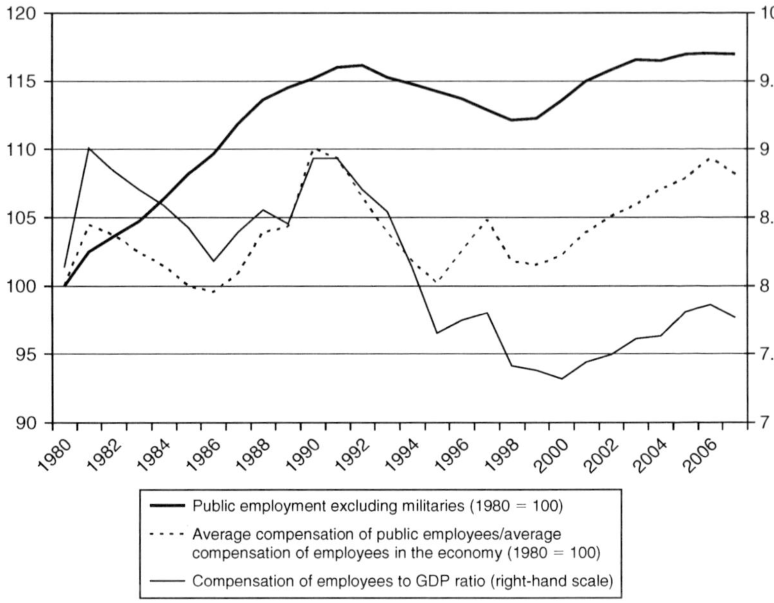

Figure 4.10 Public employment
Source: Based on ISTAT.

budget (introduced with the budget for 2008 – see Section 4.7) and the start of the spending review in 2007[23] both go in the direction of improving the quality of public spending and curbing its level in the medium term. The action begun in 2006 to control health spending moves in the same direction. It increases the constraints imposed on the regions with large deficits and envisages automatic increases in regional tax rates.

One of the main challenges of fiscal policy concerns the control of the cost of public employment (Figure 4.10). In 2000–7, both the number of public employees and their relative wage have been on an upward trend.[24]

Entrenched practices, the multiplicity of actors, and the inevitable complexity of the rules mean that expenditure reform is a long-term endeavour.[25] However, in order to bring down the debt ratio and reduce the fiscal burden, it is important to achieve results in the medium term too.[26] This would reduce the risk of having to implement corrective measures in the future in a difficult economic context, diminish uncertainty among companies and households, and avoid increases in the spread on Italian bonds.[27]

Fiscal policy should also try to remove the factors that have curtailed the growth of the Italian economy in recent years (Morcaldo, 2005 and 2007). Some policies can improve both the potential growth and the fiscal outcome. This is the case of measures postponing retirement, which can increase labour supply and reduce public spending. Since the mid-1990s the average retirement age has already increased by more than two years. However, the employment rate in the 55–64 year range (32.5 per cent in 2006) remains far below the euro-area average and the Lisbon target (50 per cent). Some policies can increase potential growth without worsening public finances. This is the case with measures reducing, in parallel, tax evasion and tax rates.[28] It is also the case of policies increasing the efficiency of public services, such as education,[29] softening the burden of legal and procedural constraints (Ferro *et al.*, 1999), and improving the efficiency in the operation of markets.

Labour market reforms show both the potential of structural policies and the complexity of the reform process. In the last decade the labour market has been widely reformed to remove some of the existing rigidities. The interventions have focused mainly on reducing institutional protections and increasing the rewards of participation. They have contributed to the sizeable increase in employment, achieved in a low-growth period, and to the decline of unemployment, which is now back to the level of the early 1980s. However, some changes have increased the complexity of the institutional framework and the dualism of the labour market, making it more segmented between different age-cohorts, between insiders and outsiders and between different types of outsiders (Boeri, 2004; Brandolini *et al.*, 2007; Rosolia and Torrini, 2007). Some of the actions required to redress the labour market situation represent a challenge for the public finances as well. Notably, reforms of employment protection need to trade labour market flexibility with more robust state-provided unemployment insurance, better job-search services and participation incentives. This suggests that social expenditure should be reformed, releasing resources from the pension system to improve welfare schemes (see also Section 4.9).

Tax policy will play a major role. Several problems remain still unsolved. First, because of tax erosion and evasion, the tax burden has long been unevenly distributed among the various groups of taxpayers. This situation largely depends on the structure of the Italian economy, with its small enterprises and army of self-employed workers, and on the difficulties of the tax administration of coping with the problems that such a structure causes for tax assessment (Reviglio, 2006b). Further progress in reducing erosion and evasion will be crucial in reducing tax rates and the distortions introduced by taxation in the economy. Second, the decentralisation of the country requires that a substantial autonomy to local authorities be granted on the revenue side. However, the increase in the tax autonomy of local administrations can hinder the reduction of tax revenue for the public sector as a whole. Moreover, the dimension and the characteristics of the tax bases to be decentralised are crucial and are hard to define. Third, there is a need to limit recourse to frequent tax reforms. Radical fiscal reforms are necessarily costly in terms of adjustment costs and uncertainty of prospective decisions, such as those concerning investment and production. In recent years, the Italian tax system has been subject to contrasting, radical changes (Balassone *et al.*, 2002).

4.6 Fiscal indicators

From 2000, the evaluation of Italian public finance trends became more difficult: the picture of the public finances one could get by looking at net borrowing was very different (and persistently so) from the picture one could get by looking at the cash borrowing requirement. Even accounting for the fact that these two indicators are calculated according to different statistical procedures, differences were sizeable and non-standard (Balassone *et al.*, 2005; 2007).

The cash borrowing requirement was the main fiscal indicator up until the mid-nineties (Balassone and Franco, 1996). Afterwards, the focus shifted to net borrowing as both the eligibility requirements for joining EMU and the European fiscal rules were defined in terms of this indicator. However, while the gap between the two indicators was very small throughout most of the 1990s, things changed from 1999, also in connection with the revision of European statistical standards which require net borrowing to be computed on an accrual basis.[30]

Since 2000 the general government borrowing requirement has been much larger than net borrowing. Initially, both the Italian statistical office and the Ministry of Finance underestimated the information coming from the evolution of cash data on the financing of budget imbalances.[31] As a result, net borrowing for 2001 and the following years had to be repeatedly revised upwards, ending up even above the 3 per cent ceiling. The revisions regarded several items, such as transfers to railways, health spending, proceeds of public property sales, receipts from lotteries and transactions with the EU. The cash borrowing requirement was also revised upwards. The changes mainly reflected Eurostat decisions on the above-mentioned securitisations, funds for a high-speed railway line to be built and the availability of data concerning private accounts with the Post Office. In the end, the average gap between the borrowing requirement and net borrowing in 2001–3 declined from the 1.6 per cent of GDP indicated in the early figures to 1 per cent. In the following years the gap between the two indicators remained basically stable and largely reflected the balance of transactions in financial assets.[32]

The underestimation of net borrowing at the beginning of the new century may have had a significant effect on Italian budgetary policy, which was based on indicators that were heavily revised afterwards. Net borrowing in 2001 turned out to be 3.1 per cent of GDP, against an initial estimate (released in March 2002) of 1.4 per cent and a primary surplus indicated at the time at 4.9 per cent (a value close to the medium-term target). These provisional outturns did not provide a strong incentive for the government to undertake adequate measures in a timely way in years in which economic conditions were relatively favourable. Moreover, had the true figures been available immediately, peer pressure from other member states would have played a greater role.

This experience suggests that budgetary targets should be expressed in terms of both ESA95 net borrowing and the cash borrowing requirement (or the change in debt). Detailed information on the gap between the two indicators should also be provided. In recent years there have been improvements in the quality of fiscal statistics, most notably in reconciling the ESA95 net borrowing and the cash borrowing requirement.[33]

Similarly, in order to avoid a distorted view of the current situation of the public finances, it is important to have a detailed evaluation of the impact of temporary measures on current and future fiscal balances and to have a report on the general government net wealth. Some progress has recently been made in the latter area (see Ministero dell'Economia e delle Finanze, 2004; Reviglio, 2007).

4.7 Budgetary rules and procedures

Over recent decades Italy has reformed its fiscal institutions and has developed a number of budgetary procedures designed to limit fiscal imbalances.[34] A specific procedure for the yearly budget was introduced in 1978 and revised in 1988 and 1999. In 1988 the introduction of the yearly DPEF aimed at introducing medium-term planning of fiscal policies. The role of the Ministry for the Economy and Finance has been strengthened by merging the Ministry for the Budget (in 1997) and the Ministry of Finance (in 2001) into the Ministry of the Treasury.[35]

A Domestic Stability Pact was introduced in 1999 (see Section 4.8). Long-term projections of age-related expenditure are made available on a yearly basis (see Section 4.10). The budgetary framework envisages the publication of several documents aimed at providing ample information about fiscal developments.

Fiscal policy discussion is largely based on the targets set for budget balance in the coming years in the DPEF, which is released in July. No quantitative targets are set for revenue and spending levels.[36] The budget for the following year (presented to Parliament at the end of September and approved at the end of December) specifies the measures to bridge the gap between the trend deficit (*tendenziale*) and the target deficit indicated in the DPEF. The update of the Stability Programme (published at the end of the year) usually confirms the targets set in the DPEF. Supplementary fiscal packages have been introduced in most years, either to make sure that the target for the budget balance is actually achieved or to make use of unexpected budgetary margins. Quarterly budgetary developments are examined in official reports based on cash figures (*Relazione trimestrale di cassa,* Rtc). Moreover, since 2004 the national statistical office releases quarterly accounts compiled according to ESA95 rules. The monthly cash borrowing requirement provides timely indications of budgetary outcomes.

These procedures have contributed to the fiscal consolidation process, but the budgetary system still presents some weaknesses.[37]

Budget formulation is still largely based on an incremental approach. A large part of public spending is extrapolated from year to year without an in-depth examination of the effectiveness of programmes. The fragmented structure of the budget, not based on programmes, has not helped to clarify the government's priorities. In order to tackle these problems, the classification system for the state budget has been modified, starting from the 2008 budget. The budget is now divided into missions and programmes. The reform aims to increase the transparency of the allocative process and shift the focus of the discussion from the new measures included in the year's budget to the policies in effect, which cover most of public spending (Ministero dell'Economia e delle Finanze, 2007b).

The budget approval process also presents some problems. The implications of the new measures included in the budget law are not always carefully examined before submission to Parliament. During the parliamentary process the text is sometimes extensively modified by the government itself. The text is also subject to a large number of amendments reflecting to specific interest groups. Changes introduced in the last phase of the process may not be properly evaluated. The discussion focuses on new measures, while the budget baseline does not attract much attention. Moreover, in spite of the fact that the budget is based on a three-year horizon, the discussion focuses on the first year. The overall impact of the budget on the general government balance does not change significantly during the parliamentary process,[38] but the composition of expenditure and revenue measures can be considerably modified. The latter features may not necessarily hamper the fiscal consolidation process in the short term. However, they can be problematic for the efficient use of public resources on a longer-term horizon.

The system of expenditure management emphasises legal and procedural compliance rather than the specification of objectives and the assessment of performance. There is relatively little analysis of results and costs. The budget is audited by the State Audit Office (*Corte dei Conti*) primarily to assess legal compliance with the approved budget. In order to tackle this issue, in 2007 the government started a process of expenditure review (as already mentioned in Section 4.5) that aims to identify efficiency gains, delete low-priority programmes and make the allocation of resources more closely related to strategic targets.[39]

Some aspects of budgetary reporting need further improvement. The 'trend scenario', which plays a fundamental role in defining the size of budgetary measures, is not fully transparent.[40] Explanation of budgetary slippages is sometimes poor. Moreover, there is scarce information on non-Maastricht debt, such as commercial debt and the liabilities of public corporations. In general, the model and the assumptions underlying the government forecasts should be made available to the public. This applies, for example, to the indicators of the long-term sustainability of public finance, which could also be revised by independent technical bodies (Franco and Marino, 2003).

Outturns for net borrowing and the primary surplus have often been worse than the estimates made in the previous year (July DPEF and its September update) and in the spring of the same year (Rtc). Part of these gaps can be explained by the often 'optimistic' official macroeconomic forecasts (CER, IRS, Prometeia, 2000; Onofri, 2001). Jonung and Larch (2006) note that, as in France and Germany, Italian official GDP forecasts in the period 1987–2005 were characterised by an optimistic bias.[41] They argue that this may be part of a strategy designed to postpone painful policy decisions. However, macroeconomic forecasts only marginally explain the distance between outturns and forecasts in the Italian fiscal projections (Banca d'Italia, 2006).[42] It is notable that in recent years official forecasts (both macroeconomic and fiscal) have been in line with those of international institutions and outcomes have been better than projected figures.[43] Further progress could be made on this issue by employing independent bodies to provide an evaluation of the government forecasts.

Action to address some of these weak points was started in 2007. It is particularly important that the spending review becomes part of the budget system and that further progress be achieved in the preparation, approval and execution of the budget (International Monetary Fund, 2007b). Monitoring of budgetary developments can benefit greatly from full operational use of the SIOPE system (*Sistema operativo dei pubblici enti*), which – once fully implemented – will collect information concerning all cash operations of central and local governments in real time. The system is based on a standardised codification of spending and revenue activities and is gradually being extended to all government agencies.[44]

While the debate on budgetary procedures has been lively, there has been little discussion so far concerning the introduction of new fiscal rules at the national level.[45] This may reflect a certain scepticism concerning the effectiveness of rules based on the experience of Article 81 of the Constitution.[46] It may also reflect the recognition that the EU framework (the 3 per cent of GDP limit for the deficit and the close-to-balance requirement) provides an adequate set of rules and the consideration that rules for sub-national governments are now the priority issue (Section 4.8). As for the last topic, the constitutional reform of 2001 introduced a provision preventing regional and local governments from incurring debt for any reason other than investment financing.

Awareness of the need to keep public expenditure under control has prompted debate concerning the introduction of some form of expenditure rule.[47] This rule should directly involve the expenditure of central government and social security institutions and indirectly the expenditure of sub-national governments (Giarda *et al.*, 2005).

4.8 Fiscal decentralisation

Until the 1980s Italy was a highly centralised country. The decentralisation process gained momentum in the 1990s. Greater spending functions and tax responsibilities were allocated to regions and municipalities.[48] However, in the 1990s when central government was confronted with the challenge of combining fiscal consolidation and fiscal decentralisation, it usually assigned priority to the former. The contribution of sub-national governments to fiscal adjustment was determined by instruments typical of a centralised institutional set-up: mandatory limits for transfers from the State, overall ceilings for health expenditure, and limits to hiring in the public sector.

At the end of the 1990s, when the decentralisation process speeded up again, the issue of fiscal rules for sub-national governments became prominent. It was apparent that there was a need for an institutional framework combining decentralisation of fiscal responsibilities with respect of EMU rules, while avoiding pro-cyclical policies and cuts in capital spending at the local level. In 1999 the Domestic Stability Pact was introduced with a view to involving sub-national authorities in the attainment of the fiscal objectives set at the European level (Balassone and Franco, 2001). Its name notwithstanding, the Pact was a central government law and did not mimic the European Pact. From its creation the Pact presented several problems: weak sanctions, targets unrelated to the budget balance used at the EU level, and exclusion of several budgetary items. In the following years, the Pact was frequently changed and gradually evolved from a regulation setting maximum ceilings on the growth of local government deficits to a tool for centralised expenditure control, not consistent with fiscal decentralisation.

Most regions and local governments have respected the Pact. Nevertheless, in the period 1999–2005 the growth rate of current primary spending of sub-national governments averaged 6.3 per cent, against 3.2 per cent for central government. In real terms, it increased by 3.9 per cent per year. This apparent inconsistency reflects the exclusions from the Pact of some major expenditure items such as, in particular, fast-growing health expenditure.

The 2001 constitutional reform greatly extended regional powers. A further constitutional reform was introduced in 2005 but was rejected by a referendum in 2006. However, several aspects of the new fiscal framework remain partly undefined (Bordignon, 2006; ISAE, 2007b). The tax responsibilities of sub-national governments are still fairly limited.[49] Transfers to sub-national governments still largely reflect the past spending of each government. The results of the decentralisation process are mixed in terms of both allocative efficiency and budgetary control. Lacking a close link between spending and revenue decisions and clear budgetary rules, the decentralisation process has not yet fully succeeded in making supply more responsive to user preferences, increasing citizen control over public administrators and fostering competition between sub-national governments (Esposito, 2003).

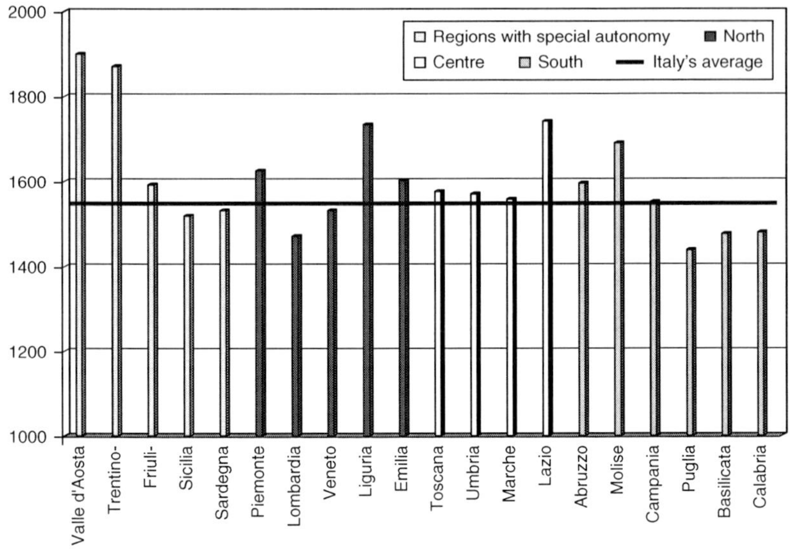

Figure 4.11 Per capita health service costs by region
Source: Relazione generale sulla situazione economica del Paese (2006). Data adjusted for interregional mobility.

Differences in the quality of the services provided by regional and local authorities remain sizeable (Figure 4.11). These differences reflect both different degrees of efficiency in running public services, with a general North-South divide, and different spending levels within all areas of the country, which partly reflect transfers based on past spending levels.[50]

These developments reflect the lack of political consensus over the end-point of the process of decentralisation. There is no consensus about some possible implications of the decentralisation process, such as the acceptable degree of differentiation in the provision of services across the country. This is borne out by the back-and-forth of policy changes and the contradictions that characterise some technical solutions, such as those concerning revenue and spending responsibilities.

The decisions on the desired degree and on the features of decentralisation should go hand in hand with the definition of budgetary rules and procedures (Giarda, 2003; Petretto, 2003). If the decentralisation process is to be followed through, at least by fully implementing the 2001 constitutional provision, the link between revenue and spending decisions should be strengthened. Otherwise, there is a risk that a soft budget constraint could turn decentralised governments into a constant threat to fiscal soundness.

Progress would be required in four main areas: i) budget rules should be based on the budget balance; ii) sub-national governments should have adequate tax bases and margins to set rates[51]; iii) transfers from the state should be predefined and based on actual needs rather than on past transfer levels; iv) budgetary procedures and monitoring systems should be strengthened; and v) all levels of government should be involved in the definition of targets and in monitoring fiscal trends (Franco *et al.*, 2004; Giarda *et al.*, 2005).

This process faces several obstacles. First, economic integration sets limits on the allocation of tax bases to sub-national governments. Second, it is politically difficult to move from transfers based on past spending to transfers based on a uniform standard of service. Losers may veto the process. This was already the case in 1992, 1997 and 2000. But if the rationale for transfers remains shaky, it is politically difficult to establish full fiscal responsibility. Third, large income differences across the country[52] require either the acceptance of large differences in per capita spending or the need for large transfers in favour of relatively poor regions (Fausto, 2003). The current situation is a mix of the two instances, the outcome being a rather opaque solution. The definition of predefined transfers would increase the transparency of differences in entitlements across the country and the size of the subsidies across regions. Some basic issues would need an explicit answer: what regional differences in public services are acceptable? Should wages be different in the public sector? Finally, sub-national governments are responsible for some expenditure programmes that are partly driven by structural factors. This is the case of health care and to some extent also for welfare spending.[53] If the dynamics of tax bases and transfers are not consistent with that of expenditure commitments, there is a risk that the central government will systematically have to bail out sub-national governments.

4.9 The search for a sustainable pension system[54]

The reform of the pension system has long been at the core of the efforts to ensure fiscal consolidation and long-term sustainability in Italy. This reflects both the structure of the Italian social protection system, largely focused on pensions, and demographic trends. Italy's fertility rate is among the lowest in Europe (1.35 children per woman of childbearing age). Life expectancy is relatively high and has been increasing fast.[55]

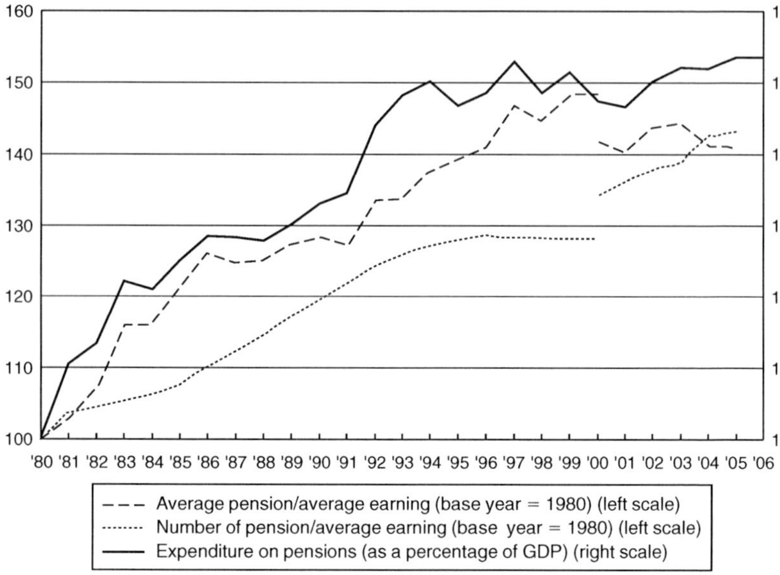

Figure 4.12 Pension expenditure, number of pensions and average replacement ratio
Source: based on ISTAT data.

The ratio of persons aged 65 and over to the working-age population is expected to rise from 29 per cent in 2005 to 36 per cent in 2020 and to 58 per cent in 2040 (ISTAT, 2006a; 2006b).

In the 1980s it gradually became apparent that the system regulating pension benefits was incompatible with demographics: the pension formula, the eligibility conditions and the indexation rules granted rates of return that were considerably higher than the rate of growth of the social security tax base. Pension expenditure increased from 5 per cent of GDP in 1960 to 14.9 per cent in 1992 (Figure 4.12). Later projections estimated that pension expenditure would have reached 25 per cent of GDP by 2030. Pension reform was also recognised as an important component of any policy to improve the functioning of the labour market, namely by increasing labour mobility and the low participation rate. Finally, since the incidence of pensions in total social spending was very high (70 per cent), pension reform was also considered a precondition for implementing policies that would increase public support for the non-elderly groups of citizens and finance additional spending on long-term care.

The reform process began in 1992 (Franco, 2002). After decades of short-sighted policy-making, prospective public-sector pension liabilities were abruptly cut by about one quarter. A second major reform was launched in 1995, gradually shifting the pension regime from a defined benefit to a notional defined contribution system.[56] The main reforms were integrated by numerous minor changes in legislation. In 2004 the eligibility conditions for seniority pensions were tightened as of 2008.[57] These measures were partly modified in 2007.

After 1992, Italian governments radically redressed the prospects of pay-as-you-go (PAYG) pension schemes. Expenditure trends have been heavily adjusted downwards. The rules applying to the different schemes were harmonised. Microeconomic incentives were improved. Distributive effects have been extensively redesigned. Moreover, several steps have been taken to develop supplementary funded pensions with a view to moving towards a two-pillar system that is more diversified and more resilient to shocks.

The reform process is not yet completed, however (Castellino and Fornero, 2001; Franco and Marè, 2002). Pension spending is still expected to increase as a share of GDP. While these increases are less dramatic than in most other EU countries (see Section 4.10), the present size of pension expenditure makes them barely sustainable. Moreover, some solutions may prove to be socially unbearable in the long run. In particular, expenditure cuts came mainly from changes in the indexation mechanisms, which may be politically unsustainable in the long run if associated with lengthy retirement periods. More generally, relying on the reduction of the transfer ratio rather than on increases in retirement age may create political pressure for discretionary increases in pensions in real terms.

One specific aspect concerns the younger cohorts, which are the most affected by the pension reforms, as well as by the changes taking place in the labour market. In a context of increased inequality of earnings (Boeri and Brandolini, 2005), these generations are experiencing a reduction in entry wages (Rosolia and Torrini, 2007) and in average job tenure. It is likely that the joint impact of pension reforms and labour market changes on the lifetime welfare of younger cohorts will soon become a critical social and political issue.

The pension system, being pure pay-as-you-go, remains vulnerable to demographic and macro-economic shocks. While a stable equilibrium contributory rate would require strong built-in stabilisers, the existing system has very limited stabilisers: the indexation of pensions is exogenous and there is only a general provision requiring a reassessment of parameters every ten years (to become three years from 2010) to take account of any change in the demographic scenario.[58] In the end, as the corrective mechanisms are incomplete, adverse demographic and economic events can determine cash deficits, which are avoidable only with ad hoc cuts in pensions and changes in the pension formula, just as in traditional PAYG systems.

Some factors may determine a systematic imbalance of the notional defined contribution (NDC) scheme. The conversion coefficients have been computed without considering part of the expenditure for disability and survivors' pensions.[59] Pensions paid to survivors of deceased workers have also been disregarded. These benefits were implicitly considered welfare benefits to be financed out of the government budget. Moreover, in a context of rising life expectancy, the method of computation of conversion coefficients may produce values that do not reflect the true life expectancy of individuals.[60]

An actuarially based pension system, such as that introduced in Italy in 1995, can deliver the expected labour market benefits only if the link between contributions and benefits is tight, transparent, easy to grasp and perceived as stable by the public (Franco and Sartor, 2005). This may not be the case in Italy, where many workers are not affected by the new pension regime, no major information campaign has been conducted, and the public expects further reforms, thus perceiving the return on the contributions as uncertain. Moreover, some recent policy developments are not consistent with the underlying philosophy of an NDC plan.[61] This situation could lead Italy to experience the problematic aspects of NDC systems (complexity, explicit pension liabilities) without their benefits (microeconomic effects, self-balancing mechanisms and flexibility in the choice of retirement age).

Ensuring adequate living standards to a growing number of elderly while restraining the growth of pension spending represents the main challenge for Italian pension policy. The main policy indications are very straightforward.[62] First, the average effective retirement age, which is now fairly low, should be raised and the public resources made available should be used to supplement the pensions and welfare benefits paid to the most elderly and the other groups of retirees at high risk of poverty.[63] This would shift the focus of expenditure control from the reduction of replacement ratios to the reduction of the ratio of pensioners to workers. The scope of such an operation is quite large: about 30 per cent of pension spending is now allocated to individuals aged under 65. Second, one should ensure the financial equilibrium of the NDC scheme and avoid the expected rise of the pension expenditure-to-GDP ratio. These targets can be achieved via parametric changes in the pension regime established by the 1995 reform.[64] Developing the funded pension pillar is also crucial (Messori, 2006). In this regard, it is important for institutional investors to come up with cheap, easy-to-understand, and relatively safe financial products, which can be attractive for low-wage workers.

4.10 The long-term outlook

The arithmetic of sustainability hinges on four elements: the structural primary budget balance (net of cyclical and temporary components); the cost of public debt; stock-flow adjustments; and growth. The reduction of the debt-to-GDP ratio after 1994 relied on high primary surpluses, a declining interest rate bill and a large privatisation programme that kept the stock flow adjustment broadly neutral. It was hampered by relatively low growth. Net of cyclical and temporary components, the primary surplus in 2006 was about 1.3 per cent of GDP. It significantly improved in 2007. This level should be further increased in the coming years in order to achieve the objective of a balanced budget.

In the coming years, the stock-flow adjustments can be expected to remain broadly neutral: while privatisation proceedings may be fewer than in the past decade,[65] hidden liabilities have already been sizeably reduced. In principle, one can expect that over the long run the cash borrowing requirement and accrual-based net borrowing would be on average about equal.[66]

As already mentioned above (see Section 4.5), the decline in the interest bill has come to a halt: in the future, interest expenditure reductions will only come from the reduction in the size of the debt. If public finances are kept under control, participation in EMU and the share of long-term bonds are likely to prevent the large fluctuations in the cost of the debt which took place in the past.

In the future, the major source of budgetary imbalances will be represented by the ageing process.[67] Raising dependency ratios is likely to increase expenditure on pensions, health care and long-term care and thus gradually worsen the primary balance.

The State Accounting Office estimates that expenditure associated with the ageing of the population will grow slowly in proportion to GDP until 2020 and accelerate thereafter (Ministero dell'Economia e delle Finanze, 2006b).[68] Between 2005 and 2040, increased spending on pensions (1.8 points), health care (1.6 points) and long-term care (0.3 points) would be partly offset by savings on education (0.7 points).

This implies that, on the basis of current legislation, the primary surplus is set to decline gradually. Projections show that the pressure of ageing is gradual and apparently manageable. The decline in the debt ratio ensuing from the commitment to balance the budget would provide budgetary room for greater age-related expenditure. Lower interest spending would largely offset greater spending on pensions and health and long-term care.

However, it is likely that, without specific intervention, age-related expenditure could rise more sharply and sooner. In fact, the forecasts for health spending focus mainly on the effects of the changing age structure of the population. Other factors, such as the rising cost of medical treatment, have largely contributed to health spending growth in recent decades in Italy and throughout the industrial world (Pammolli and Salerno, 2006). As for long-term care, the changes in family structure and the increase in female employment could prompt greater demand for public assistance (Beltrametti, 2003). The estimates of pension spending account for the effects of current legislation, which only envisages indexation to price increases and include the regular revision of the coefficients for converting the contribution base into the annual pension entitlement (see Section 4.9).

The importance of the budgetary policy choices of the coming years emerges clearly from three simple simulations of the performance of the debt-to-GDP ratio in the period 2007–50, based on scenarios that differ only with regard to the medium-term budgetary adjustment (Figure 4.13). All the simulations assume the average cost of the debt to be constant from 2010 onwards and equal to 4.8 per cent;[69] a growth rate of real GDP of 1.5 per cent (in line with the estimates of the potential growth rate); inflation set at 2 per cent; and a gap between the cash borrowing requirement and net borrowing equal to half a percentage point of GDP every year (see Section 4.6).

In the first simulation the primary surplus is kept at the level targeted for 2007 until 2020,[70] after which it is allowed to deteriorate as a consequence of the ageing of the population. In this case the debt-to-GDP ratio declines over the coming years to just above 90 per cent between 2025 and 2030, after which it rises again.

In the other two simulations it is assumed that budgetary balance is achieved in 2010. In the second simulation the primary surplus is kept at the level necessary to ensure budgetary balance up to 2020, falling from just under 5 per cent of GDP in 2010 to about 3.5 per cent in 2020, thanks to the savings in interest payments from the reduction of the debt. Subsequently, as in the first simulation, the primary surplus deteriorates

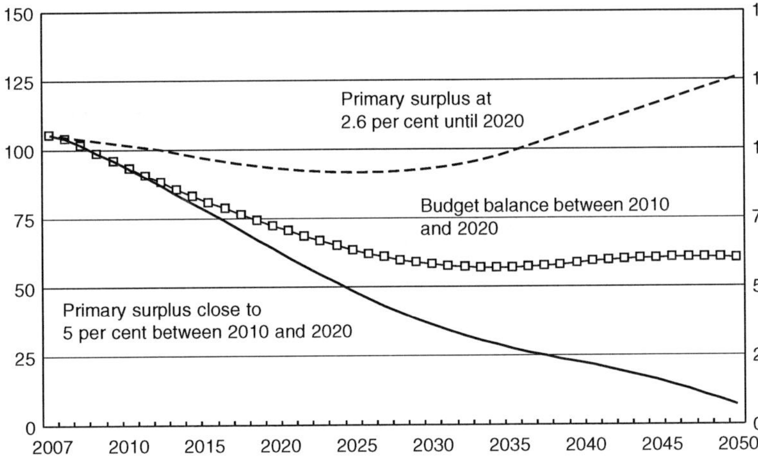

Figure 4.13 The evolution of the debt-to-GDP ratio in different scenarios

as a consequence of the ageing of the population. In this case the ratio of debt to GDP declines to about 80 per cent by the middle of the next decade and to below 60 per cent before 2030, after which it stabilises at this level.

If the effects of the demographic evolution on the public finances were greater than those described above, it would be necessary, in this second simulation as well, to take additional measures to attenuate the expenditure growth in the long run. These interventions would nonetheless be on a much smaller scale than that required in the first simulation: keeping the budget balanced in the next decade allows increasing savings on interest payments, amounting to almost 3 per cent of GDP in 2050.

In the third simulation the primary surplus remains at the level necessary to ensure budgetary balance in 2010 (just below 5 per cent of GDP) and up to 2020 (which determines an overall surplus), and then deteriorates as a consequence of the ageing of the population, as in the two other simulations. In this case the ratio of debt to GDP declines to below 60 per cent before 2025 and continues to decline thereafter.

The 2007 update of the Stability Programme (Ministero dell'Economia e delle Finanze, 2007b) points to similar results. It shows that the achievement of the target set in the programme (a structural primary surplus of 4.9 per cent of GDP in 2011) would ensure a gradual and continuous reduction in the debt ratio in spite of the increase in age-related expenditure. In this scenario the decline in the debt ratio ensuing from the commitment to balance the budget would provide budgetary room for greater age-related expenditure. Lower interest spending would largely compensate for greater spending on pensions and health and long-term care. On the contrary, a primary surplus of less than 4.2 per cent would not prevent the debt from rising after an initial phase of decline.

4.11 Conclusions

Italy has run unsustainable fiscal policies for many years. High deficits fuelled the accumulation of public debt. Compared to other European countries, Italy took longer to redress the fiscal path. In the first half of the 1980s, while fiscal consolidation prevailed elsewhere in Europe, in Italy imbalances increased even further. The fiscal results changed radically between 1992 and 1997, first under the pressure of external constraints, then in order to qualify for EMU. In the first years of EMU the stance of fiscal policy relaxed. In the following years the slowdown in economic growth contributed to an increase in budgetary imbalances. The primary balance shrunk to virtually nil. Overall, the large dividend of EMU in terms of lower interest expenditure was not used to run down the debt level. Most of the reduction of the gross debt ratio was achieved by means of operations of debt restructuring and sales of assets.

In 2006 and 2007 the structural primary balance improved, although it still remains well below the levels recorded in the late 1990s. The improvement was primarily driven by the increase in revenues. This reflects better cyclical conditions, the effects of fiscal drag and government measures, including efforts to reduce tax evasion. Current primary expenditure has remained nearly constant in terms of GDP, while public investment has declined slightly. Driven by a sizeable reduction in the borrowing requirement, in 2007 the debt ratio again shifted to a downward trend, after having increased in the previous two years.

While displaying some of the weaknesses highlighted in the consolidation phase of the 1990s, the improvement in fiscal outcomes clearly represents a second opportunity to take Italy's public finances onto safer ground, where the focus of budgetary policy could shift from short-term deficit control to stabilisation, allocation and distribution functions.

Italian fiscal policy in the coming years will face several important challenges. It will have to cope with the large public debt, population ageing, the impact of globalisation, an unfinished decentralisation process, a relatively large irregular economy, the unbalanced structure of social protection, and sizeable income differences within the country. The persistence of a context of sluggish economic growth would obviously aggravate the difficulties.

Among helpful policy actions, the following are probably the most important.

A balanced budget

The debt ratio and the demographic prospects suggest that close-to-balanced budgets should become a permanent feature of fiscal policy in the coming decade. This would help Italy to meet the budgetary impact of the ageing of the large generation born before the mid-1960s. It would also provide room for the stabilisers to operate fully and would reduce uncertainty among companies and households by removing the necessity for frequent corrective measures.

EU fiscal rules were very important in guiding the fiscal consolidation process in the 1990s and in more recent years. However, once the excessive deficit procedure started in 2005 expires, the external pressure towards fiscal consolidation may diminish. There is now a need to recognise that fiscal soundness is primarily in the national interest and that it would be advisable to pursue targets at least as ambitious as those indicated in the SGP framework.

A growth-oriented strategy

Over the last decade, the growth of the Italian economy has systematically lagged behind that of the other euro-area countries. Slow growth is a continuous source of stress for public finances. Italy risks being trapped in a vicious circle: the difficulty of constraining the growth of current expenditure below the GDP growth rate may lead to an increase in the tax-to-GDP ratio and cuts in capital spending which can negatively affect growth.

Fiscal policy should contribute to increasing potential growth by removing some factors which hamper total factor productivity, such as the unsatisfactory quality of some public services, especially in certain regions, and cumbersome regulations. It should also foster labour market participation, especially among women and older generations, for which participation rates are far below the Lisbon targets. It should contribute more intensively to the accumulation of both physical capital and human capital. In this regard, it would be important to achieve educational outcomes in line with those of other EU countries.[71] The reduction of the overall tax burden on firms and households has a crucial role.[72] Bridging the gap between the Centre/North and the South, where per capita GDP is 56 per cent of that of the other regions of the country, remains one of the main challenges of public policy.

Expenditure control

The ability of the government to restrain the growth of current primary expenditure will be crucial for achieving a close-to-balanced budget and for providing some room for tax cuts and capital spending increases. The size of the adjustment calls for an extensive correction based on structural reforms. The challenge of reducing the rate of growth of spending significantly over several years should not be underestimated. Past experience shows that public expenditure control is extremely difficult: the dynamics of spending reflect structural factors, decisions taken in the distant past, the actions of several levels of government and tough political competition. Action to reduce overspending in some sectors or areas often meets with harsh opposition. Moreover, it is frequently difficult to disentangle legitimate social needs from the pressure of interest groups.

For all these reasons, it is important that the spending review process becomes part of the budget system and contributes to improving the effectiveness and efficiency of public-sector operations. This may also require changes in the organisation of public bodies and in the incentives for civil servants. Curbing the size of public spending may also require revising the scope of public action: the public sector may have to stop providing some services and transfers.

Decentralisation

The unfinished decentralisation process tends to blur the allocation of responsibilities. It can become an unending source of tensions. There is a need for budgetary arrangements that are better suited to a decentralised system: sub-national governments should be responsible for their spending decisions, additional spending should be matched by additional taxes. This may entail difficult choices, especially regarding the flow of funds across regions and the differentiation of services and wage levels. The only alternative option is fiscal centralisation. The current intermediate solution may otherwise combine the weak points of the centralised and decentralised frameworks without their benefits.

Social protection

Distribution targets may also have to be reconsidered. In spite of several reform projects, the social protection system still concentrates its resources on pensions, while limited resources are devoted to family support, unemployment benefits and welfare services. In the end, only a sizeable increase in the average retirement age can allow both adequate pensions and the development of a broader welfare system.

Budgetary procedures

Several reforms have been introduced in the budgetary framework in the last two decades. Fiscal transparency has increased, the role of the Ministry for the Economy and Finance has been strengthened, and EMU rules are widely accepted. However, many aspects of the current fiscal framework remain those of the period of high fiscal imbalances: expenditure policy is largely incremental, fiscal responsibilities across levels of government are not clearly defined, and *ex-post* evaluation of results is weak. Moreover, targets for the budget balance seem to be more easily met by increasing revenues than by reducing spending.

The introduction of an expenditure rule can be considered as a means to tackle this issue. In a decentralised framework the rule should apply to spending by central government and social security institutions, while sub-national governments could be asked to balance their budget, net of investment expenditure. A limit on investment expenditure financed by market borrowing should be set for sub-national government finances as a whole. Sub-national government finances should be closely coordinated within the national general government framework, specifying their targets in the DPEF.

Fiscal transparency

Providing the public with better information concerning the current situation and the prospects of the public finances can improve fiscal policy.[73] The gross debt statistics could be supplemented with periodic estimates of the net asset position, taking into account assets and liabilities excluded from the EMU debt definition (Balassone *et al.*, 2005). Long-term projections could consider a broader range of assumptions and could be made available to the public more systematically. The availability to the public of more information at the micro level on the cost of public services and the quality of the services provided by different units (schools, hospitals, etc.) would help to improve the management of the public sector.

Notes

1. See Francese and Pace (2007), Ministero del Tesoro (1988) and Toniolo (1988). De Cecco (1989) noted that 'heavy fiscal pressure and huge national debt were the two birthmarks of the new Kingdom of Italy'.
2. See Baldassarri and Briotti (1990), Bosi *et al.* (1990), Franco (1993), Giavazzi and Spaventa (1989), Morcaldo (1993) and European Commission (1993).

Italian fiscal policy is regularly examined in the Annual Reports and the Economic Bulletins of Banca d'Italia.

3. For a broader analysis of Italian economic policy in the 1970s and in the 1980s see respectively Basevi and Onofri (1997) and Arcelli and Micossi (1997). On the interaction between fiscal policy, monetary policy and financial market regulation, see Galli and Giavazzi (1992), Giovannini (1988), Spaventa (1988) and Tabellini (1988). Rossi (2007) examines economic policy in the period 1968–2007. Visaggio (1997) examines Italian fiscal policy from 1963 to 1995 with a special focus on the relationship between fiscal and monetary institutions.
4. In European Commission (1993, p. 1) it is noted that: 'Public finances form the area in which convergence between Italy and its ERM partners has been most conspicuously missing. ... unless these problems are tackled energetically, Italy may soon face a situation of fiscal unsustainability.'
5. The management of public debt in the long period of fiscal imbalances is examined by Paesani and Piga (2002).
6. The fragmentation of Italian governments may have had a bearing on the outcomes. For a review of the literature on the political and institutional determinants of budget deficits see Alesina and Perotti (1995) and Balassone and Giordano (2001). Padovano and Venturi (2001) model the effects of government fragmentation on deficits and find evidence that this played a role in determining Italy's fiscal policy in the 1970s and 1980s. Hallerberg (2004) argues that the improvement in fiscal outcomes in the 1990s is largely attributable to changes in the form of fiscal governance following the change in the electoral system from proportional representation to a mixed system. According to Hallenberg, Italy moved from a fiefdom form of governance (in which spending ministers are largely independent) to a delegation form under a strong finance minister.
7. See Amato (1990), Barucci (1995) and Monorchio (1996).
8. See Degni *et al.* (2001), Ferrera and Gualmini (1999a), Onofri (2001), Reviglio (1998) and Verzichelli (1999). Different authors place the take-off of Italy's consolidation process at different times. The analyses by Alesina and Perotti (1997) and Zaghini (2001) begin, respectively, in 1989 and 1991. Spaventa and Chiorazzo (2000), while noting the efforts made in the late 1980s, put the start of the adjustment in 1990–1. Degni *et al.* (2001), taking into account the effects of the cycle on the budget, attribute crucial importance to the measures taken in the second half of 1992.
9. A two-step budget adjustment amounting to about 3 per cent of GDP was implemented, mainly in the form of revenue increases. Substantial use was made of temporary measures, which amounted to approximately 1.5 per cent of GDP and mainly concerned one-off taxes. These included the 'Europe-tax', which was a progressive surcharge on personal income tax. The economic and political aspects of Italy's admission to EMU are examined by Spaventa and Chiorazzo (1999; 2000). They note that: 'Still in the middle of 1996 the prevailing opinion was that the participation of Italy in the Monetary Union was impossible, given the existing distance from meeting, in 1997, the condition set in the Maastricht Treaty' (2000, p. 9).
10. On the basis of the public accounts for 1990, the gap between the net taxes paid by the latest-born generation (on the basis of current policies) and those

paid by future generations (taking into account policy actions to restore government solvency) was extremely wide and comparatively larger than in the other western countries (Franco *et al.*, 1994). In the following years the gap closed considerably and came into line with that of the other countries (Leibfritz, 2000; Cardarelli and Sartor, 2000).

11. Momigliano and Siviero (2002) examine the impact of fiscal policy on the Italian economy.
12. This outcome seems in line with the evidence provided by Alesina and Perotti (1997) that fiscal adjustments which rely primarily on tax increases and cuts in public investment tend not to last long and lead to a contraction.
13. See Ferrera and Gualmini (1999b), Kostoris Padoa Schioppa (2001), Reviglio (1998), Salvati (2000) and Spaventa and Chiorazzo (2000).
14. The average rate of growth of real GDP in the period 1998–2001 was about 2.2 per cent.
15. The average rate of growth of GDP in real terms in the period 2002–5 was about 0.4 per cent.
16. The Finance Bill for 2002 aimed to raise additional resources for approximately 1.2 percentage points of GDP; temporary measures on net borrowing amounted to around 0.9 per cent of GDP, those with an effect on the cash borrowing requirement and public debt respectively to over 2 and about 4 per cent. The Finance Bills for 2003 and 2004 were supplemented by corrective measures implemented during the same year: overall budgetary interventions amounted to 1.2 and 1.5 per cent of GDP respectively; temporary measures can be approximately quantified respectively at 2.0 and 1.5 per cent of GDP.
17. A centre-left coalition was in power in the period 1998–2001, while from 2001 to 2006 a centre-right coalition ran the country. The rate of growth of current primary expenditure in real terms was respectively 2.2 per cent and 2.0 per cent per year.
18. In this paper structural figures are net of the effects of the economic cycle and temporary measures, both computed using the methodology developed within the European System of Central Banks. Changes in structural figures are also decomposed in order to distinguish the effect of discretionary measures, fiscal drag and decoupling between tax bases and GDP growth. For detailed references see Bouthevillain *et al.* (2001) and Kremer *et al.* (2006).
19. For a detailed analysis see Momigliano and Rizza (2007).
20. This applies, in particular, to tax amnesties. See Bernasconi and Lapecorella (2006).
21. The transfer to INPS (the National Social Insurance Institute) of part of the contributions previously assigned to employers' severance pay funds is the main temporary measure introduced recently. This operation (started in 2007) is a *de facto* loan, with an implicit burden on the budget that is potentially greater than that of government securities. INPS must pay back the portions of severance pay that go into the Fund plus the amount of their revaluation, currently equal to about 3 per cent per year. From 2008 on, this burden will be compounded by the compensation planned for firms in terms of lower social security contribution rates.
22. With the budget for 2008 the Italian government introduced a cut in the statutory tax rates on corporate income (including IRAP) of about 6 percentage points (to 31.4 per cent) to be compensated by an increase in the tax

base. In Germany and Spain large reductions in corporate income tax rates are effective from 2008.

23. Commissione Tecnica per la Finanza Pubblica (2007b) presents some preliminary results for the first group of ministries taken into consideration. (Justice, Infrastructure, Interior, Education and Transport). Its report shows that there are significant margins for improving the allocation of resources in the country and reducing the number of public-sector employees. It also points to several solutions for improving procedures and the organisation of work.
24. See Faini *et al.* (2006) and Reviglio (2006b). On the use of public employment as a redistributive device, see Alesina *et al.* (1999).
25. Potential risks for the public finances also come from agencies not included in the general government. The cancellation of the national railway company's debt to central government, which had a large negative impact on net borrowing in 2006, is an example of these risks.
26. See Faini *et al.* (2006).
27. The recent trends in financial markets do not seem to indicate the risk of an increase in interest rate spreads between Italy and the other euro-area countries. However, it is worth noting that even a small increase in the risk premia could pose a problem in a country like Italy which, compared to the country it was in the 1980s, is now characterised by lower growth, a higher fiscal burden and an older population. Additionally, the empirical literature suggests that the reaction of the financial markets is initially slow and moderate, later becoming rapid and severe (Balassone *et al.*, 2004). Therefore, it is fairly dangerous to assume that the risk premia will in any case stay at their current levels (Faini, 2004).
28. On this topic, see Papp and Takats (2008).
29. The margins for increasing the quality of services are significant. For instance, the OECD's PISA survey found sizeable regional differences in the test scores of 15-year-old students: the performance of students in the South is much worse than that of students in the Centre and North (Banca d'Italia, 2007). See also Giannini and Onofri (2005). The issue of the efficiency of public services is examined in Banca d'Italia (2002).
30. In 1999 ESA95 replaced ESA79.
31. The decline initially reported in the deficit between 2000 and 2001 (from 1.7 per cent to 1.4 per cent of GDP) was in sharp contrast with the dynamics of the debt. According to the data available in March 2002, the latter rose from 1.6 per cent of GDP in 2000 to 3.5 per cent in 2001.
32. This balance measures the net acquisition of financial assets with the exception of the changes in the Treasury's deposits at the Bank of Italy and privatisation receipts. In 2006 it was equal to 0.8 per cent of GDP, lower than in 2005 (1.3 per cent) and also lower than the average for 1999–2004 (1.1 per cent, excluding in 2003 the effects of the transformation of Cassa Depositi e Prestiti into a company limited by shares). In 2003–5 the build-up of claims on the railways in connection with the financing of the high-speed railway network had contributed to keeping the balance of financial transactions high.
33. The progress was recognised in the 2007 update of the Report on the Observance of Standards and Codes (ROSC) carried out by the IMF in 2002. See International Monetary Fund (2007a), which nevertheless notes that the responsibility for compiling and disseminating a comprehensive and

integrated set of general government statistics must be established and stresses the usefulness of preserving inter-agency cross-checking of fiscal figures. Banca d'Italia (2006) provides detailed information on the reconciliation between net borrowing, borrowing requirement and debt variation in Table 11.7 of the *Annual Report* for the year 2006.

34. See De Joanna (1993), Salvemini (2003), Giarda *et al.* (2005) and Camera dei Deputati (2007a).
35. The strengthening of the powers of the Ministry of Treasury was one of the proposals of Alesina *et al.* (1998). They also suggested radically simplifying procedures and documents in order to increase transparency and shift the focus from *ex-post* formal controls to better incentives in the execution of the budget.
36. The DPEF usually indicates the levels of public expenditure and revenue – together with a detailed breakdown of public accounts – only in the trend scenario. It sets targets only for the overall balance, the primary balance and the debt ratio.
37. See CER (2006) and International Monetary Fund (2007b).
38. This reflects the reform of 1988: contrary to previous years, from 1989 the parliamentary process does not significantly modify the impact of the budget on the balance (Giarda *et al.*, 2005). In the 2008 DPEF, targets for the five years of the planning scenario have been set also in terms of the detailed expenditure and revenue items.
39. Commissione Tecnica per la Finanza Pubblica (2007b) and Ministero dell'Economia e delle Finanze (2007b).
40. Until 1999 the trend scenario was based on criteria of unchanged policy. Thereafter, it has been based on criteria of unchanged legislation. The change was designed to make decisions more visible (Camera dei Deputati, 2007b). The new approach leaves less room for discretion but can underestimate expenditure commitments. In order to evaluate better the state of the public finances, in 2007 the Ministero dell'Economia e delle Finanze (2007a) provided indicative estimates of expenditures that are very likely to be made but are not included in the trend scenario. These expenditures are connected with commitments entered into by the government, with established practices (such as appropriations for future labour contracts and transfers to the National Road Agency and the State Railways) and with new initiatives that the government intends to enact.
41. Their results are in line with those of Strauch *et al.* (2004).
42. For instance, in 2000–5 the preliminary outturns for net borrowing and primary balance (included in the spring notification to the EU) were on average 0.6 and 0.7 percentage points of GDP worse than indicated in the March RTC (with 0.3 points, due to lower GDP growth), in spite of corrective measures introduced after the RTC. The gap is even larger taking into account the revisions of the figures implemented after the first notification.
43. The December 2005 and December 2006 updates of the Stability Programme indicated GDP growth rates respectively for 2006 and for 2007 which turned out lower than the outcomes. In particular, in 2006 the GDP grew at 1.8 per cent against the 1.5 per cent expected in December 2005; in 2007 the GDP growth rate is currently reported at 1.5 per cent against the 1.3 per cent expected respectively in December 2005 and December 2006.

44. SIOPE (General Government Transactions Information System) is managed by Banca d'Italia on behalf of the Ministry of the Economy and Finance. The operations are recorded by the banks carrying out the transactions for government bodies.
45. CER (2006) considers a possible revision of article 81 of the Constitutional Law.
46. Article 81 requires that any additional spending must be covered by offsetting expenditure cuts or additional revenues. This provision – which applies to the central government budget – has been circumvented in several ways (Pisauro, 2003). However, the main problem lies in the fact that it cannot ensure the financial equilibrium of spending programmes operating over long periods of time (Pedone, 2005). Ensuring that new programmes do not increase the deficit is not sufficient when the spending for existing programmes is rising due to structural factors or because of the way benefits have been designed a long time before.
47. In Ministero dell'Economia e delle Finanze (2007a) the proposition is made that the parliamentary resolution concerning the DPEF should indicate a ceiling for primary expenditure. Galeotti *et al.* (1998) suggest that the government formulates targets for both expenditure and revenue levels and that in the parliamentary process any proposal to increase spending should be matched by an expenditure cut.
48. On fiscal relationships among different government levels in Italy, see Arachi and Zanardi (2000), Buglione (1999), Fausto and Pica (2000) and Franco *et al.* (2004). See also the yearly reports by ISAE (for instance ISAE, 2003).
49. In 2002 the government set up a High Commission on Fiscal Federalism with the purpose of defining new rules for decentralised government. The commission (see Alta Commissione sul Federalismo Fiscale, 2005) noted that sub-national governments should primarily rely on sharing national taxes and pointed to the need to increase tax autonomy based on the benefit principle. The indications of the Commission were not followed by policy action.
50. In 2002–5, in ordinary-statute regions, health spending in the North ranged from €1,402 per capita in Lombardy to €1,659 in Liguria; in the Centre it ranged from €1,481 in Marche to €1,623 in Molise and in the South from €1,354 in Puglia to €1,494 in Campania. In special-statute regions, per capita health spending ranged from €1,459 in Sicily to €1,813 in Valle d'Aosta. In 2003, current per capita spending in municipalities ranged in the North from €790 in Lombardy to €1,051 in Liguria, in the Centre from €614 in Abruzzo to €953 in Lazio, and in the South from €567 in Puglia to €676 in Campania. In special-statute regions, per capita current spending ranged from €777 in Sicily to €1,444 in Valle d'Aosta.
51. The budget for 2007 moved in the direction indicated in point i) and ii). As to the former aspect, see Ministero dell'Economia e delle Finanze (2007b).
52. According to the Alta Commissione sul Federalismo Fiscale (2005), the revenue from Irap ranges from €116 per capita in Calabria to €700 in Lombardy; the revenue from the 0.9 per cent personal income tax surcharge ranges from €52 in Calabria to €116 in Lombardy. Current per capita spending in Calabria is €1938, against €2360 in Lombardy.

53. The issue of public expenditure control in the health sector is closely related to the issue of funding of regional governments (Muraro, 2003). In 2000 the central government (centre-left coalition) introduced new legislation aimed to gradually move towards a funding based on standardised needs (rather than past spending level). In 2001 the government (centre-right coalition) reached an agreement with regions, according to which the central government would allocate 6 per cent of GDP to health services and regions would fund additional spending. Both reforms failed. In 2006 and 2007 the central government (first the centre-right coalition, then the centre-left coalition) imposed automatic increases of regional taxes in case of overspending. The new approach has proved more effective, but the issue is still open. It is still uncertain whether health policies will be further diversified at the regional level or will move back to a more uniform and centralised framework.
54. This chapter does not consider the issue of the evolution of the welfare system and the debate concerning welfare reforms. See Commissione per l'analisi delle compatibilità macroeconomiche della spesa sociale (1997), Boeri and Perotti (2002) and Giannini and Onofri (2005).
55. From the early 1930s to 2004, life expectancy for males increased by 6.2 years at the age of 60, 4.7 years at the age of 70 and 2.9 years at the age of 80; for women, the improvement was even greater: 9.7, 7.6 and 4.6 years. About two-thirds of the increase in life expectancy of males and about one half of that of females took place after 1980.
56. See Banca d'Italia (1995), Rostagno (1996), Peracchi and Rossi (1998), Sartor (2001), and Gronchi and Nisticò (2005).
57. According to official assessments, the measures taken in 2004 to tighten retirement requirements with effect from 2008 would have reached their maximum expenditure-curbing effect of 0.7 percentage points of GDP in 2012. The effect would have then remained basically stable (0.6–0.7 percentage points) for the next two decades. The effects would have become negative in the period 2040–50, when higher pensions would begin to be paid as a consequence of longer contribution periods.
58. The revision of the conversion coefficients is essential to maintain the long-term equilibrium between the expenditure and revenue of the pension system. When life expectancy increases, changing the coefficients reduces the income replacement rate while keeping pension wealth unchanged; the worker is entitled to a smaller monthly pension but for a larger number of years. When the retirement age is flexible, this creates an incentive to work for a longer time.
59. More specifically, it has not been considered that disabled workers will receive benefits in excess of those awarded on the basis of their contributions. Gronchi (1998) tentatively estimates that this expenditure may represent 2 percentage points of earnings.
60. As shown by Morcaldo (2006), this reflects the 10-year pattern of revisions (to become three years from 2010), the delayed publication of mortality tables, and the fact that life expectancy is computed on the basis of the currently observed survival rates, rather than on the basis of the survival rate that each cohort will experience in the remaining part of its life.
61. There has been no updating, so far, of the coefficients for converting accrued contributions into benefits. In 2007 the government and trade unions agreed

to adjust the coefficient in 2010. This will be 15 years after the introduction of the coefficients, which, in any case, were based on the 1990 mortality tables. Some of the solutions envisaged in the agreement risk moving the system further away from the basic principles of a notional defined contribution system: equal treatment of workers and a close link between contributions and benefits. More specifically, the agreement allows for the possibility that the coefficients be no longer the same for all workers, with distinctions being made according to the sector of activity. The possibility is also mooted that some workers may be guaranteed a minimum income replacement ratio of 60 per cent, independently of the contributions paid, the growth of the economy, or demographic developments.

62. On the recent debate see Fornero (2006).
63. For analysis of the distribution of income and the incidence of poverty among retirees in 2004 see Franco *et al.* (2008).
64. In particular, it would be advisable to fix a higher minimum retirement age than the one introduced in 1995 (57 years) and the one now foreseen for women (60 years) and allow for more flexibility by raising the maximum retirement age. The minimum level of pension benefits that allows for early retirement under the system (which is presently set at 1.2 times the welfare pension) could also be increased. The introduction of partial indexation of pensions to increases in real wages compensated by a reduction in the replacement rate at retirement can also be considered, keeping in mind that the overall stock of implicit pension debt would not change.
65. Guarino (2007) outlines a plan for a large-scale sale of public assets with a view to rapidly curbing the debt ratio. The plan raises some problematic issues; see De Cecco (2007).
66. The gap between the two indicators widened in 1999, peaked in 2001 (1.8 per cent of GDP) and has averaged about one percentage point over the last decade.
67. The ongoing integration of the single European market and the process of globalisation can exert a downward pressure on tax rates. However, so far there is little quantitative evidence concerning the possible importance of this factor.
68. For a survey of pension expenditure projections in Italy and their role in the pension policy debate, see Franco and Marino (2003).
69. This is in line with the December 2006 update of the Stability Programme. The November 2007 update indicates a slightly higher rate.
70. The simulation refers to the primary surplus indicated by the government in March 2007 (2.6 per cent of GDP). The outturn for 2007 was 3.1 per cent of GDP. However, in June 2008 the government indicated a primary surplus of 2.6 per cent for the year 2008.
71. The issue is examined in Ministero dell'Economia e delle Finanze and Ministero della Pubblica Istruzione (2007).
72. This is not a new issue. On 31 January 1903, *The Economist* noted that: 'The great need of the present moment in Italy is not only to safeguard her strong financial position, but to reduce and redistribute taxation in such a way as to promote her industry and the social welfare of people.'
73. Kopits (2001, p. 74) notes that there is some evidence that 'transparency is conducive to successful fiscal policy whether in the context of rules-based or of discretionary policymaking'.

Comment on Chapter 4

*Martin Larch and Lucia Piana**
European Commission – Bureau of European Policy Advisors and Directorate-General for Economic and Financial Affairs

Introduction

The chapter by Franco and Rizza is a very comprehensive account of the eventful history of public finances in Italy since the mid-1960s. It provides a detailed and accurate analysis of the different stages of development starting with the long period of rising fiscal imbalances up until the early 1990s when, on the back of decade-long primary deficits, the government debt ratio went above 100 per cent of GDP. The trend started to reverse after the financial crisis in 1992–3, which brought to light the unsustainable nature of fiscal policy and forced policy-makers to react. In those days, debt repudiation was openly discussed in the financial and non-financial press as a possibility to get to grips with the debt problem. The crisis marked the beginning of a season of comparatively harsh consolidation episodes, which managed to move Italy's public finances away from the brink into somewhat safer territory.[1]

The Italian experience of fiscal imbalances and high public debt had attracted the attention of the economics profession a couple of years before the financial crisis of 1992–3 ultimately exposed the gravity of the fiscal situation of the country. A book edited by Giavazzi and Spaventa (1988) collected a series of papers examining the build-up of fiscal imbalances from various angles and pointing to patterns and implications the relevance of which went beyond the case of Italy. The book called attention to two questions: i) is the observed path of debt accumulation sustainable?; and ii) how can debt be controlled or reduced? As regards the first question there was a general and genuine feeling that difficult times would be ahead. The discussion of the second question essentially

*The opinions expressed in these comments are those of the authors. They do not necessarily represent the views of the European Commission.

revolved around 'traditional' policy measures or instruments such as debt management, the role played by capital markets and controls.

What was missing from or only marginally touched upon in the discussion at the time was the issue of fiscal governance. More specifically, the political economy factors explaining the accumulation of fiscal imbalances and possible improvements in the governance that would curb the consistent deficit bias that lay at the origin of the crisis stayed in the background of the discussion. The analysis of the link between fiscal performance and the main dimensions of fiscal governance was still in its infancy and would reach its heyday a couple of years later, when a whole new branch of literature emerged. Some early papers were published in the late 1980s and early 1990s, for instance Grilli *et al.* (1991), who tested whether institutional arrangements play a role in the accumulation of debt in some OECD countries, including Italy. In the 2000s, by contrast, fiscal governance features prominently in the analysis of fiscal policy performance. Establishing or strengthening elements of governance has become the standard recipe to tackle the notorious deficit bias, which was particularly strong in Italy but which afflicted, to varying degrees, many countries forming the Economic and Monetary Union (EMU).

Loose reins: weak fiscal governance

When going through the various phases of fiscal policy developments in Italy, the chapter repeatedly and duly touches upon a number of governance dimensions, such as budgetary rules, institutions and procedures. To pick just one very indicative example, the chapter identifies a particularly problematic legacy of the heavy adjustment process following the financial crisis of the early 1990s, namely that fiscal consolidation was achieved without adequately changing prevailing budgetary institutions and procedures.

In light of the evidence produced by the empirical literature on fiscal governance this legacy weighed heavily on the years following the adoption of the euro. Two points deserve to be noted. Firstly and most importantly, the deficit of effective fiscal rules and institutions in Italy was certainly not the only reason for the accumulation of fiscal imbalances, but definitively one of the main ones. The pitfalls of the budgetary framework introduced in the 1978 reform soon become evident and were only partially addressed in 1988 by introducing new budgetary procedures aimed at setting deficit targets ahead of the budgetary session and at assessing the cost of new legislation. Less extensive reforms of the budgetary process were carried out in the second half of the 1990s. In a country known for its fragmented political system where a polyphonic choir of vested interests puts pressure on the budget, the clear lack of effective expenditure rules is a serious issue. By not effectively tackling the lack of rules or the credibility gap of the existing rules, it was only a question of time before the seeds of the previous trends would sprout again. Anything other than a systematic tendency to overspend would have been a surprise and a critical exception to the predictions of the common-pool problem in budgetary policy.[2]

Secondly, and related to the first point, the series of fiscal adjustments of the 1990s followed a recipe which, on the basis of available evidence, generally does not lead to a lasting correction. The adjustment was mainly revenue-based and also relied on one-off measures. It also benefited from a substantial drop in interest expenditure as interest rates declined during the convergence process. The remaining, rather limited, part of the fiscal adjustment carried out on the expenditure side was mainly achieved through cuts in public investment. As recalled in the chapter, a broad range of studies, starting with the seminal work of Alesina and Perotti (1995) consistently show that fiscal corrections with such a composition are typically doomed to fail. They do not tackle the main reasons for fiscal imbalances, namely expenditure overruns, and stifle economic growth.

It is probably true that in the light of the prevailing circumstances the outcome was a sort of constrained optimum, but the renewed tensions in Italian public finance in the early 2000s simply confirmed the considerable lack of effective fiscal governance. Even the adjustment carried out through expenditure items that generally prove more conducive to successful consolidations, in particular compensation of employees, has been reversed, starting from 2000. The relapse also confirms the findings of the European Commission (2007a), which revisited the determinants of successful fiscal consolidation. Specifically, on top of the traditional recipe for success laid out by Alesina and Perotti (1995) and others, the likelihood of achieving a lasting fiscal correction increases with effective fiscal rules and procedures.

Against this backdrop and also taking into account the specific expertise that the Directorate-General for Economic and Financial Affairs (DG ECFIN) of the European Commission has accumulated in the field of fiscal rules, institutions and procedures, in the following paragraphs we will take a closer look at how Italy compares with the rest of the euro area in this respect. The graph below reports Italy's score along four different dimensions of fiscal governance: fiscal rules in general, expenditure rules, budgetary procedures and the quality of medium-term budgetary

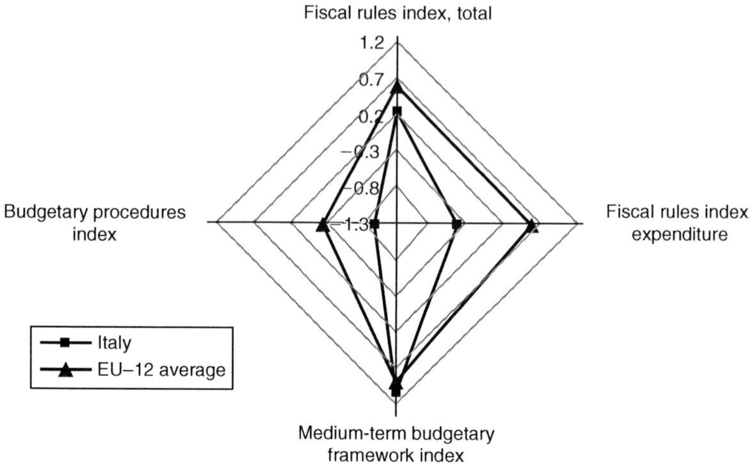

Figure 4.14 Fiscal governance: Italy in the euro area

frameworks.[3] Except for the latter, Italy fares below the average of the euro-area member states.

As regards numerical fiscal rules in general, Italy ranks only eighth, chiefly in view of a relatively small share of public finances covered by the existing rules.[4] Among the four arrangements documented for Italy (the domestic stability pact for local entities, a budget balance rule for health-care expenditure, a golden rule for local government, and an expenditure ceiling for pharmaceuticals) the coverage reaches at most 35 per cent of total public finances. Another noteworthy point to highlight is that the existing rules are rather new and subject to a number of teething problems, notably a lack of enforcement, limited coverage and/or frequent changes in definitions of key variables. A particularly evident case in point is the so-called Domestic Stability Pact (see Section 4.8). In the wake of a progressive devolution of public expenditure and – to a smaller extent – taxation to the regions since the early 1990s, the Pact was put in place only towards the end of that decade with a view to better involving regions and municipalities in the attainment of the objectives for the general government budget under the Stability and Growth Pact requirements. By comparison, a large number of EU member states had already started introducing fiscal rules in the early or mid-1990s generally coupled with the signing of the Maastricht Treaty and its numerical thresholds for the government deficit and debt ratio. Furthermore, in the light of a mixed track record, the Pact was repeatedly revised by successive budget laws. The revisions were far from minor: they involved piecemeal changes in the objectives ranging from ad hoc deficit measures (not consistent with ESA95 definitions) to a variety of expenditure caps. In particular, continued health-care overruns lead to exclude health-care outlays from the definition of the deficit concept used for Pact in 2000. The attempt to control health-care expenditure which is the lion's share of regional finances, has been pursued, through separate agreements. While the latter have been consistently violated, and resulted in *ex-post* funding of regional deficits, the objectives set by the Pact have been respected by most regions and local governments. Nevertheless, the targeted reduction of local government deficit has not been achieved (ISAE, 2007b).[5]

On top of the low coverage of existing fiscal rules and their 'young age', Italy compares particularly badly in terms of a specific type of numerical rule which, based on available evidence, is particularly instrumental in keeping the lid on deficits, namely expenditure rules. Based on the experience accumulated in the EU fiscal surveillance framework, the main reason for not achieving budgetary targets is expenditure overruns. Although lower-than-projected economic growth contributed to the breach of the 3 per cent of GDP deficit threshold already in 2001, in subsequent years it was the inability to enact the planned expenditure savings necessary to finance discretionary tax cuts that hindered public finance consolidation.

Empirical evidence shows that the effectiveness of fiscal rules crucially hinges on the share of expenditure actually covered by the arrangement (see European Commission, 2006d). In the case of Italy, two of the four existing fiscal rules target expenditure, yet relate, as mentioned before, to a rather small part of total government outlays. In particular, expenditure rules do not encompass expenditure for compensation of employees, which represents over 40 per cent of current primary expenditure, net of pensions. Hiring freezes imposed in successive budget laws constantly failed to be enforced. As for the Domestic Stability Pact, whereas originally it applied to all municipalities, entities with fewer than 5,000 inhabitants were later excluded.[6] Even the much advertised 2 per cent cap on nominal expenditure growth foreseen by the 2005 budget law envisaged so many exceptions, again including expenditure on compensation of employees, that its significance was substantially watered down.

While there is no one-size-fits all fiscal rule that may work well for all countries, the public finance developments in Italy portrayed in the chapter clearly show that the main difficulties in the past were expenditure dynamics, and more specifically the recurrent or at least frequent overshooting of expenditure targets. In light of this, and also taking into account the findings of the existing literature on fiscal rules, according to which among the different types of rules those focusing on expenditure seem to deliver a better fiscal performance, Franco and Rizza rightly conclude that what Italy needs are intelligent ways to better control the expenditure side of the budget. However, Franco and Rizza's prescription is more detailed and complex than just identifying the need for effective expenditure rules. Their specific understanding of the institutional setting of public finances in Italy, especially the interactions between the different levels of government, gives rise to more differentiated suggestions. In particular, when it comes to the lower levels of government Franco and Rizza express a clear preference for budget-balance rules over rules targeting expenditure. This preference echoes the experience of recent years, where unfinished decentralisation lacking a close link between spending and revenue decisions, went along with rising expenditure overruns by regions and municipalities.

Besides the issue of choosing the right type of fiscal rule, what is equally important for the effectiveness of any fiscal control mechanism is its enforcement. Franco and Rizza explicitly argue that as soon as external pressures, coming first from the financial markets and then from the decision to qualify for the euro, faded away, both expenditure and revenue developments gradually returned to their original trends.[7] This pertinent assessment relates to at least two of the main weaknesses of the budgetary procedures in Italy: lack of ownership and far from effective budgetary procedures. One of the main lessons learned from the 2003 crisis of the Stability and Growth Pact and the subsequent reform of the EU fiscal surveillance framework was precisely that, in the absence of an external enforcement mechanism, rules will remain ineffective unless there is an understanding or conviction on the side of the national authorities that rules and institutions are necessary. As long as this understanding is not there enforcement will be very difficult. The lack of ownership appears particularly surprising in the case of Italy, where, as remarked in the chapter, the achievement of a balanced budget is pressing also from a purely national point of view – in order to reduce the very high government debt which acts as a burden on the Italian economy. The second element that can be further enhanced, and where Italy compares particularly badly with the rest of the euro area are budgetary procedures, that is, the set of arrangements governing the planning, implementation and monitoring of the budget. The gap between Italy's score and the euro-area average actually epitomises a well-known problem which is also highlighted in more detail in the outside view presented by Leipold in Chapter 5.[8] Among the seven characteristics[9] captured by the composite indicators reported in our graph the main weak spots of Italy's budgetary procedures are a low degree of centralisation[10] and the low reliance on performance budgeting techniques.

The degree of centralisation generally increases with the size of an economy and, linked to it, the size and complexity of government. This is, *inter alia,* the reason for a comparatively high degree of centralisation in Germany, France, Spain and the UK. Italy is an exception: centralisation, including top-down budgeting techniques whereby the planning process starts with a binding decision on the budgetary aggregates that cannot be changed in following budgetary steps, plays a relatively weak role. The common-pool problem surfaces at a very early stage of budgetary planning: the deficit targets set at the end of June in the medium-term macroeconomic and financial planning document (the DPEF) introduced by the 1988 budget reform are negotiated among the numerous political parties typically forming the coalition government. Until the budgetary session for 2009, no quantitative objectives were set for total expenditure and the tax burden. Constrained only by the agreed deficit targets, Parliament massively exploits its right to introduce amendments to the draft budget law for the following year submitted by the government at the end of September. Following decades of lenient implementation, the constitutional obligation, in force since 1948, to compensate the budgetary impact of any additional expenditure and/or lower revenue measure with offsetting measures has eventually received increasing attention. In particular, the rule has been substantially strengthened: The State Accounting Office tries to ensure it complied with not only on the basis of domestic accounting rules, but also in accordance with the European System of Accounts. Nevertheless the proposed compensatory measures (typically spur-of-the-moment expenditure cuts) often prove ineffective. A further major weakness of Italian budgetary procedures is the lack of commitment to medium-term budgetary objectives. They are moving targets: revised annually in the light of the budgetary outturns, especially slippages. A medium-term budgetary framework, which effectively steers public finances towards a target set beyond the year covered by the budget, is missing. This is also reflected in the budget discussion: even though the budget is structured with a three-year horizon, it focuses narrowly only on the first year.[11]

A further notable element of Italy's budget procedures with scope for improvement is performance budgeting, that is, techniques that aim to improve the effectiveness of government spending. Performance budgeting has received increasing attention, especially in view of the impending budgetary impact of an ageing population and, not to forget, a rising discontent among the general public with the quality of public services. The budget process does not include specific mechanisms assessing whether and to what extent the implementation of the budget has achieved individual objectives. Instead, it supports an incremental approach. The parliamentary discussion focuses on a draft budget law which introduces new fiscal measures, whereas the bulk of appropriations is allocated by simply forecasting the budgetary impact of spending programmes linked to legislation which was approved in the past (Montanino and Nicoletti Altimari, 2007). These programmes are not subject to a systematic revision aimed at assessing their efficiency and their relative value.

Where is fiscal governance heading?

The information underlying our assessment of budgetary procedures refers to the year 2003. Since then, a number of initiatives have been taken to improve fiscal governance in Italy. The flaws or shortcomings of the past are gradually being exploited to learn lessons for the future. For instance, the repeated failure to implement the agreements with regions which were supposed to constrain health-care expenditure led the government to enshrine in the 2006 budget law an automatic increase in regional taxes for non-compliant regions. After many years when regions incurring deficits in health-care accounts obtained *ex-post* higher transfers from the central government, the introduction of such an automatic mechanism aims to make the rule actually binding. By contrast, the gradual weakening of the sanctions for local governments violating the Domestic Stability Pact in the face of slightly more challenging expenditure ceilings has contributed to the opposite result.[12] These effects suggest that, more in general, Italy could benefit from mechanisms incorporating effective and credible sanctions. As a matter of fact, the 2007 budget law envisages that, as from 2008, an automatic increase of taxes also applies to municipalities that breached the domestic stability pact in the previous year. The actual implementation of this sanction will represent a crucial test for the credibility of the rule. Clearly, mechanisms of this kind are more likely to be applied by the central government to curb local government expenditure rather than that at the central level itself, where politicians can simply change the law imposing the sanctions. This is especially true in a country where the reputation cost attached to deviating from rules is very low. The idea of enhancing the credibility of rules by delegating some of the fiscal policy decision powers to an independent fiscal committee has thus been considered. In this regard, the Italian experience with independent authorities is mixed, with the degree of independence varying substantially according to the procedures followed to appoint and finance them, but also being subject to revisions of the degree of delegation. The 2007 budget law established a Technical Committee on Public Finance, the role of which was limited to carrying out analysis and studies. This committee was abolished in 2008.

The chapter recalls that several initiatives aimed at improving transparency and performance budgeting were undertaken in 2007. Notably, with advice by the IMF and input of the Technical Committee on Public Finance, a programme-based budget classification was prepared and promptly tested in the budgetary session; a pilot project of spending review was carried out in five ministries;[13] and a green book highlighting the need to improve the quality of public expenditure was released (Commissione Tecnica per la Finanza Pubblica, 2007a). In particular, the reform of the budget classification enhances the transparency of government priorities in terms of allocation of resources by organising the state budget in 34 overarching missions, which are aligned with the government's strategic objectives, ranging from public safety to fiscal relationships with local authorities. Within each mission, different programmes, 168 in total, identify homogeneous activities managed by one ministry in order to achieve specific objectives. Another significant step towards improving fiscal governance was taken in July 2007, with the presentation to Parliament of a draft framework law on fiscal federalism. After years of vacuum, the adoption of legislation coherent with the constitutional reform, which in 2001 stepped up decentralisation, would be important for enhancing local government accountability, and hence political commitment to budgetary targets. As stressed by Franco and Rizza, this objective can only be achieved if the legislation strengthens the link between revenue and spending decisions, which implies a degree of differentiation in the provision of services across the country.[14]

The aforementioned measures are intended only as the first steps of a more comprehensive budget reform process. Specifically, the DPEF covering 2008–11 (Ministero dell'Economia e delle Finanze, 2007a) points to the willingness to increase the use of performance budgeting. Initiatives adopted in 2008 tackle other characteristics of the budget procedures, which would also need urgent enhancement. As highlighted in the chapter, and confirmed by the 2008 budget law, there is a high risk that Italy's fiscal policy would return to a short-term focus once the pressure coming from the excessive deficit procedure is removed. The risk could be mitigated by significant improvements in fiscal governance so as to provide the right incentives or disincentives for policy-makers, for instance by strengthening the medium-term budgetary framework, which, in its current form, is not conducive to centralising the spending demands coming from fragmented coalition governments. The technical assessment of the annual updates of Italy's stability programme carried out by DG ECFIN repeatedly highlighted the fact that domestic planning documents provided little information about the composition of the fiscal adjustment.[15] This shortcoming essentially reflects the lack of an underlying strategy on how to achieve the adjustment, or at least the lack of an open endorsement of a strategy. Against this background, the invitation of the ECOFIN Council, included in its opinion on the 2007 update of the stability programme, to spell out the budgetary strategy with a medium-term perspective is meant not only to enhance compliance with the data requirements of the code of conduct of the Stability and Growth Pact.[16] It rather addresses a main weakness of the budgetary framework in Italy, namely the absence of a reliable multi-annual fiscal programme as a part of the coalition contract among the ruling parties. Eventually, the DPEF covering 2009–13 (Ministero dell'Economia e delle finanze, 2008) approved in June 2008 set detailed yearly targets for single expenditure and revenue items.

In an attempt to improve top-down budgeting techniques, in July 2007 the Prime Minister issued instructions for preparing the draft 2008 budget law. Ministers were required to accompany every proposal for higher expenditure with a corresponding reduction of resources allocated to other programmes. The limited response to this request highlights: i) the lack of effective medium-term expenditure ceilings set at the top; and ii) comparatively weak incentives for the line ministries to come forward with proposals for expenditure cuts within the spending programmes of their competence. While the absence of detailed targets for the medium-term appropriations was addressed in the 2008 DPEF,[17] Considerable progress could still be made by tackling the 'excessive' flexibility of the medium-term framework, which allows for revisions of the overall objectives from year to year not only as a result of changes in economic developments, but also in the fiscal policy agenda. A framework articulated around a medium-term projection for government expenditure that cannot be revised yearly, unless exceptional events occur, could provide a stronger degree of political commitment to the medium-term adjustment path, and the connection to the annual budget needed to achieve a turning point in the history of Italian public finances.

The very few empirical works examining the factors that shape budgetary institutions and rules (see, for instance, Fabrizio and Mody, 2007) seem to suggest that one determinant that typically brings about change is negative economic shock. Clearly, this conclusion is not particularly encouraging. It leaves us with the dreary prospect of waiting for the next merciful crisis. The initiatives taken by the Italian government since the beginning of the 2000s, aimed towards improving fiscal governance, can be read as an indication that the political leadership has started tackling the issue so as to pre-empt the more painful, even if cathartic, experience of a crisis. As Franco and Rizza put it, this represents a second opportunity to take Italy's public finances onto safer ground. Forward-looking discipline is crucial to avoid taking the risk of discovering the cost of a third opportunity.

Notes

1. For a wide-ranging analysis of Italian economic policy based on a review of official planning documents, including the economic policy carried out in the face of the 1992–3 financial crises, see Crescenzi (2007).
2. In budgetary policy, a 'common-pool' problem arises as politicians representing the interests of individual groups tend to overestimate the net social benefit from policies targeted at their constituency; they perceive the full social benefit of these policies, but only part of the cost, which is incurred not only by their voters, but spread over all taxpayers (von Hagen and Harden, 1996).
3. The figures presented in the graph are composite indicators which incorporate the information collected via specific surveys carried out by DG ECFIN, mostly in 2005, focusing on fiscal rules, budgetary procedures and medium-term budgetary frameworks. The technical details of the individual indicators and the related empirical work are presented in European Commission (2006; 2007a).
4. The definition of 'fiscal rules' underpinning the indicators constructed by DG ECFIN builds upon the work of Kopits and Symanski (1998). Fiscal rules are taken to be a permanent constraint on fiscal policy, expressed in terms of a summary indicator of fiscal performance. Numerical fiscal rules therefore specify numerical targets or limits for key budgetary aggregates such as annual budget balance, expenditure, revenue or debt.
5. According to Cimbolini (2008), in 2004 and 2005 the budget balances of municipalities substantially deteriorated despite compliance with the domestic stability pact.
6. ISAE (2007) reports that, in 2005, more than 17 per cent of the total expenditure carried out by municipalities related to entities with fewer than 5,000 inhabitants. An attempt to extend the coverage again in 2005 to municipalities with more than 3,000 inhabitants was abandoned the following year.
7. See also Faini *et al.* (2006).
8. See also International Monetary Fund (2007e).

9. Transparency, a multi-annual planning horizon, centralisation, top-down budgeting, prudent economic assumptions, performance budgeting, and centralisation during execution.
10. The centralisation of the budget process relates to the creation of institutions forcing the authors of individual decisions to recognise the true marginal costs and benefits of the projects financed by the general tax fund, and thus to internalise the externalities related to the common-pool problem (von Hagen *et al.*, 2002).
11. In terms of the numerical indicator measuring the quality of existing medium-term budgetary frameworks reported in Figure 4.14, Italy does not score too badly, which suggests that our assessment of the DPEF may be too pessimistic. However, two elements need to be taken into account. Firstly, the scale of the indicator is not metric and hence the distance along the axis cannot strictly be taken as a gauge of quality. The relative position is more important. Secondly, and looking at the individual criteria underpinning the aggregate indicator, Italy scores badly when it comes to the coordination mechanism across levels of government prior to setting the medium-term budgetary plans. This seems to be particularly problematic given that a large part of the slippages tend to occur at the lower level of government.
12. As pointed out in the contribution by Franco and Rizza, most local governments respect the Domestic Stability Pact; however, the number of non-compliant entities over the 2004–6 period points to an increasing trend, even though these entities are small in number. In particular, in 2006, a year for which sanctions were eventually abrogated by the 2007 budget law, non-compliant municipalities increased to around 15 per cent of the total, more than three times as much as the percentage recorded, on average, before 2005.
13. The ministries involved in the pilot project of spending review are: Education, Infrastructure, Interior, Justice and Transport. An interim report of this exercise (Commissione Tecnica per la Finanza Pubblica, 2007b), released in December 2007, presents some broad indications for actions that will need to be specified in detail and implemented.
14. Bibbee (2007) illustrates how fiscal federalism can complement structural reforms and budget consolidation.
15. In accordance with the Stability and Growth Pact, euro-area member states have to submit to the Council and the European Commission an annual update of the stability programme, which Italy submitted for the first time in December 1998. The updated programmes are assessed by the Commission and examined by the Economic Financial Committee. The Council can adopt an Opinion of the update programmes based on a recommendation by the Commission.
16. The lack of information on the composition of the planned budgetary adjustment in the stability programme updates is not in line with the Stability and Growth Pact and its code of conduct, which require not only a breakdown of the revenue and expenditure components in line with the budgetary targets, but also a description of the broad measures backing the budgetary targets throughout the programme period.
17. Before the novelty represented by the 2008 DPEF, a detailed evolution of taxes and government spending was projected on the basis of an unchanged legislation scenario, but targets were set only for the budget balance.

*Vito Tanzi**
Former IMF, Under-Secretary of State of Italy

Introduction

I should start my comment with the statement that fiscal policy is a messy area that cannot be captured by a few graphs or parameters as is often done in academic papers. There are simply too many aspects to it. The chapter by Daniele Franco and Pietro Rizza tries to capture some of these aspects and reaches conclusions with which I am broadly in agreement, although with qualifications and nuances. In this comment, I will first summarise briefly the main points made by Franco and Rizza and then add some personal views on Italian fiscal policy over the years.

For 20 years, until 1994, the Italian fiscal deficit, *as conventionally measured,* averaged about 10 per cent of GDP leading to a fast growth in public debt. The public debt, that in 1970 was about 40 per cent of GDP, increased to about 120 per cent of GDP in the 1990s. Because of my interest in Argentina, I will point out that between 1965 and 1985 Italy made the same mistake as Argentina in the 1946–54 period, during the first Peron administration: it attempted to create a large public-sector role (a kind of welfare state) without accompanying it with the ordinary revenue necessary to fully finance it. In this period primary spending increased from 29 per cent of GDP in 1964 to 42 per cent of GDP in 1985, or about the same increase as in Argentina (Tanzi, 2007). Naturally to this increase one has to add the servicing of the rapidly rising public debt.

The chapter indicates that the main contributors to the spending increase were: public pensions (about 8 per cent of GDP); transfers to enterprises (about 2.5 per cent of GDP); public health (about 2 per cent); and education (about 1 per cent). It should be noted that most of the increase in public spending *came from cash and not from real* (or 'exhaustive') *spending*. Health and education spending accounted for only 3 per cent of GDP, a relatively modest increase. In spite of this, the number of public employees rose from 1.5 million to 3.4 million, thus more than doubling. Of course, not too many public employees are needed to make cash payments. The large increase in public employment was politically

* This is an edited version of comments delivered on occasion of the seminar on: 'Can Italy Adjust and Grow?', in memory of Riccardo Faini, Brussels, 2 March 2007.

motivated. This helps in part to explain the high teacher-to-student ratio and possibly the high doctor-to-nurse ratio that characterises these programmes in the Italian public sector. Interest payments increased sharply between 1964 and 1985, going from 1 per cent to 8 per cent of GDP and thus contributing to a large part of the fiscal deficit.

The sharp increase in public spending was first financed largely with debt and later, but not completely, with taxes. The tax ratio had been almost constant and low until 1975, during the years of the 'Italian economic miracle'. Then it started rising at a record pace. It rose by about 1 per cent of GDP per year, reaching 38 per cent of GDP in 1985 and almost 45 per cent of GDP in the 1990s. If one believes that increasing taxes reduces economic growth, one should look no further than Italy for some evidence. The tax increase was needed to pay pensions to retired but still young people, and subsidies to inefficient enterprises. Given that the ownership of financial assets is often concentrated among older people, the interest payments on the public debt were probably going in large part to the same groups (and often to the same persons) that were getting the public pensions.

I will now add more specific and personal comments to Franco and Rizza's useful description of events.

Once established, the primary spending could not be reduced because legal or political 'entitlements' had been created. It became legally and politically difficult – especially for governments that were aggregations of many groups, each reflecting particular constituencies and vested interests – to change the legislation that had created the legal entitlements or expectations of public assistance. The few attempts, especially in later years, made to reduce spending were often administrative rather than substantive measures aimed at reducing entitlements. The *decreto taglia spese* was a classic example of this approach. This decree instructed the administrators of public programmes to spend less without changing the fundamental nature of the programmes. It was no surprise that these attempts were not successful. They tried to contain the steam coming out of the pot by holding the cover of the pot tighter and not by reducing the flame that created the pressure.

The situation described in the last paragraph had also implications for counter-cyclical fiscal policy. That policy could be pursued mainly, if not only, in one direction. It was far easier to relax fiscal policy than to tighten it. This asymmetry in countercyclical fiscal policy, combined with a trust in that policy, was a major factor in the rise of the public debt.

As already said, there were huge increases in the tax level after 1975. In a Keynesian framework (accompanied by Haavelmo's balanced-budget theorem) the tax increases would not affect economic growth, at least not in the short run, if the higher taxes are accompanied, as they were, by higher public spending. In fact, they would be expansionary, as Haavelmo's theorem argues. However, in a supply-side framework, when the economy is closer to a full utilization of its resources, the higher tax rates could not fail, over the longer run, to damage economic growth. The effects of high taxes might be, and probably were in Italy, delayed by the presence of rigid labour markets and unemployment that gave dependent workers little opportunity (except perhaps that of going to the underground economy) to avoid the higher taxes by changing working hours or by other means.

Because of tax evasion and underground economic activities, the tax burden *in the official economy* was higher than indicated by the ratio of taxes to GDP. Large and random evasion must have reduced the efficiency of the economy. Also the cost of complying with the progressively more complex tax system – that created an industry of tax consultants – must have affected economic growth and sharply raised the marginal cost of additional public spending. One additional lira or euro of spending must have cost, in real terms, much more than that additional lira or euro of public spending. It should be recalled that at one point President Scalfaro declared that the tax return that Italian taxpayers had to present must have been designed by 'lunatics'. It is not likely that the tax system became less complex or less inefficient in later years.

The fiscal consolidation of 1992–7

The chapter refers to the attempt at fiscal consolidation made in 1992–7, when the fiscal deficit fell from 11.4 per cent of GDP to 2.7 per cent of GDP. A fiscal adjustment of 8.7 per cent of GDP in five years would appear a remarkable achievement and the governments that were in control during these years have received high praise for it. While some of the praise is merited, because a genuine effort was made to reduce the deficit, the real or true adjustment was somewhat less impressive than these numbers suggest. The reasons for this divergent view are several.

First, the fall in inflation during those years led to a sharp reduction in *nominal interest rates*. As it is known, inflation, through the Fisher effect, leads to higher *nominal* interest rates. This converts part of the higher interest payments into an unplanned repayment of the principal on the debt, thus swelling the measured (but not the real) deficit. When the size of the public debt is large (as it was in Italy) and the rate of inflation is significant (as it was in Italy in the early 1990s), this distortion of the measured deficit can become important. This issue was discussed in detail by Tanzi *et al.* (1987).[1] Thus a large part of the 8.7 per cent of GDP adjustment in the fiscal deficit was a statistical illusion and not a genuine change in the fiscal situation.

Second, the move toward Maastricht led to falls in *real* interest rates that contributed to a genuine, and not just an accounting, reduction in the fiscal deficit. While real, this reduction could not be attributed to fiscal actions taken by the governments in power at that time. However, the government should, of course, receive praise for making Italy part of the Maastricht agreement.

Third, the impact on the deficit of the widespread judicial investigations that followed the corruption scandals known as *tangentopoli* has not been recognised. These reduced significantly the costs of public investment projects, by removing the bribes that had up to that time increased these costs. It also made policy-makers more cautious in starting new projects, thus reducing real public investment. The net result was that spending on public investment fell significantly during the 1992–7 period. This contributed to a reduction in public spending and in the fiscal deficit. Some would also argue that it reduced the rate of growth of the Italian economy.

Fourth, Italy was undergoing a period of privatisation of many public enterprises that contributed to large, but 'one-off', public revenue. This revenue contributed to the reduction in public debt that took place over the period.

Finally, as in other countries on the way to Maastricht, Italy made recourse to various accounting tricks and other 'one-off' measures. The 'tax for Europe', for example, was one of these but there were other less visible ones. At a time when the *cash* measure of the deficit was still the norm, simply postponing some payments, such as the reimbursement of VAT refunds, could contribute to the lowering of the reported cash deficit. These postponements of payments may have contributed to the difference, in later years, between '*fabbisogno*' and '*indebitements netto*', that is, between cash and accrual measures.

There were, of course, some important attempts at real reform, especially in the pension area. These reduced significantly, but unfortunately not enough, the future costs of pensions. By 1999, however, bad habits had returned or, perhaps, had become more transparent. As an article in *The Economist* at the time put it, the government ran out of ideas or courage.

The Berlusconi period

The Berlusconi government, of which I was part for the first two years (May 2001–July 2003), came with many expectations and with some naïve views of how economies operate.

One such a view was what I would label the *teoria della scossa* (shock theory). This theory was never articulated in a clear or explicit way but it influenced policy decisions, especially during the first year of the new government, that set the stage for future years. Putting it bluntly, the view was that since a new government, led by managers who had been very successful in their private sector activities, had taken over, the annual growth rate of the economy would, almost magically, rise to perhaps as much as 4 per cent, up from the low rates of the previous years. This sharp rise would be a reflection of psychological factors and of anticipated future policy changes, such as the promised tax reform. This reform would significantly reduce the tax burden on enterprises and individuals. There were also various less significant measures that some political leaders felt would have a major impact on the economy. This belief led to unrealistic promises about tax reductions for future years and to weak attempts at preventing primary spending from rising. A faster-growing economy can of course more easily finance higher public spending. The Economic and Financial Planning Document (DPEF) of 2001 (Ministero dell'Economia e delle Finanze, 2001) reflected to some extent this *teoria della scossa*. The latter led to a reluctance to accept realistic growth forecasts even in the face of clear evidence. And, of course, over-optimistic forecasts encouraged or justified higher public spending requests by ministries.

A second problem faced by the Berlusconi government, at least at the beginning, was the confusion about the actual current fiscal situation. For a realistic fiscal policy to be followed, a government: i) must know what the current real fiscal situation is; ii) must have a clear idea of where it wants to go; and iii) must be confident that it knows how to get there. There were difficulties on all three grounds. At least at the beginning there was genuine confusion as to what the actual situation was. The office that should have known, the General Accounting Office – Ragioneria Generale dello Stato – was asserting, as late as September 2001, that the fiscal deficit for 2001 would be around 1 per cent. (For a brief discussion of this issue see Tanzi, 2006.) When Minister Tremonti, in the autumn of 2001, started talking about a *buco* – a hole in the public accounts – he was sharply criticised and not just by the opposition. He turned out to be more than right. The deficit in 2001 turned out to be three times as large as the Ragioneria had believed in September. The new government could not be blamed for much of this deterioration because its first budget law (the so-called *finanziaria*) would only come later that year.

To get where it wanted to go, while, perhaps, still waiting for the favourable effects expected from the *scossa*, the government started to rely significantly on measures such as tax amnesties, sale of assets, and various manoeuvres of social engineering that made the current deficit look better than it was while doing little for a real solution to the structural, long-run fiscal problem. My impression at the time was that the new policy-makers did not fully appreciate the difference between permanent and 'one-off' measures because in the short run the difference does not appear significant. A belief in the expansionary power of fiscal deficits did not help. The public debt, that had fallen in previous years, started rising again and so did primary spending. The earlier promise to cut the tax level was largely forgotten.

In conclusion, neither the governments that had represented the centre-left (until May 2001) nor the one that represented the centre-right (after May 2001) was able to make a real and sustainable difference to the precarious fiscal situation. In 2006, after the change in government, the fiscal accounts improved unexpectedly and mysteriously. This improvement was interpreted by some as a signal that the fiscal emergency was over. Pressures started again to increase spending by using the so-called *tesoretto*, that is, the resources from the unexpected improvement in revenue. The sudden, unexpected large change in revenue raised again questions the ability of the relevant offices to forecast fiscal variables.

Necessary reforms

I shall end this comment with a brief discussion of necessary reforms, separating technical and procedural issues from more structural or even cultural ones. Some of the reforms suggested below are similar to those mentioned, much more diplomatically, by Franco and Rizza. I shall start with the technical issues.

First of all there is a need to remove biases from forecasts (both of the economy and of budgetary outcomes). At times politics may drive forecasts, thus compromising the assessment of the policies that need to be enacted. Politically independent non-governmental institutions should play a larger role in this context because of inevitable biases that may influence those who make the official forecasts. Those who make official forecasts should be given full independence. However, at times this is difficult when the budgets of these offices are decided by the government in power. I should add that I consider the forecasts made by the Bank of Italy as unbiased but it would be good to have several institutions making forecasts.

Second, there is a need to give more clarity to the fiscal accounts. There is too much confusion in this area and over the years there has been little interest on the part of the relevant bureaucracies to make these accounts more transparent and easier to understand. The problem may be that clarity would reduce the power of some high-level bureaucrats.

Third, there is a need for a comprehensive and more timely exchange of information among the constituent parts of the public sector. The timely availability of some information is still missing, requiring frequent and embarrassing *ex-post* revisions of the fiscal accounts.

Fourth, and related to the above, there must be a better public diffusion of all available data. At times particular data are given only to a minister, in sealed envelopes, and are not available to others, even within the government, until later.

Fifth, in my view it would be worthwhile to abolish the DPEF (the *libro dei sogni* – book of dreams). It does not serve a useful purpose and it distracts policy-makers from the real discussion that should be focused on the presentation of the budget, a document that should include proposed changes now presented in the *finanziaria*. There is in any case too much time between the discussion of the DPEF and that of the *finanziaria*. Six months is too long for a fast-changing world.

Finally, budgetary procedures must be streamlined and a much simpler and clearer version of the budget should be made available to parliament and to the public on a more timely basis. Few individuals understand the budget; and the *finanziaria* has become an unwieldy document that few read carefully and fewer understand.

Let me now turn to structural issues. Here the starting point for the future equilibrium of the fiscal accounts must inevitably be public pensions. The pension system needs to be reformed to reduce its future burden and to improve its sustainability. Pension payments now absorb more public resources as a share of GDP than the whole public sector did in 1913. Future demographic changes in Italy are among the most worrisome among countries (long and rising life expectancy, low birth rates, low labour-force participation). The retirement age is much too low (perhaps by as much as ten years) and the proposed changes will not be sufficient to make much difference if life expectancy keeps growing as it has in recent decades. The official projections of pension data are very sensitive to the assumptions made. Future developments could be much worse than officially projected. A problem is that labour unions now represent more pensioners than workers. While unions continue to have much political power, the number of pensioners or near-pensioners who would oppose changes keeps growing all the time.

A second reform should be the acceleration of the disposal of publicly held assets. Estimates made by the Cassa Depositi e Prestiti indicate that the Italian public sector continues to own and use (or often misuse) huge stocks of publicly owned assets. According to these estimates, it uses about three times as much as the United Kingdom. The use by the public sector of these assets often contributes little to GDP or to taxes and leads to an underestimation of the cost of the public sector. The national and the local governments should continue to sell these assets *but not to generate cash to be spent*. The objective should be to improve the rate of return to *all* assets in the economy, whether they are public or private, and to use the revenue so obtained to reduce the public debt so that the servicing of the debt decreases over time.

A third reform should be to clarify the rules related to fiscal decentralisation, to abolish the provinces, and possibly to consolidate the number of local governments or administrations. The provinces are not needed in the presence of regions and municipalities. They inevitably add to the costs of public-sector operations by duplicating some functions. Furthermore, provinces are an Italian peculiarity. Other federal countries have three and not four levels of government. It will be important to bring finality and clarity to the fiscal arrangements among the different levels of government. Half-completed reforms are rarely satisfactory and often contribute to inefficient outcomes.[2] Additionally, the number of municipalities is too high in Italy and this contributes to higher public spending.

A fourth area of reform should be the coordination of the Lisbon objectives (that require a sharp rise in the employed share of the population and especially of the female population) with the needs of the very old. This reform will probably increase public spending but it is a necessary one. The fastest-growing age group in Italy is the over-eighties. Now these old people are, for the most part, taken care of by their daughters or stepdaughters or by granddaughters. If the latter go to work in much larger proportions (as the Lisbon agenda recommends), who will take care of the very old? How expensive this can be can be learned from Sweden, a country that already spends about five per cent of its GDP on this social function against an insignificant amount in Italy.

There are other areas that require attention. Some concern arrangements in the area of education, health, research, security and others. The reforms in these areas should aim at making some of them more efficient and less costly and thus increase the efficiency of public spending. Some of these reforms have been described in specialised studies but relatively little has been done so far.

Other reforms of a technical-structural-cultural nature would reduce public spending and increase the efficiency of the public sector. Some are mentioned below without elaboration.

There is first the need for serious (and not cosmetic) pruning of the Byzantine regulations that continue to exist in Italy and that make life difficult for many citizens and require the time and effort of many public employees. Anybody who has spent a lot of time in a country such as the United States becomes aware of how many operations are unnecessarily complicated in Italy. They absorb a large share of the time of citizens and require the attention of many public employees. The greater the number of these regulations, the larger must be the number of public employees needed to deal with them. A cut in the number of public employees, without reducing the number of, or simplifying, regulations, may simply result in longer response times for getting permits, documents and so on. It must be realised that many public employees are not engaged in providing useful services to citizens but in administering often useless regulations. The response times to citizens' requests for authorisations to engage in particular activites (opening enterprises, making investments, obtaining passports, etc.) have been reported to be already much longer than in other countries.

There is a need for greater mobility in government jobs so that the real effort required from public employees is equalised. Some work very hard while others do very little, and certainly very little of social or economic value. Job mobility could allow some reduction in public employment.

Third, as already mentioned, there is a need for deep reform in sectors such as education, security, justice and health. Justice, especially, is a disaster area with damaging implications for the working of the economy because of the impact that it has on the rule of law, the timely enforcement of contracts and the efficiency of some markets, such as housing and credit.

There is also a need to introduce a *culture of austerity* in the public sector, a culture that is badly missing in Italy. Evidence of the lack of such a culture can be seen from: i) the use of blue cars by a large number of public employees; ii) the use of planes by ministers for travel even to places well served by commercial airlines; iii) the number of members of the Senate and the House; iv) the number of employees who work for the *Quirinale*; v) the resources that go into parliamentary activities (including pensions), resources that have been growing at a fast pace in recent years; and vi) the resources that go into parades, such as the 2 June parade in Rome, and similar events, such as the huge number of publicly financed festivals and so-called 'cultural activities'. The expenses in some of these areas have been reported to have grown rapidly in Italy and to be much greater than in other countries. In France, Germany and the United Kingdom these 'cultural' expenses are more limited than in Italy.

There is also a need for paying more attention to what I have occasionally called 'institutional externalities', that is, how failures in one institution (say the justice system) affect the operation and the efficiency of important sectors of the economy (such as the housing or credit market), as mentioned earlier.

Finally, it is important that policy-makers come to believe that what the public sector provides can often be provided more efficiently by a private sector made more efficient by good regulations and well-focused regulators. Thus, the generation of good regulations and the appointment of good regulators must be seen as one of the most essential roles of the State. A lot of what the public sector provides by taxing the citizens and spending the money on their behalf could be bought directly by the taxpayers from a better-regulated private sector. For an attempt to quantify the degree of efficiency in delivering social objectives, see Afonso *et al.* (2005).

Having spent a lot of time with Riccardo Faini, both at the IMF and at the Italian Treasury, I am confident that he would agree with much, but not necessarily all, of what I have written above. His premature death removed one of the important agents of change from the Italian scene.

Notes

1. See also Tanzi (1980).
2. It should also be pointed out that Italy has already too many regions and far too many municipalities for its size. China has the same number of regions as Italy and Brazil has a little more than half the municipalities of Italy. Both are huge countries.

5

Italy Viewed from the Outside*

The OECD View

Alexandra Bibbee
Organisation for Economic Co-operation and Development (OECD)

Italy has been recovering from a long period of economic near-stagnation, but the durability of the turnaround is not yet assured. A productivity slowdown since 1995, with even an absolute decline in total factor productivity after the turn of the millennium – a rare event in the OECD context – continues to hobble potential growth. Ageing meanwhile is starting to bite as the size of the working-age population steadily erodes. Per capita income growth in recent years has been sustained mostly by rising total hours worked, thanks to major labour-market reforms. The achievement of simultaneous robust growth in employment and productivity has thus proved elusive thus far, but is vital in order to confront Italy's longer-run challenges. This chapter discusses key supply side issues in Italy as seen by the OECD.*

Boosting productivity to better cope with globalisation

The export engine has stalled

Between 1995 and 2006, nearly half of Italy's substantial export market shares evaporated, while Italy's share of world trade in value terms declined by one-third. This reflects an apparent severe loss of international competitiveness, as relative unit labour costs over the same period jumped by more than 50 per cent (Figure 5.1). Though relative consumer prices appreciated only by about half as much, their gap *vis-à-vis* relative

* This chapter was submitted to the editor in September 2007. It is based upon the *OECD Economic Surveys: Italy* published by OECD in 2007. It has benefited from the valuable inputs and comments of Benoît Bellone, Sylvie Foucher-Hantala and Patrick Lenain.

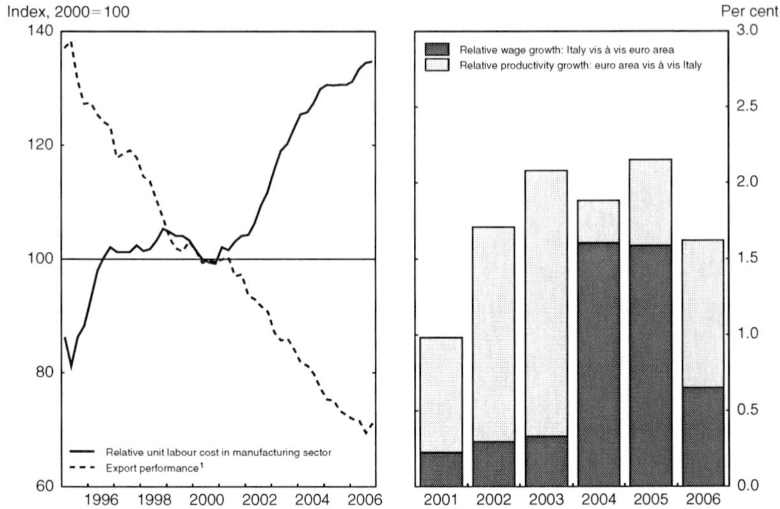

Figure 5.1 Competitiveness indicators
1. Defined as the ratio between export volumes and export markets weighted by Italian trade shares.
Source: OECD *Economic Outlook* No. 81 database (June 2007).

labour costs nonetheless suggests a marked profit squeeze. As deteriorating export performance coincided with dismantling of trade barriers between OECD and non-OECD countries and the entry of Italy into EMU at an irrevocably fixed exchange rate, it would seem that Italy has found it difficult to cope with the shock of globalisation solely via structural flexibility, without the aid of monetary independence as in the past.

Italy has been especially vulnerable to the globalisation shock in part because of a production structure quite similar to emerging market competitors, that is, heavily based on traditional low-skill products, with a large price elasticity of demand. As noted in Chapter 1, Italy even reinforced this disadvantage by shifting its relative specialisation even more toward such products as the shock deepened. Countries that seem to be coping better with globalisation have been shifting resources toward areas less sensitive to low-cost competition, notably high-tech goods and services or other niche areas. Other euro-area countries (though less so Spain) appear to be in this category and have better preserved their overall market shares. They have also been moving much more rapidly than Italy toward higher shares of university-educated people in the population in order to not only supply the knowledge base for high-tech production but also to adequately diffuse new technologies throughout the economy. Furthermore, deindustrialisation elsewhere in the OECD triggered processes leading to an increasing specialisation in dynamic service sectors, something that is indeed called for in the massive shift in the internal terms of trade.

Some signs of adjustment

To be sure, there are signs of adjustment. Export prices are rising relative to general product prices more in Italy than elsewhere, allowing substantially better export performance in value than in volume terms. Hence, the share within each sector of firms producing higher value-added seems to be growing, either because such firms themselves are upgrading and able to exercise greater market pricing power, or because lower value-added firms are dropping out of the market. There could also have been more pricing to market in the recent strong global upswing. Indeed, average price rises have been especially sharp in the luxury high ends of traditional goods, for which there is a growing demand by an emerging middle class in non-OECD countries. There is corroborating evidence of a higher variability of profit outcomes in Italian industry, along with a descending mean value (Figure 5.2). Larger firms in particular seem much better able to outsource and innovate in order to survive than smaller ones. This dichotomy may be aggravated by the fact that small firms find it difficult to grow to medium (later large) size in Italy as a means of adjusting.

Another way to view the situation is that rising stars such as India and China are themselves shifting into high-tech areas and investing in human capital. New OECD areas of comparative advantage may before long become contested and overcrowded. Export prices of such goods have in fact been falling, also because of technology, so that the terms of trade for countries specialising in them are an income loser. Italy may one day look to be better placed for the long run: it has a solid export base featuring high-grade consumer items and the machinery to make them, much prized by China and others. Italy, for all its export woes, has avoided current account balance deterioration after netting out oil imports (Banca d'Italia, 2007), while the extra-euro-area trade balance has held up better than that *vis-à-vis* the euro area (Cotis, 2006). It is probably wise to build upon traditional strengths even while restructuring.

It was argued in Chapter 3 that difficulties in recording illegal immigrants and their output may have exaggerated the extent of the competitiveness problem (see also Chaney, 2006 and Gros, 2007). This

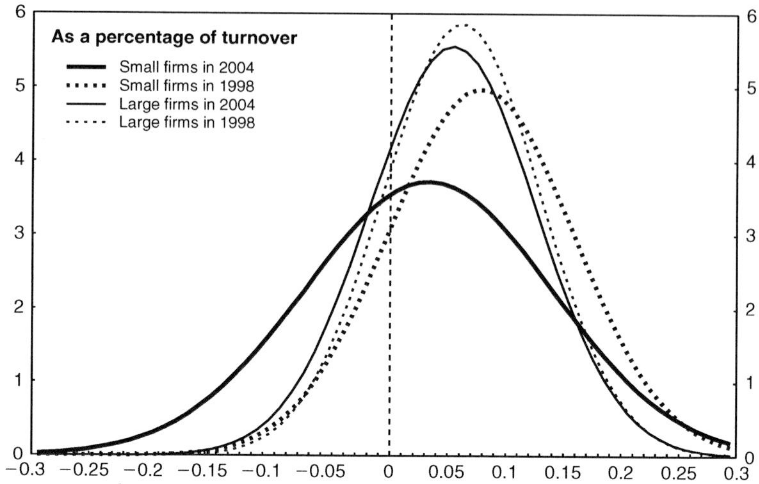

Figure 5.2 Restructuring is under way with evidence of rising variability in profitability (Earning before interest and tax (EBIT) on turnover distribution according to firm's size)

1. Small firms are firms with less than 2 billion euros turnover. Large ones have a turnover of more than 50 billion euros.
Source: Confindustria.

hypothesis relies on a twofold data distortion. First, large periodic immigrant regularisation programmes imply that the earlier level of productivity in Italy may have been exaggerated insofar as ISTAT understated the size of the underground economy on the output side in relation to the factor input side; hence, the productivity collapse is really a process of adjustment to the 'true', lower productivity level. Second, the collapse of export volume market share which on the surface appears wholly consistent with the published productivity series (via competitiveness indicators), must also be incorrect. The culprit here is using export unit values to proxy export prices,[1] and the volume/unit value split is notoriously difficult to make because of the difficulty of allocating quality improvements which are erroneously being put into unit values rather than volumes. Hence, the proper export performance measure to look at is value market shares where, as seen, Italy is doing much better.

Low TFP growth is the core problem

But the fact that export market shares are still being lost, and at a significant rate, suggests that at the aggregate level the adjustment is still unsatisfactory; more export firms are exiting than staying in and thriving.[2] Even though labour is being released by less efficient traditional-sector firms, itself a sign of adjustment, such resources are apparently not yet being used productively enough in the sheltered sectors. All in all, an inability to adjust the structure of production to the demands of globalisation suggests a fundamental problem with structural dynamism normally associated with total factor productivity (TFP). Inadequate public infrastructure following years of budget cuts could also play a role.

A standard OECD growth accounting analysis substantiates that Italy experienced an unusually sharp deceleration in TFP in the last decade (Figure 5.3). At the same time, however, Italy forged ahead of other countries (except the United States) in terms of labour utilisation, thereby limiting the absolute and relative decline in its potential rate of growth. Capital deepening slowed only marginally, and further analysis shows that this reflected a steady growth in the capital to labour ratio along with a slowly falling rate of return to capital. This suggests that the productivity slowdown cannot be attributed to any large extent to 'labour deepening' endogenous to labour-market reforms themselves. Nor can it be traced mainly to temporary composition effects, notably as atypical contracts bid lower-skill people into jobs, as shown by a more refined estimate of TFP that controls for changes in labour quality.[3]

Human capital indicators for Italy further support the conclusion of weak TFP growth (Figure 5.4). Italy has one of the OECD's lowest proportions of researchers and engineers in total employment, and its innovation performance (private R&D spending, patents, ICT diffusion) ranks poorly in international comparison. A relative lack of research skills weakens the ability not only to initiate innovations locally but also to absorb knowledge and adapt inventions from abroad. Poor innovation performance can be traced back to deficiencies of the tertiary education system. Currently, less than 15 per cent of a generation obtains a tertiary diploma, far below the 40 per cent and upwards reached in top OECD performers. But technological progress also requires broader human resources in terms of a skilled workforce capable of implementing the needed organisational changes. In this respect, a major weakness for Italy is the very high share of the workforce having little or no formal qualifications beyond compulsory schooling – the mirror image of the productive structure.

Sheltered sectors must be opened up to competition

TFP is calculated as a residual but is thought to reflect managerial efficiency and innovative activity, the creative process that gives rise to

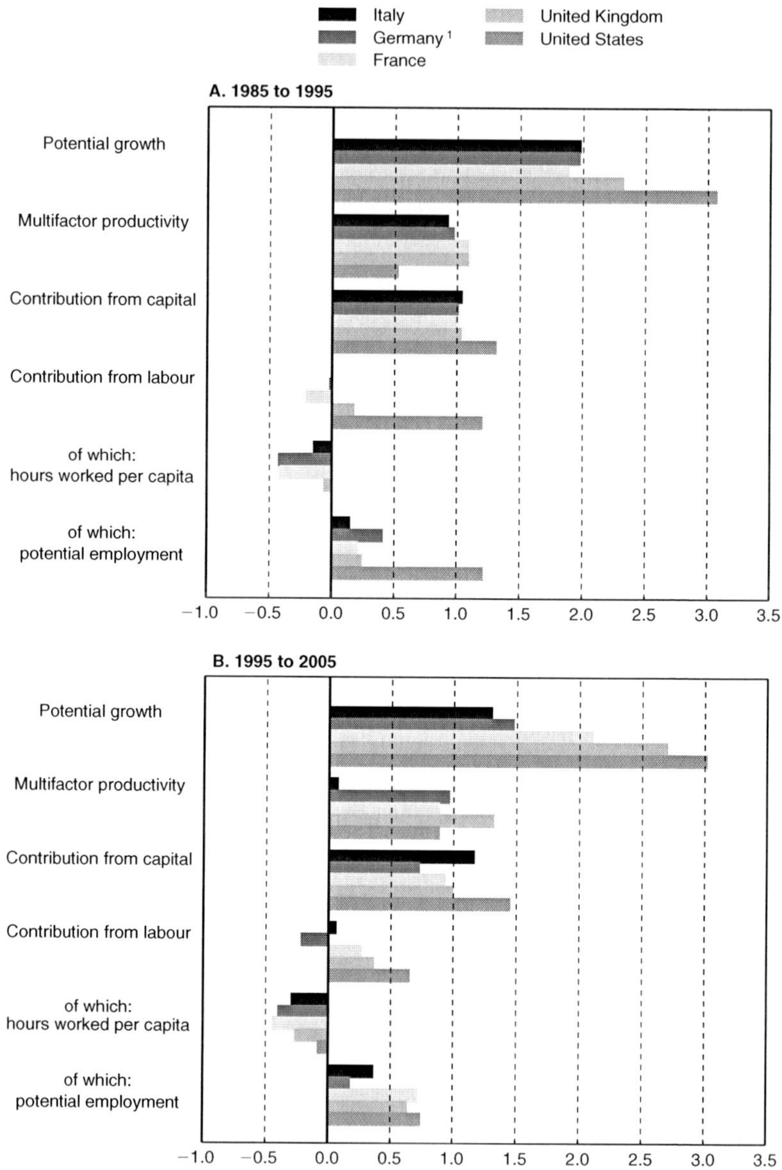

Figure 5.3 Decomposition of potential growth: an international comparison (annualised growth rate)

Note: 1. 1991–5 for Germany.

Source: OECD *Economic Outlook* No. 81 database (June 2007).

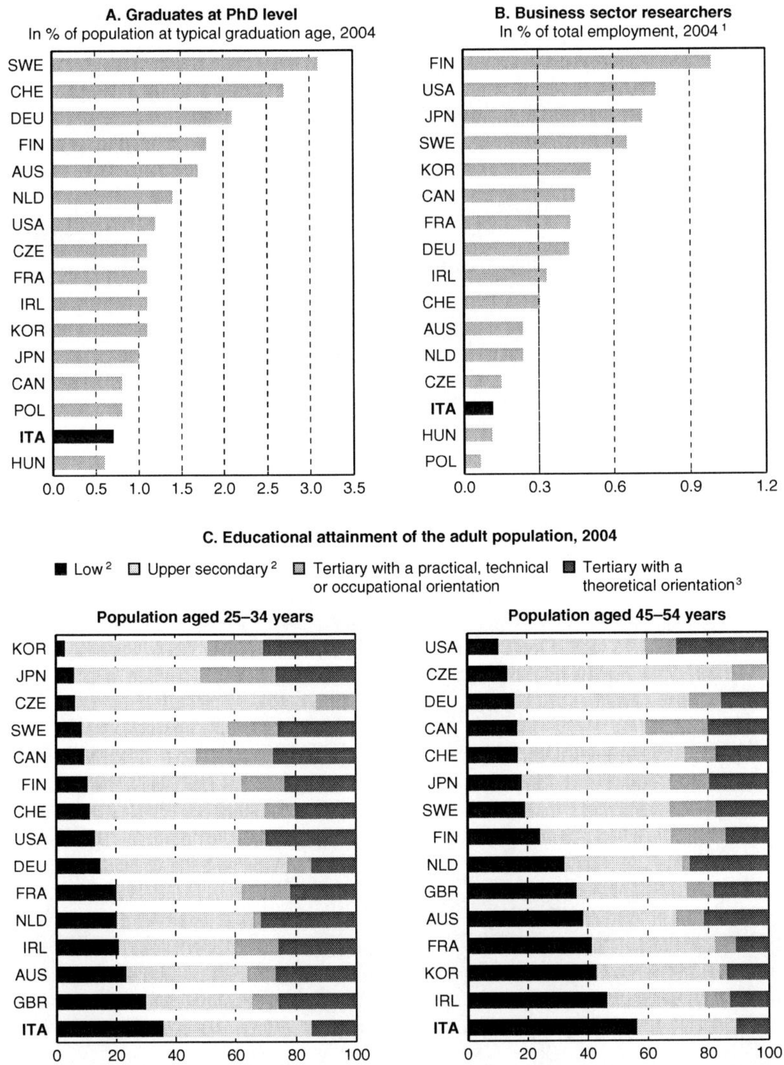

Figure 5.4 A low-skill bias in Italy

Notes: 1. 2003 for Netherlands and Sweden, 2002 for Canada and United States.

2. Low comprises persons having primary school, lower secondary school or ISCED 3C short programmes as their only formal qualification; upper secondary includes also post-secondary-non-tertiary programmes.

3. Includes tertiary with a practical, technical or occupational orientation for Italy.

Source: Cotis (2006).

value-added. A strong human capital endowment is obviously needed to supply the requisite skills. But the demand for such skills is just as critical. Competition is the main stimulus to innovation demand by firms, especially if accompanied by a deep and efficient financial system to cushion the risks involved and accelerate the development of small and medium enterprises.

Ironically perhaps, in Italy it is the exposed manufacturing sector that explains virtually all of the past decade's aggregate TFP growth collapse. In the services sector, largely sheltered from either foreign or domestic competition, TFP slowed down much less. However, the more salient fact is that TFP growth in the services sector has been dramatically slow for a long time,[4] and this may itself have played a role in the economy's difficulty in adapting to global competition. The United States by contrast experienced an important surge in services productivity – finance, ICT services and retail and wholesale trade, from low rates of growth traditionally, which is at the heart of that country's much vaunted 'productivity miracle'. This suggests a global technology that was available, and a missed opportunity for Italy.

A growing body of OECD research suggests a significant link between service-sector competition and economy-wide productivity. There is evidence that product-market competition is a key to promoting productivity and employment simultaneously, by reinforcing incentives to innovate and improve efficiency (Conway *et al.*, 2005; Nicoletti and Scarpetta, 2005). Another key finding is that services are major suppliers of inputs to other industries in Italy, notably in the exposed sector, and that the impacts of deregulation in non-manufacturing on the manufacturing sector would be stronger in Italy and Greece than in other OECD countries (Conway and Nicoletti, 2006).[5] Competition-restraining regulations furthermore slow the rate of catch-up to the technological frontier (Conway *et al.*, 2006). Hence, over the past decade labour productivity may have accelerated in lightly regulated economies, but decelerated in highly regulated countries such as Italy, which fell even farther behind the high-productivity frontier (Figure 5.5).

Acknowledging increasing evidence that competition-restraining regulations contribute to sluggish macroeconomic performance, the Italian government has moved recently to ease entry barriers in professional services, cut bureaucratic red tape, expand consumer choice, diminish sheltered sector rents, and reinforce the competition framework – all welcome steps. Yet, market forces could be strengthened further. Supporting competition at local levels, with a view to protecting consumers' rather than local vested interests, could stimulate the retail and wholesale trade

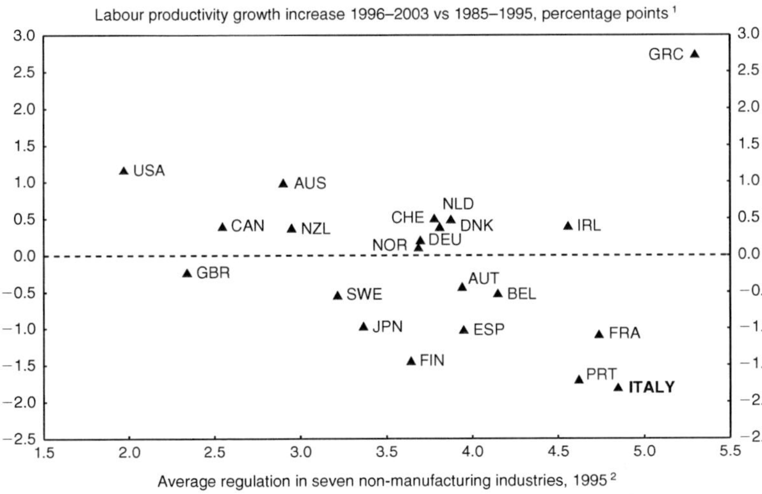

Figure 5.5 Cross-country differences in product market regulation may have contributed to divergent productivity growth (the scale of the indicators is 0–6 from least to most restrictive)

Notes: 1. Labour productivity is defined as output per hour worked. In absence of sufficient retropolation at the time of publication, data for Greece do not take into account the 25 per cent upwards revision to the level of GDP announced in 2006.

2. The seven non-manufacturing industries are airlines, telecommunications, electricity, gas, post, rail and road freight.

Source: OECD (2007c).

sector besides inducing greater efficiency in the supply of local public economic services. The consolidation process of the banking industry is promising, but Italy might need more competition to spur productivity in this area. The country would also surely benefit from a more market-based financing system to allow firms to grow and innovate. The bankruptcy reform at the end of 2005 was a long overdue and critical step in this direction.

Making the most of labour resources in an ageing society

On top of being exceptionally exposed to the globalisation shock, Italy is among the OECD countries to be most severely hit by population ageing. This vulnerability reflects very low fertility rates and lengthening life-spans of its relatively large post-war baby boom generation, together implying a sharp rise in the dependency ratio over the next 30 years (to 62 per cent, at the EU's high end[6]). Participation rates of females and older workers and youth employment rates have improved, but are still well below corresponding European and OECD averages (Table 5.1). Italy has substantial scope to boost its growth rate by converging to these norms. But labour market and fiscal distortions hamper its ability to do so.

Impressive job growth, but also growing duality

Labour-market reforms over the past decade or so, featuring atypical contract liberalisations, have clearly succeeded in creating employment: 90 per cent of new jobs have been on a part-time basis, and over 40 per cent on a fixed-term basis.[7] Thanks to these jobs, unemployment has sharply fallen, benefiting household confidence and consumption. First-time and less-skilled workers have also been able to get a toehold in the job market. This is nonetheless a second-best solution. Flexibility is consigned to the margins of the market. Youth, women and other marginals lack unemployment insurance, yet face a high risk of intermittent unemployment.[8] Meanwhile, strong employment protection for the bulk of workers with tenured contracts is firmly in place, including the right to judicial recourse for individual unfair dismissals. Larger firms provide such workers with unemployment insurance. This creates a dual labour market, and a rebalancing of protections seems in order. Employment protection (EPL) for permanent contracts should be eased, even if that requires modest universal unemployment insurance, once budget conditions permit.[9]

EPL is likely to impede innovation and growth, moreover (OECD, 2007c). Excessive job protection makes it costly for firms to restructure and reduces the incentives for employees to exert effort, besides making employers reluctant to hire in the first place. This is an important reason why atypical contracts have been such a success: they greatly reduce firing costs and permit restructuring, besides enabling greater flexibility in the use of labour in response to fluctuations in demand. As the strictest part of EPL legislation kicks in only above a certain threshold (15 employees) it may favour small firm size to some extent, whereas innovation tends to occur at larger scales. EPL on open-ended contracts may be an obstacle to productivity growth and job creation as it slows down the creative-destructive process in Italy.

A relatively large underground economy

A relatively large underground economy in Italy[10] is but an extreme form of the insider-outsider dichotomy. To be sure, it is better to be working in the informal sector than not at all, so that many Southern youth, women and early retirees may actually be participating in this way. Given that immigration quotas are far below the needs of firms (in the North), the

Table 5.1 Labour market performance: international comparisons

	1985–1995			1995–2005			2005		
	Italy	**EU–15**	**OECD**	**Italy**	**EU–15**	**OECD**	**Italy**	**EU–15**	**OECD**
Employment rate[1]	52.1	60.3	52.5	54.1	62.9	54.9	57.5	65.2	65.5
Of which:									
Men	69.2	72.7	76.5	68.3	72.1	75.6	69.7	72.9	75.0
Women	35.3	48.1	52.5	39.9	53.7	54.9	45.3	57.5	56.1
Unemployment rate	11.4	10.0	7.3	10.2	9.1	6.9	7.8	8.4	6.8
Of which:									
Men[1]	8.0	8.6	6.8	7.9	8.1	6.5	6.3	7.7	6.5
Women[1]	17.3	12.0	8.0	14.0	10.4	7.4	10.1	9.2	7.1
Long term[1,2]	81.8	67.8	48.3	75.9	64.4	47.5	67.7	60.4	46.9
Young[3]	32.6	19.4	14.2	28.7	17.3	13.1	24.0	16.6	13.3
Participation rate	58.8	66.9	69.5	60.2	69.2	69.9	62.4	71.1	70.2
Of which:									
Men	75.2	79.5	82.0	74.1	78.4	80.8	74.4	78.9	80.3
Women	42.6	54.3	57.2	46.3	60.0	59.2	50.4	63.3	60.3
Older persons[4]	32.5	40.4	49.3	30.1	42.8	51.2	32.6	50.6	54.5
of which:									
Men	51.6	55.7	32.5	44.0	53.7	30.1	44.3	57.2	32.6
Women	15.1	26.3	35.2	17.2	31.9	39.5	21.5	38.3	43.9
Hours worked[5]	1906	1543	1448.2	1847.7	1665.8	1669.5	1791.0	1634.0	1541.2

1. Refers to population aged 15 to 64.
2. Share of unemployment for 6 months and over.
3. Refers to population aged 15 to 24.
4. Refers to the population aged 55 to 64.
5. Refers to annual average, including self employed persons, unweighted average for OECD.

Source: OECD (2006).

informal sector also provides an entry point for the required extra immigrants, easing labour-market pressures. A high tax wedge (47 per cent not counting the labour component of the company value added tax, IRAP) and labour regulations (EPL, safety standards, benefits) imply 'rents' to the employer of such workers, which may be shared, whereas risk of prosecution has been low. Big firms make use of undeclared labour through a system of subcontracting. Globalisation may have aggravated informality by intensifying cost competition, though also providing a safety valve insofar as firms can more easily move operations to EU countries such as Romania in order to cut costs.

Widespread informality does not seem propitious for the development of a modern market economy, however. First, it narrows the tax base, imposing a higher tax rate on those who pay. This distortion is estimated to amount to nearly 5 percentage points of GDP – a 32 per cent effective tax rate on the formal economy compared to a 27 per cent overall tax burden (Ministero dell'Economia e delle Finanze, 2006a). In the end, lower-skill people are likely to enter work through the informal door, as the economy gets stuck in a sub-par equilibrium. The rapid rate of public spending growth observed since EMU entry exacerbates the syndrome by further pushing up tax pressure. Second, it undermines the development of human capital because informal workers, being consigned to second-class status, are rarely trained or promoted.

The new atypical contracts are one policy answer to the informality problem as these should serve as a bridge to better jobs in the formal sector and ease transition costs for firms. Pension reforms have introduced actuarial mechanisms that provide incentives to stay in formal work longer. The government has vowed to 'get tough' with tax evaders. But it is still necessary to remove the fundamental policy distortions that feed the underground economy. More rational immigration quotas (with fewer amnesties) are called for. A reduction of high public spending is essential, to reduce fiscal pressure. Formal employability of low-skilled workers should be fostered by lowering their social charges and easing EPL, not raising charges on atypical jobs and forcing their conversion into protected ones.

The persisting North-South gap

In the southern part of the country, per capita GDP levels are around one-third lower than in the North, mainly reflecting a productivity gap; unemployment, highly concentrated among youth, is triple that in the North, and the female employment rate, extremely low among all age groups, accounts for virtually all of Italy's lag *vis-à-vis* Europe; the bank system is less developed and the shadow economy more widely diffused; and there is a substantial lag in scholastic performance. Most discouraging, southern Italy's gap *vis-à-vis* northern Italy has hardly narrowed since unification 150 years ago, despite large government transfers until recently. This situation reflects some historically weak fundamentals in the South, notably the fragile quality of public administration and infrastructure, and weaker property rights and security. Italy highlights the paradox that convergence across countries is often faster than that within countries, where regional differences can become deep-seated.[11] But the regional policy has changed dramatically to better assist the catch-up. Southern growth rates could potentially be high, lifting Italy's average.

In light of Italy's need to mobilise the labour force, regional segmentation of the labour market is particularly worrisome. Tight labour markets in the North coexisting with abundant slack in the South reflect low labour mobility and a skill mismatch. Immigrants typically arrive in the South but migrate to the North where the jobs are, leaving southern Italy's own unemployed youth behind (OECD, 2005). Italian firms outsource jobs abroad, often bypassing the South. A national *de facto* minimum wage imposes a strong competitive disadvantage on the South beyond that faced by Italy as a whole. Relatively higher wage rates in the North, including skill premiums, could ease pressures there, while relatively lower wages in the South, together with a programme to improve public infrastructure and services, could attract private investments and provide jobs for lower-skilled youth, and encourage emigration northward. Greater wage differentiation to reflect quality could also improve the incentives to stay in school and study hard.[12]

Conclusion

Given the need to find social consensus for deeper structural reforms, public advocacy of reform benefits will be of the utmost importance to Italy. It is thus useful to look clearly both at what has been achieved and what critical failures remain. Italian firms are no longer adjusting to competitive crises by massive lay-offs as in the past: labour is a resource to be treasured, not discarded. This in itself reflects a deep structural reform that benefits social welfare remarkably. As to the productivity puzzle, it has been suggested here that structural failings still untouched by reforms are dominant factors. Cyclical factors could also have played a role after 2000, when low interest rates may have facilitated labour hoarding.[13] Remaining labour-market rigidities still impede the full use of labour potential. 'Framework conditions' for innovation may be deficient: human capital may be limited by a lagging educational system; capital quality may suffer from infrastructure weaknesses; the financial system may not support risk-taking and firm growth. Sheltered service sectors may see no need to innovate anyway, enjoying extensive public protection explicitly or through professional *ordini*. Privatisation may have preserved monopoly positions, with low efficiency and high rents the result. A key problem is high public spending and tax pressure. An analysis by the OECD (OECD, 2007c) shows that the high tax wedge is a major factor explaining low labour-market participation, especially by women. Thus, dealing with such issues so as to further liberate Italy's full business potential will be necessary in order to assure sustainable high growth.

Notes

1. For evidence that export unit values overestimate the growth of export prices, and hence lead to understated export quantities, see Bugamelli (2007).
2. The same could be inferred from simulation of a standard export volume growth equation by the OECD (Cotis, 2006). After around 2000, the fitted values of the equation – fully accounting for Italy's price competitiveness as well as market growth – were substantially above the actual ones. This suggests a lack of quality adjustments to compensate for the price disadvantage.
3. Bassanetti and Zollino (2007) provide a more refined decomposition of labour productivity. It suggests that labour composition effects merely reduced the rate of rise in labour quality otherwise implied by cohort effects, which themselves have been decelerating. By the same token, a large part of the strong TFP growth of the 1980s and early 1990s disappears when correcting for these cohort effects; hence the slowdown in TFP correcting for such effects is smaller, though still substantial. Taking into account capital composition effects, moreover, suggests that around 20 per cent of the manufacturing TFP decline in the 2000s has been offset by intra-sector shifts as Italian manufacturing firms are successful in upgrading their products as a strategy against increasing competition from emerging market economies.
4. Manufacturing TFP growth declined from around 1.75 per cent per year on average during 1980–95 to −0.9 per cent during 1996–2006; that in services fell from around 0 per cent to −0.8 per cent (Bassanetti and Zollino, 2007).
5. Using an inverted Leontief Matrix at a two-digit ISIC level, the authors calculate how many units of an industry's output have to be produced at any stage of the value chain to produce one unit for final demand. Those weights are then used to calculate a weighted average index, so-called regulation impact indicators.
6. See European Commission Economic Policy Committee (2006), Tables 3–6.
7. Cipollone and Guelfi (2006) estimate that firms value the possibility of hiring 1 per cent of new workers on a fixed-term contract as much as a cut in the labour cost of an open-ended worker of 1.3–2.8 per cent. IMF (2005) estimates

that the advent of flexibility in the Italian labour market explains between 40 per cent and 80 per cent of the decade-long employment rise.

8. Such groups account for 12 per cent of total employment but around one-third of unemployment at any moment of time. See Mandrone and Massaselli (2007).
9. The unions do not seem to be pushing too hard for a UI scheme since they perhaps see no need for one so long as EPL stays so strong and its coverage widespread.
10. ISTAT estimates that in 2004, 17–18 per cent of total output and 11.5 per cent of employment were in the underground economy, not counting illegal activity. See ISTAT (2006). Outside estimates usually go higher.
11. By comparison, Spain started out with a similar gap *vis-à-vis* Italy when it joined the EU but then mostly caught up in a matter of decades, and the Irish case is well known.
12. Employers, though, are generally not pushing for such a decentralisation of wage formation as they evidently fear that higher wage pressure in the North could be the result.
13. In other words, labour market reforms may have expanded the supply curve of labour but not that of demand, so that employment merely expanded at a lower real wage (Daveri and Jona-Lasino, 2005).

The IMF Perspective

Alessandro Leipold
International Monetary Fund (IMF)

Italy and the IMF: an overview

Italy's relations with the IMF enjoy a comparatively high profile. To be sure, the days of IMF financial arrangements with Italy (the late 1970s) are long gone. But significant economic challenges, central to the IMF's mandate – notably, a large public debt and competitiveness weaknesses – have been at the centre of our bilateral dialogue. This has contributed to the considerable attention devoted to the Fund's periodic 'check-ups' of the Italian economy in the national policy debate and media coverage. Needless to say, the Fund's analysis has benefited immensely from the pool of dedicated Italian professionals who have chosen to work at its headquarters. Among these, Riccardo Faini stands out, and his years at the Fund were warmly remembered by colleagues in Washington on the day of his funeral.

Over the past decade, the theme of low growth dominated discussions of economic performance in Italy. Lacklustre growth hampered progress in resolving the country's major fiscal imbalances and prompted a continuous search for causes and solutions, against the background of a similar, albeit milder, growth malaise affecting other European economies. The Fund's recommendations regarding these challenges have been similar to those of other external observers, reported elsewhere in this volume, while evolving in focus over time.

On the growth challenge, the Fund has long viewed broad-based liberalisation as key. Initially, labour market rigidities stood out (see Decressin, 2000). As labour market reform progressed and employment growth picked up, there was a relative shift in emphasis from labour issues toward addressing slumping productivity growth by means of product market reforms. Still, with our cross-country research

(International Monetary Fund, 2004) suggesting that *joint* labour- and product-market liberalisation is optimal for growth (as well as for political economy reasons), further labour-market flexibility – affecting primarily highly protected 'insiders' – remains needed in Italy. More recently, we have highlighted a complementary growth dividend from greater financial liberalisation and development of the financial sector, in Italy and Europe (Decressin *et al.*, 2007); see also the first European Regional Economic Outlook (International Monetary Fund, 2007d), where Italy is a case study.

On the fiscal position, the Fund, as others, has long propounded the need for accelerated consolidation toward overall balance. This is an objective common to all euro-area countries. But, for Italy, with its legacy of large fiscal deficits and related accumulation of a colossal public debt, the pay-off stands to be particularly handsome – especially so in the case of the recommended expenditure-based adjustment. Such consolidation would contribute to growth not only by boosting credibility and reducing uncertainty, but also by creating the 'fiscal space' needed to alleviate a stifling tax burden and redirect resources to productive spending.

While the Fund's policy advice has largely overlapped with the authorities' own broad strategy as set out in public documents, implementation has been mixed (see Table 5.2). Two areas – labour-market and pension reform – saw appreciable advances, but these remain incomplete. Some notable, if incremental, steps were made in several other areas, including the so-called Bersani liberalisations, but overall progress has so far been clearly insufficient both on the liberalisation and consolidation fronts. Anaemic growth, persistent fiscal deficits, and slow debt reduction to date indicate that more decisive action remains needed.

The reasons for the lack of greater progress have been many, but one element, common to the IMF's work in many countries, stands out as key. While our recommendations are generally seen as reasonable and shared at a technical level, motivating such reforms to broader society has remained an elusive goal. This is evident for structural reforms, which have all too often been thwarted by 'special interests'. But the lack of motivation also undercut the goal of fiscal consolidation, whose benefits – with euro adoption and, at least until recently, benign financial markets – have not been immediately perceptible. There are two aspects to advancing the reform agenda worth highlighting. In both, Riccardo Faini played a vital role.

First, *economic pedagogy*, i.e., educating society about a country's economic challenges and solutions. This goal indeed defined much of Faini's work. For example, politicians have often been tempted to ascribe Italy's

Table 5.2 Italy: IMF policy recommendations and implementation (through 2008)

Policy area	Fund recommendations	Implementation
Fiscal Policy		
Fiscal consolidation	Adopt and begin implementing credible medium-term consolidation plan to achieve the medium-term objective of fiscal balance, relying on targeted measures to contain spending	Consolidation efforts had largely relied on unsustainable across-the-board expenditure cuts and one-off revenues. Some deficit reduction achieved in 2006–07, but it was mainly revenue-based and the deficit will likely increase in 2008
Pension reform	Curtail long-term spending pressure from population aging by reforming the pension system	A series of pension reforms has significantly improved long-term fiscal sustainability, but some key reform elements have not yet been implemented and there has been some backtracking
Public financial management	Enhance transparency and timeliness of fiscal reporting; modernise budget preparation and execution	Some progress on narrowing the historically large stock-flow discrepancy. Reform of the tortuous and nontransparent budget process has begun, but results are too early to assess
Structural reforms		
Labour market	Build on previous labour market reforms to strengthen unemployment support and relax employment protection	First round of labour market reforms successful. No action on Fund calls for a second round
Product market	Pursue comprehensive product market reforms to spur competition and growth	Various reforms over the years, yet overall progress has been slow and surveys still point to high levels of regulation and shortcomings in the business environment
Financial sector	Address structural weaknesses including limited banking market contestability; high operating costs; and undersized corporate bond and equity markets	Appreciable progress, particularly in banking market contestability and other recommendations, but further progress needed in enhancing corporate bond and equity markets, and reducing bank costs

woes to 'outside' forces – clearly not a route to generating understanding for domestic reforms. So one of the many themes of Faini's writings was that Italy's problems were 'made in Italy' and needed a domestic solution (Faini, 2007).[1] As to the elements of the solution, the medium-term planning document (DPEF) presented in 2006 (Ministero dell'Economia e delle Finanze, 2006a), which bore Faini's imprint, was a masterful piece: lucid in its analysis and compelling in its motivation for reforms, highlighting their benefits for consumers and society at large.

But good analysis and plans are not enough: a second necessary ingredient for reform success is *implementation capacity*, without which the best of plans can be derailed.[2] And here the Italian public administration falls short. As further elaborated below, a basic weakness of the Italian civil service stems from its low attractiveness to talented individuals. As a result, it is common to add talent through people 'on call'. Brought in by ministers as trusted advisors, they depart when political fortunes turn, with the career civil servants left behind consequently feeling uninvolved and demotivated. As a result, the administration is constantly 'reinventing the wheel'. Studies – some very good – are not carried forward through successive administrations. Reforms thus take longer to define and elaborate, and often remain only partially enacted. Fiscal federalism and budget reforms are cases in point.

Riccardo Faini was a person 'on policy-makers' call' par excellence, contributing substantively to better day-to-day decisions. It was striking, but also telling of the shortcomings of Italy's civil service, that his passing was seen not only as a loss of a friend and inspiration for many of us, but also – in commentators' analysis – as a blow for the Italian public administration itself, and indeed potentially for the reform process as well.

The remainder of this chapter dwells in more detail on the challenges of reforming public employment and, more broadly, public spending – a subject on which Faini was working intensely and was set to contribute even more. On these aspects, the IMF provided technical assistance and advice in 2007. As the prospective chairman of the Advisory Committee for the Public Finances (Commissione Tecnica per la Finanza Pubblica) set up in March 2007, Faini was slated to be a central figure in ensuring the success of our joint technical cooperation on budget process reforms and expenditure reviews. This work was, encouragingly, carried on, and it is to be hoped that it will continue going forward, as such reforms are multi-year in character.

Taming public spending

The quality-cum-quantity of public expenditure may well be the single most important issue in addressing Italy's enduring dual challenge of fiscal deficits and low growth. And, to be effective on both fronts, the quality and quantity of public spending have to be considered in tandem. The Green Book on public spending (Commissione Tecnica per la Finanza Pubblica, 2007) makes a persuasive case for an ambitious effort to improve the quality of expenditure. By illustrating the disparities and the low quality of spending in certain areas in a comparative perspective, the report offers a good, if yet incomplete, platform for specific policy efforts to tackle the more glaring spending problems.

Among the broad areas for improving expenditure and its control, two stand out as particularly pertinent for Italy. First, the *reform of budget procedures* has the potential to comprehensively address, and rationalise, all key determinants of spending, by facilitating a rules-based and performance-oriented budget process. Second, *public employment reform* would address the largest single determinant of spending that can be regularly affected by the government's action and policies. These areas are briefly addressed below.

Reforming budget procedures

As noted by many observers, Italy's budget system is afflicted with a number of maladies. Briefly, these regard: i) lack of transparency – including a weak information base on the cost side, an overly fragmented budget presentation, and an inadequate medium-term framework; ii) excessive rigidity – including an incremental approach to budget formulation and a plethora of *ex-ante* controls on budget execution; and iii) weak orientation and accountability for results – including scant focus on budget outturns and on broader spending performance and results.

The reforms initiated by the authorities, with technical input from the Fund (see International Monetary Fund, 2007e), are intended to gradually tackle these problems, along three main avenues. First, the development of a programme-based classification of the budget, aimed at enhancing its legibility, and the grouping of some 170 programmes into 34 missions to facilitate political decisions and assessments. Second, the initiation of spending reviews for selected ministries, helping prioritise spending and measure its effectiveness. Third, the pursuit of other specific reforms connected with the various stages of the budget process (preparation, approval, execution, monitoring and reporting).

The 2008 budget incorporated some of these reforms, notably the presentation of the budget in the new classification – though budget appropriations may still be made based on the previous forecasting units (UPBs). Spending reviews resulted in an interim report with some broad indications of policy action and in a White Notebook on the school system, with a wealth of information, including various performance indicators.[3] A comprehensive assessment of Italy's budget system reform is beyond the scope of this chapter, but a few initial considerations appear in order.

First, a number of observers noted that the 2008 budget was more legible and understandable in terms of strategic priorities – a conclusion that emerges clearly from comparisons with prior-year budgets. At the same time, pending substantial improvements in the costing of programmes, it may well be reasonable to continue appropriating on the basis of the old classification.

Second, generating appreciable macroeconomic effects from spending reviews takes time and a gradual improvement in implementation capacity. Cross-country experience suggests that results in terms of expenditure outcomes take some four to five years, or longer. In the meantime, spending reviews should become an integral part of the budget process and be aligned with incentives in line ministries, including through a rule that allows the latter to keep part of the savings identified in the spending review. Importantly, the review should cover all, including mandatory, expenditures. Here, Italy presents some particular challenges for implementing a spending review that may not have been present in similar reforms conducted in, say, an Anglo-Saxon context, such as the need to systematically review and rationalise the plethora of laws, potentially developed over many years, impinging on a single spending programme and reducing managerial flexibility.

Third, the reform of the various stages of the budget process should continue, leveraging the benefits of a more transparent budget classification to secure improved outcomes. The extensive *ex-ante* controls on budget execution should be streamlined and performance indicators for programmes steadily developed and tested. The rigidity of the underlying laws, notably of the mandatory spending categories that constitute over 90 per cent of central government spending, constitutes a major stumbling block for results-based budgeting. To the extent that the ordinary budget process, including its parliamentary stage, is unable to deliver the needed flexibility, a broader legal reform may be in order. Developing more realistic forward estimates (compared to the ongoing assumption of 'unchanged legislation') is also essential for the new budget process to be effective and provide the right incentives.

Finally, it is crucial to maintain an intensive, steady, and well-sequenced pace of reforms, avoiding the delays that characterised the aftermath of the Ciampi reform of the late 1990s.[4] The lack of follow-up to the latter stands in contrast to the experience of Italy's neighbours, whose capacity for technical implementation is not nearly as vulnerable to political transitions. In France, for example, work on the Loi Organique, introducing a performance-based approach to budgeting, began as far back as 1998, with a proposal put forward by Laurent Fabius, then President of the National Assembly. The reform was approved in 2001, with a calendar of gradual implementation over five to six years – these changes cannot be done overnight. Inevitably, in the meantime, governments and ministers changed (indeed there were as many as five ministers at Bercy over this period, and three different prime ministers at Matignon), but the civil service carried on undeterred, implementing the measures, reorganising spending categories, introducing performance indicators, undertaking ministry-by-ministry performance audits, and so forth – so that finally the 2006 budget could be presented fully in line with the new system. A similar experience marked the introduction, and more recent modification, of the Budget Stability Law (Ley de Estabilidad Presupuestaria) in Spain.

Reforming the civil service

As noted, a key weakness of Italian public administration is that the pool of available talent does not measure up to the country's requirements. This is exacerbated by the high turnover among the most talented. A comparison of the broad quality of the civil service between, for example, France, Spain and Italy is unflattering for the last-named. This is not to say, of course, that there are not excellent individual civil servants throughout Italy's ministries, but what is lacking is *a strongly qualified and committed permanent civil service cadre*, providing that essential backbone of technical support on an ongoing, continual basis.

A fundamental determinant of these differences is that, in Italy, employment in public administration is not generally seen as a prestigious professional achievement for a young graduate. This stands in contrast with the reality in France and Spain, where working at the Direction de la Prévision or at INSEE, or being an Economista del Estado, are coveted and esteemed positions. There, entry is subject to rigorous and difficult examinations, and is a highly competitive process. It is true that,

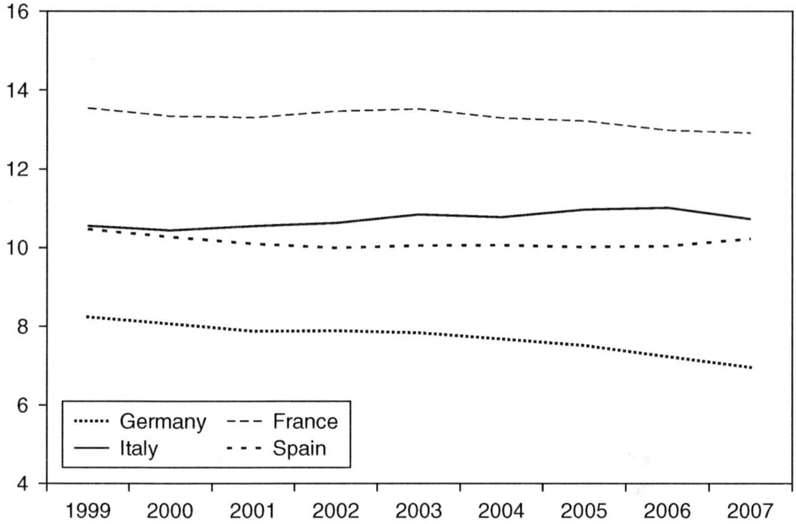

Figure 5.6 The public wage bill (per cent of GDP)

once hired, one is potentially a civil servant for life: job security is virtually unassailable. But both systems have selection processes for existing staff that function effectively in rewarding merit. In France, for example, there is a required mobility scheme for mid-career staff every three to four years, with job fairs and interviews. Supervisors are well aware of the stronger performers, and these individuals progress accordingly. In Spain, to advance from one career level to another, one needs to pass a further exam, and those already in the administration are obliged to compete with new entrants. They are thus perforce kept on their toes, including in terms of lifelong learning.

By contrast, in Italy, as noted by Carlo Dell'Aringa (2006), the marked increases in public wages in recent years were largely due to promotion-related increases – promotions negotiated with the trade unions and decided, save for some commendable exceptions, on criteria not based on individual merit but rather largely on seniority.

The absence of a merit-based approach to wage increases, and the reduced mobility of public employees, may well be already weakening Italy's ability to contain budget spending on compensation. While public spending in Italy is not particularly higher than elsewhere, the public wage bill, at 11 per cent of GDP (if adjusted for one-off factors that influenced the 2007 outcome), is now appreciably above the euro-area average (just over 10 per cent of GDP). In Italy, it rose in 2000–7, while in Germany it declined continuously by a cumulative 1.1 percentage points over the same period. Interestingly, Italy's increase in the wage bill was higher at the central than at the local level: a counter-intuitive development, indicative of further rigidities, since control should in principle be easier on the former.

Public administration reform thus rightly continues to be on the policy agenda. There, too, durable results are unlikely to come quickly, and should be safeguarded against a propensity to grant further uniform wage raises as the 'budgetary situation permits'. Mobility and productivity-encouraging measures are constrained by the very tight room for manoeuvre offered by centralised bargaining, and by the long history of nearly uniform wage increases. Beyond relaxing these restrictions, a break in public service culture – toward merit-based outcomes – still needs to be made. This is in turn itself crucial for the successful implementation of budget process reform, as it is difficult to overcome the incremental focus of Italy's budget formulation without addressing the rigidities and misplaced incentives in public employment – a key area of mandatory spending.

A still large agenda

Italy's fundamental challenges of low growth and fiscal imbalances persist. Despite the modest recovery of 2006–7, and increasing evidence of economic restructuring, the economy weakened since late 2007 and potential growth remains anaemic. On the fiscal front, the medium-term objective is still distant – disappointing given the highly favourable revenue trends in 2006–7. In large swathes of public and political opinion, there remains an ingrained belief that high levels of public spending are needed to support growth. But – as the IMF staff asked rhetorically at the conclusion of the last Article IV consultation in late 2006 – how much growth have years of rising public expenditure brought to Italy?[5] On the contrary, the legacy of Italy's high spending is a massive debt load and a heavy tax burden that divert resources from families and enterprises to the public sector, sapping growth. Jumpstarting the reform momentum and advancing fiscal consolidation are thus as topical as ever.

Thus, a focus on the level and quality of public spending – an effort that Riccardo Faini was spearheading – promises a large payoff to reforms. But spending trends are unlikely to be significantly altered without changing their fundamental drivers, which are linked to broader structural factors and economic incentives. Moreover, as in other countries, and perhaps even more so in Italy, such progress will not come quickly and will take time and continued improvements in implementation capacity.

To this end, public administration reform is crucial in Italy, as well illustrated by Pietro Ichino in his numerous interventions on the subject.[6] Reform is clearly needed to deliver efficient services to the citizenry, but perhaps more importantly to attract and retain the talent required for the technical work and tenacity over time needed to carry forward complex reforms, particularly so in a country so exposed to political vicissitudes. Without a stronger civil service, the answer to the question 'Can Italy Adjust and Grow?' that was addressed at the March 2007 seminar that stimulated this book is most likely a disappointing 'Yes, but ...' Yes, because – as is known and indeed increasingly observed – entrepreneurs do over time adjust and restructure; but they also need the public sector to be a lever for growth by providing favourable 'framework conditions'. On this front, Italy is not there yet.

Notes

1. Incidentally, one of the Fund's research papers (Sgherri, 2006) dovetails with the same theme.
2. There is of course also the need for political consensus, which remains elusive in Italy, itself a reflection of the insufficient reach of economic pedagogy.
3. Commissione Tecnica per la Finanza Pubblica (2007b) and Ministero dell'Economia e delle Finanze and Ministero della Pubblica Istruzione (2007).
4. Legislation approved in 1997 merged the Ministry of the Budget and Economic Planning with the Ministry of Treasury and introduced important changes in the structure of the budget, in particular by reducing considerably the number of budget items. Another budget reform was approved in 1999, which amended the content of both the budget law and the DPEF, and provided a basis for improved costing, performance measurement, and results orientation of the budget process. However, while some work on initial indicators that track performance was done in the aftermath of these reforms, performance measurement remained quite 'underdeveloped' (see International Monetary Fund, 2007e).
5. See International Monetary Fund (2006; 2007c).
6. See, for instance, Ichino (2006).

The Italian Conundrum: Pundits Condemn, Capital Markets Nod

Eric Chaney
Morgan Stanley

The close to zero growth performance of Italy in 2007 (on a fourth quarter to fourth quarter basis), following its credit downgrade in 2006, reinvigorated a theory that has some popularity in the financial markets, namely that Italy could be the first casualty of an ill-conceived monetary union. In addition, the growing tension between a dovish US Federal Reserve and a hawkish European Central Bank, which has propelled the euro in unchartered overvalued territory, is bringing back reminiscences of another period of similar tensions, 1991–2, which had resulted in the devaluation of the lira and caused the 'black Wednesday'.

Although the underperformance of the Italian economy in 2007 had nothing to do with competitiveness issues and, instead, was entirely explained by a large-scale fiscal tightening that cut the Italian public deficit by over two percentage points in 2006–7, the theory is alive and well. In short, it says that Italy has suffered from a huge loss of competitiveness, that its productivity is stagnant and its public debt is running out of control. As the story goes, real life has allegedly demonstrated that this country cannot compete with her neighbours on a level playing field, that is, without the repeated 'shots in the arm' provided by devaluations. According to this line of reasoning, investors should ultimately impose a higher risk premium and, as debt servicing becomes more costly, their pessimism would turn into a self-fulfilling prophecy: Italians would start dreaming of 1992-style devaluation as the only way to bail out their flagging economy, at the expense, of course, of their main trading partners.

I think that the script of this horror movie is based on flawed macroeconomic analysis and poor use of dubious statistics. On the contrary, I believe Italy is on the mend and likely to attract more foreign capital than it has done in the past. Besides, it strikes me that the performance of Italian financial markets, relative to its EMU peers, is quite honourable, especially in risk-adjusted terms.

Some facts that do not square with Italy bashing

Let me start with four hard facts that fly in the face of this 'Italy-bashing' analysis.

1. Since EMU inception and until the end of 2007, the average performance of the Italian equity market, as measured by the MSCI index that includes net dividends[1] (what investors really get) was 5.5 per cent per annum vs. 4.9 per cent for Germany and 6.9 per cent for France. Are capital markets totally blind?
2. Over the same period, Italian GDP has increased by 1.4 per cent per year versus 1.5 per cent for Germany and 2.2 per cent for France and the EMU bloc. In the race to win the crown of the sickest economy, I wonder which one is the winner.
3. Despite a sharply rising oil bill, Italy's current account posted a 2.6 per cent of GDP deficit in Q3 2007, vs. −4.7 per cent for the UK, which has no oil bill to foot, and −10.1 per cent for Spain. From this perspective, the UK, not Italy, could be considered as part of the so-called 'Club Med'.
4. The Italian harmonised unemployment rate dropped from 11.4 per cent just before EMU started, to 6.1 per cent in 2007, one percentage point lower than the euro-area average. It is now similar to the UK rate. The decline of unemployment in Italy since 1999 was much faster than in France or Germany and came second only to Spain.

At pains to explain how a lame duck could manage to reduce unemployment so massively without fuelling wage inflation, Italy bashers may question the quality of unemployment statistics. However, these measures are based on large-sample household surveys and are therefore more reliable and consistent than claimant counts, which are dependent on national unemployment insurance systems. They have nevertheless some idiosyncratic features on which I will comment later.

The indicators that seem to seal the fate of Italy

So why are so many analysts convinced that Italy has been priced out of the game by super-competitive Germany? Because they look at measures

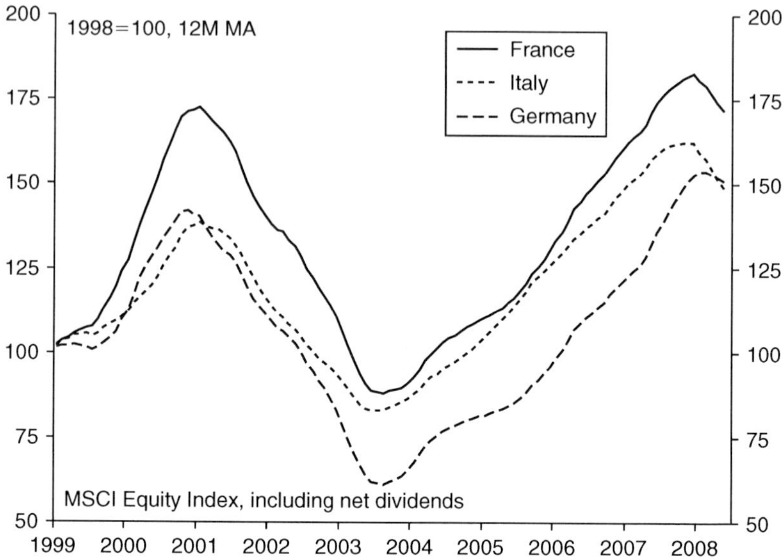

Figure 5.7 Since 1999, Italian equities have performed equally as well as German equities
Source: MSCI–Barra.

of competitiveness such as unit-labour costs or export volumes. On these criteria, the Italian situation looks truly desperate. Take for example the relative unit-labour costs in the manufacturing sector calculated by the European Commission. On this measure, Italy's competitive position relative to its euro-area partners has declined 22.7 per cent since 1999 while Germany's position has improved by 18.8 per cent. There is worse to come: on the OECD measure of real export market performance, Italy has lost 27 points of market share since 1999, twice as much as France, while Germany has gained 4.1 points. Clearly, something must be wrong: how could an economy suffering enormous losses of competitiveness boast a falling unemployment rate and a balanced non-oil trade account?

Zero productivity growth in six years: this is just not credible

In my view, both unit-labour costs and export volumes are tainted by serious statistical uncertainties. Starting with unit-labour costs, the weak link is not the measure of costs, but that of productivity, a notorious headache for statisticians. On data gathered by the US Bureau of Labour

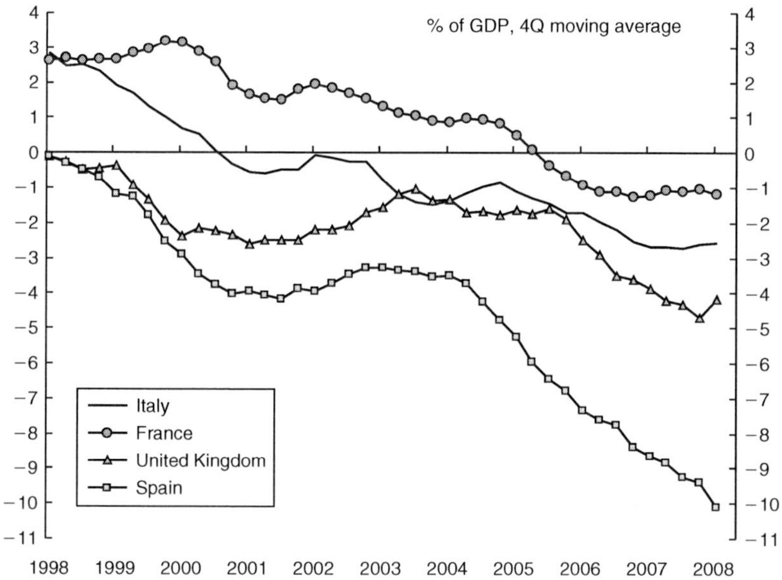

Figure 5.8 The Italian current account does not point to significant imbalances
Source: OECD *Economic Outlook*.

Statistics, Italian hourly productivity in manufacturing was the same in 2005 as it was in 1999, while it increased by 27 per cent in Germany and France over the same period. I find it hard to believe that Italian hourly productivity has really stagnated for six years and suspect that a combination of large-scale regularisation of illegal immigrants and tax incentives for employers to hire employees who were working without being recorded in payrolls have distorted productivity data. In short, hundreds of thousands of workers in Italy have moved from the black to the legal economy, artificially bringing down productivity data and probably flattering unemployment numbers as well: it is likely that black economy workers answered 'No' when asked the question 'Are you working?' in the household survey, and now say 'Yes' if they have been hired legally in the meantime.

Productivity and unemployment were overestimated

In fact, since the output of the underground economy is included in GDP as measured by ISTAT, it is fair to say that both past productivity and past unemployment levels were artificially inflated and that current data are closer to reality. From this angle, the fact that a four-point cut in the unemployment rate did not fuel wage inflation becomes less intriguing: in reality, unemployment has declined less than official measures suggest. Back to productivity, the rate of growth was underestimated because of these changes in the structure of the labour market. In the real world, hourly labour productivity has probably increased in Italy about as fast as in the average of mature economies, as a result of technological progress and capital deepening. The problem is that we do not know exactly at what rate.

The export conundrum: Italian exporters have outperformed euro-area peers

Turning to exports, here is the conundrum: standard indicators say that Italy's competitiveness has been seriously eroded and yet Italian exports are doing well, compared with those of its peers. On OECD data, Italy's market share of global trade, measured in current dollars, was 3.7 per cent in 2005, versus 4.1 per cent in 1999, a 10 per cent decline. The OECD bloc suffered from the same loss – its market share dropping from 74.5 per cent to 66.9 per cent over the same period, in favour of China and oil-exporting countries. A more relevant measure of Italy's export performance is to compare its nominal exports with those of the euro area. On this yardstick, the only one that really makes sense in a currency union, Italy actually outperformed its peers: Italian nominal exports have increased by 7 per cent more than average EMU country exports since the inception of the monetary union. Here, I believe that the statistical flaw is in the measure of prices. In reality, for lack of a direct measure, ISTAT is using unit values, that is, export values divided by quantities. When the euro shot up in 2002–3, a counterintuitive fact was that Italian export 'prices' (in fact unit values) increased. In my view, this point, which escaped analysts' attention, reveals the underlying and hidden truth: Italian producers have reacted to globalisation by off-shoring production centres to low-cost countries such as Romania and Tunisia and, more importantly, by upgrading their product mix toward more expensive products, in the fashion sector to take a well-known example. This might have been the result of a 'creative destruction' process within the Italian corporate sector.

Here again, the problem is that there is convincing indirect evidence, such as the export performance, that corporate Italy has changed for the better, even though direct and reliable statistics are lacking.

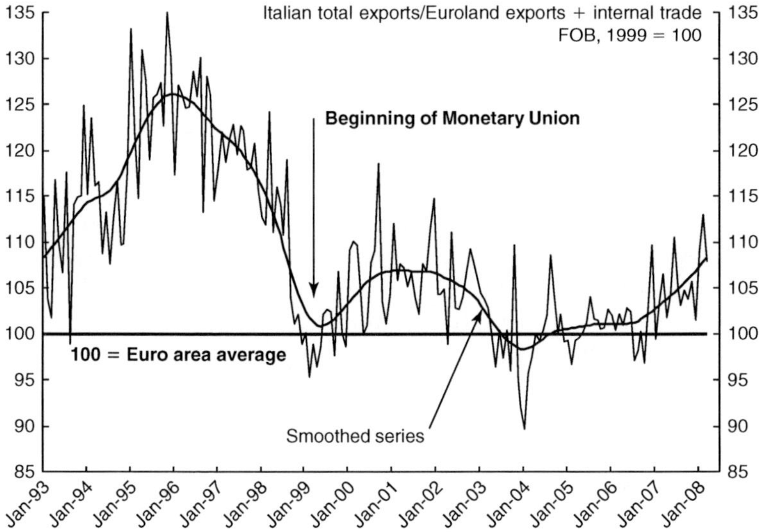

Figure 5.9 Total exports: Italy did 7% better than Euroland
Source: ISTAT, Eurostat, Morgan Stanley Research.

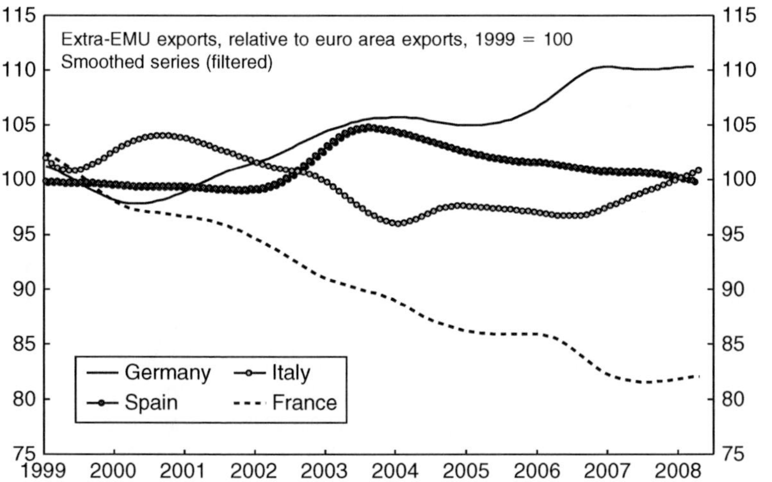

Figure 5.10 Italian exporters are faring much better than French exporters
Source: ISTAT, Insee, Destatis, Eurostat, Morgan Stanley Research.

A possible explanation for the export price conundrum

As already mentioned, Italian export prices, as measured by unit values, went up in euro terms in the aftermath of the 2002–3 appreciation of the single currency. Using the lenses of modern trade theories may help understand this counterintuitive observation and also why, in the end, the Italian export sector has apparently suffered less from the appreciation of the euro than the French one. I am referring here to a pass-through model presented by Raphael Auer and Thomas Chaney at a recent Federal Reserve Board seminar[2] (Auer and Chaney, 2007: 'Exchange Rate Pass-Through in a Competitive Model of Pricing-to-Market'). The authors consider two different types of goods, one homogeneous and the other a continuum of quality-differentiated goods. Consumers have heterogeneous preferences for quality and markets are perfectly competitive. Among other interesting conclusions, such as the incomplete pass-through of exchange rate shocks on to importers' CPIs, they show that, following a real appreciation of the currency, lowest-quality firms pull out of the export market (because of fixed costs for market access), so that the average price of exports increases even more than individual prices. In the case of Italy, I find reasonable to risk the idea that the 30 per cent real appreciation of the euro since 2001 has fuelled a tough selection process among exporters, or even between various departments within the same firm, which has led to a shift toward higher-quality goods. Note that such a shift is not easy to apprehend through trade data, even at a very detailed level: the shift toward quality might have happened within each product category.

Not the next Eldorado but a good bet for investors

Don't get me wrong. I'm not saying that Italy is the new corporate Eldorado or the next stellar macro performer in Europe. The public debt inherited from the past is a permanent sword of Damocles. Labour laws, especially redundancy rules, are rigid, corporate governance is weak, the internal market is inefficient, especially for services, the commercial property market is opaque and in the hands of a small club of investors, bureaucrats and their love affair with *documenti* are not particularly business-friendly, the population is ageing, pension reform is a 'work in progress' and health-care reform is still in limbo. And yet, at the margins, Italy might be one of the places in Europe where changes are happening.

Notes

1. The MSCI equity indices, developed by MSCI–Barra, weight companies' market capitalisation according to their free float, and are used by most fund managers in order to benchmark their performances. We have selected country indexes that include net dividend payments, in order to reflect the actual performance of country stocks, seen from an investor angle. MSCI–Barra is a provider of equity, fixed income and hedge funds indices. MSCI stands for Morgan Stanley Capital International, an independent company listed on the NYSE.
2. The Federal Reserve Board, Domestic Prices in an Integrated World Economy, 27–28 September 2007, sponsored by Federal Reserve Board and the *Journal of Money, Credit, and Banking*. See Auer and Chaney (2007).

References

Abramovitz, M. (1956) 'Resource and Output Trends in the United States Since 1870', *American Economic Review,* May.

Acemoglu D. (1996) 'A Microfoundation for Social Increasing Returns in Human Capital Accumulation', *Quarterly Journal of Economics,* 111, pp. 779–804.

Acemoglu, D. (2003) 'Factor Prices and Technical Change: from Induced Innovations to Recent Debates', in Philippe Aghion *et al.* (eds) *Knowledge, Information and Expectations in Modern Macroeconomics: In Honor of Edmund Phelps* (Princeton: Princeton University Press).

Afonso, A., L. Schuknecht and V. Tanzi (2005) 'Public Sector Efficiency: An International Comparison', *Public Choice,* 123, pp. 321–47.

Aghion, P., C. Meghir and J. Vandebussche (2005) 'Distance to Frontier and Composition of Human Capital', CEPR Discussion Paper, No. 4860 (London: CEPR).

Alberola, E., S. G. Cervero, H. Lopez, and A. Ubide (1999) 'Global Equilibrium Exchange Rates: Euro, Dollar, "Ins," "Outs", and Other Major Currencies in a Panel Cointegration Framework', IMF Working Paper No. WP/99/175, available at www.imf.org/external/pubs/ft/wp/1999/wp99175.pdf

Alesina, A. and R. Perotti (1995) 'Fiscal Expansions and Fiscal Adjustment in OECD Countries', NBER Working Paper No. W5214.

Alesina, A. and R. Perotti (1995) 'The Political Economy of Budget Deficits', *IMF Staff Papers,* 42 (1), March, pp. 1–31.

Alesina, A. and R. Perotti (1997) 'Fiscal Adjustment in OECD Countries: Composition and Macroeconomic Effects', *IMF Staff Papers,* 44 (2), June, pp. 210–48.

Alesina, A., M. Marè and R. Perotti (1998) 'Le procedure di bilancio in Italia. Analisi e proposte', in F. Giavazzi, A. Penati and G. Tabellini (eds) *La costituzione fiscale,* (Bologna: Il Mulino), pp. 13–78.

Alesina, A., S. Danninger and M. Rostagno (1999) 'Redistribution through Public Employment: the Case of Italy', NBER Working Paper Series, No. 7387.

Allegra, E., M. Forni, M. Grillo and L. Magnani (2004) 'Antitrust Policy and National Growth: Some Evidence from Italy', *Il Giornale degli Economisti,* 63 (1), April.

Alta Commissione sul Federalismo Fiscale (2005) *Relazione sull'attività svolta dall'Alta Commissione per la definizione dei meccanismi strutturali del federalismo fiscale* (Rome: Ministero dell'Economia e delle Finanze).

Amato, G. (1990) *Due anni al Tesoro* (Bologna: Il Mulino).

ANCE (2005) *Rapporto sulle infrastrutture in Italia* (Rome: Associazione Nazionale dei Costruttori Edili).

Arachi, G. and A. Zanardi (2000) 'Il federalismo fiscale regionale: opportunità e limiti', in L. Bernardi (ed.) *La finanza pubblica italiana – Rapporto 1999* (Bologna: Il Mulino).

Arcelli, M. and S. Micossi (1997) 'La politica economica negli anni Ottanta (e nei primi anni Novanta)', in M. Arcelli (ed.) *Storia, economia e società in Italia 1947–1997* (Bari: Laterza), pp. 263–322.

Auer, R. and T. Chaney (2007) 'Exchange Rate Pass-Through in a Competitive Model of Pricing-to-Market', The Federal Reserve Board, Domestic Prices in

an Integrated World Economy conference, Washington, DC 27–28 September, available at: http://home.uchicago.edu/~tchaney/research/QualityPricing.pdf
Balassone, F. and D. Franco (1995) 'La difficile riforma del welfare: il settore della sanità', *Stato e mercato*, No. 1.
Balassone, F. and D. Franco (1996) 'Il fabbisogno finanziario pubblico', Banca d'Italia, *Temi di discussione*, No. 277.
Balassone, F. and D. Franco (2001) 'Fiscal Federalism and the Stability and Growth Pact: A Difficult Union', in Banca d'Italia, *Fiscal Rules*, Rome.
Balassone, F. and R. Giordano (2001) 'Budget Deficits and Coalition Governments', *Public Choice*, 106 (3/4), pp. 327–49.
Balassone, F., D. Franco and R. Giordano (2004) 'Market Induced Fiscal Discipline: Is There a Fall-back Solution for Rule-failure?', in Banca d'Italia, *Public Debt*, Rome.
Balassone, F., D. Franco and S. Zotteri (2005) 'EMU Fiscal Indicators: A Misleading Compass?', *Empirica*, 33, pp. 63–87.
Balassone, F., D. Franco and S. Zotteri (2007) 'The Reliability of EMU Fiscal Indicators: Risks and Safeguards', Banca d'Italia, *Temi di discussione*, No. 633.
Balassone, F., D. Franco, S. Momigliano and D. Monacelli (2002) 'Italy: Fiscal Consolidation and its Legacy', in Banca d'Italia, *The Impact of Fiscal Policy*, Rome.
Baldassarri, M. and M. G. Briotti (1990) 'Bilancio pubblico ed economia italiana negli anni '70 e '80: dalle radici del debito alla manovra di risanamento, una "ristrutturazione" da fare', *Rivista di politica economica*, July–August.
Baldwin, R., Barba Navaretti, G. and Boeri, T. (eds) (2007) *Come sta cambiando l'Italia* (Bologna: Il Mulino).
Banca d'Italia (1995), 'La riforma del sistema pensionistico', *Bollettino Economico*, No. 25, October.
Banca d'Italia (2002) *L'efficienza nei servizi pubblici*, Rome.
Banca d'Italia (2006) *Annual Report*, Rome.
Banca d'Italia (2007) *Annual Report*, Rome.
Banca d'Italia (2007) *Bolletino Economico*, No. 48, April.
Barba Navaretti, G., M. Bugamelli, R. Faini, F. Schivardi, and A. Tucci (2007) 'Le imprese e la specializzazione produttiva dell'Italia. Dal macrodeclino alla microcrescita?', Fondazione R. De Benedetti report for the conference 'I vantaggi dell'Italia', Rome, March.
Barrell, R., S. Gottshalk, D. Holland, E. Khoman, I. Liadze and O. Pomerantz (2008) 'The Impact of EMU on Growth and Employment', European Commission, Directorate General for Economic and Financial Affairs, Economic Paper No. 318, April.
Barro, R. and J. Lee (2000) 'International Data on Educational Attainment', NBER Working Paper, No. 7911.
Barucci, P. (1995) *L'isola italiana del Tesoro. Ricordi di un naufragio evitato 1992–1994* (Milan: Rizzoli).
Basevi, G. and P. Onofri (1997) 'Uno sguardo retrospettivo alla politica economica negli anni Settanta', in M. Arcelli (ed.) *Storia, economia e società in Italia 1947–1997* (Bari: Laterza), pp. 185–261.
Basile, R. (2000) 'Export Behavior of Italian Manufacturing over the Nineties: the Role of Innovation', *Research Policy*, Vol. 30, pp. 1185–1201.

Basile, R., S. De Nardis and A. Girardi (2006) 'Pricing to Market of Italian Exporting Firms', ISAE Working Paper, No. 78.

Basile, R., S. De Nardis, A. Girardi and C. Pappalardo (2007) 'Le politiche di prezzo degli esportatori italiani: un'analisi su dati d'impresa', in A. Lanza and B. Quintieri (eds) *Eppur si muove, Come cambia l'export italiano* (Soveria Mannelli: Rubbettino).

Bassanetti, A. and F. Zollino (2007) 'La produttività totale dei fattori in Italia negli anni recenti: evidenze di stime preliminari per il totale del settore privato e dei principali comparti', Banca d'Italia, mimeo.

Bassanetti, A., J. Doepke, R. Torrini and R. Zizza (2006) 'Capital, Labour and Productivity: What Role Do They Play in the Potential GDP Weakness of France, Germany and Italy?', *Deutsche Bundesbank Working Papers*, No. 9.

Bassanetti, A., M. Iommi, C. Jona-Lasinio and F. Zollino (2004) 'La crescita dell'economia italiana negli anni novanta tra ritardo tecnologico e rallentamento della produttività', Temi di discussione della Banca d'Italia, No. 539.

Bassanetti, A. and Zollino, F. (2007) 'The Effects of Housing and Financial Wealth on Personal Consumption: Aggregate Evidence for Italian Households', Bank of Italy, S.A.Di.BA. Conference on Italian Household Wealth, Perugia, 16–17 October.

Bassanetti, A., J. Döpke, R. Torrini and R. Zizza (2006) 'Capital, Labour and Productivity: What Role Do They Play in the Potential GDP Weakness of France, Germany and Italy?', Discussion Paper Series 1: Economic Studies, No. 09/2006, Deutsche Bundesbank, Frankfurt am Main.

Basu, S., J. G. Fernald and M. Kimball (2006), 'Are Technology Improvements Contractionary?', *American Economic Review*, 96 (5), pp. 1418–48.

Beaudry P., and F. Collard (2002) 'Why Has the Employment-Productivity Tradeoff Among Industrialized Countries Been So Strong?', NBER Working Papers, No. 8754, February.

Beltrametti, L. (1996) *Il debito pensionistico in Italia* (Bologna, Il Mulino).

Beltrametti, L. (2003) 'Long Term Care: una prospettiva di politica economica', in M. C. Guerra and A. Zanardi (eds) *La finanza pubblica italiana – Rapporto 2003* (Bologna, Il Mulino), pp. 257–97.

Bernardi, L. (2000) 'La finanza pubblica e l'aggiustamento strutturale degli anni '90', in L. Bernardi (ed.) *La finanza pubblica italiana – Rapporto 2000* (Bologna, Il Mulino).

Bernasconi, M. and F. Lapecorella (2006) 'I condoni nel sistema tributario italiano', in M. C. Guerra and A. Zanardi (eds) *La finanza pubblica italiana – Rapporto 2006* (Bologna, Il Mulino).

Bibbee, A. (2007) 'Making Federalism Work in Italy', OECD Economics Department Working Paper, No. 590, Paris.

Blanchard, O. (2004) 'The Economic Future of Europe', *Journal of Economic Perspectives*, 18 (4), Autumn, pp. 3–26.

Blanchard, O. (2005) 'European Unemployment: the Evolution of Facts and Ideas', NBER Working Paper Series, No. 11750.

Bloom, N., R. Griffith, and J. van Reenen (2002) 'Do R&D Tax Credits Work? Evidence from an International Panel of Countries 1979–1997', *Journal of Public Economics*, 85, pp. 1–31.

Boeri, T. (2004) 'Reforming Labour and Product Market: Some Lessons from Two Decades of Experiments in Europe', background paper for the IMF World Economic Outlook, 2004.

Boeri, T. (2006) 'La risorsa in più', Confindustria Centro Studi, *Quaderni di Ricerca*, No. 2, December.

Boeri, T. and A. Brandolini (2005) 'The Age of Discontent: Italian Households at the Beginning of the Decade', in *Giornale degli Economisti e Annali di Economia*, 63 (3/4).

Boeri, T., R. Faini, A. Ichino, G. Pisauro and C. Scarpa (2005) *Oltre and Declino* (Bologna: II Mulino)

Boeri, T. and P. Garibaldi (2007) 'Two Tier Reforms of Employment Protection Legislation. A Honeymoon Effect?', *Economic Journal*, 117 (521), pp. 357–85.

Boeri, T. and R. Perotti (2002) *Meno pensioni, più welfare* (Bologna, Il Mulino).

Bordignon, M. (2006) 'Il decentramento in Italia: motivazioni, strumenti, evidenti difficoltà', in G. Brosio amd G. Muraro, *Il finanziamento del settore pubblico* (Milan: Franco Angeli).

Borin, A. and M. Lamieri (2007) 'Misurare la qualità dei beni nel commercio internazionale', in A. Lanza and B. Quintieri (eds) *Eppur si muove, come cambia l'export italiano* (Soveria Mannelli: Rubbettino).

Bosi, P., R. Golinelli and A. Stagni (eds) (1990) 'Le origini del debito pubblico e il costo della stabilizzazione', in *Un modello a medio termine dell'economia italiana: Hermes-Italia* (Bologna, Il Mulino).

Bouthevillain, C., P. Cour-Thimann, G. van den Dool, P. Hernandez de Cos, G. Langenus, M. Mohr, S. Momigliano and M. Tujula (2001) 'Cyclically Adjusted Budget Balances: An Alternative Approach', European Central Bank Working Paper No. 77.

Brandolini, A., P. Casadio, P. Cipollone, M. Magnani, A. Rosolia and R. Torrini (2007) 'Employment Growth in Italy in the 1990s: Institutional Arrangements and Market Forces', in N. Acocella and R. Leoni (eds) *Social Pacts, Employment and Growth. A Reappraisal of Tarantelli's Thought* (Heidelberg: Physica-Verlag).

Brandolini, A. and P. Cipollone (2003) 'Una nuova economia in Italia', in S. Rossi (ed.) *La Nuova Economia: i fatti dietro il mito* (Il Mulino: Bologna).

Brunetta, R. (2003) *Il coraggio e la paura* (Milan: Sperling & Kupfer).

Bugamelli, M. (2001) 'Il modello di specializzazione internazionale nell'area dell'euro and dei principali paesi europei: Omogeneità e convergenza', Temi di discussione, No. 402, Banca d'Italia, Rome.

Bugamelli, M. (2007) 'Prezzi delle esportazioni, qualità dei prodotti e caratteristiche d'impresa: un'analisi su un campione di imprese italiane', in A. Lanza and B. Quintieri (eds) *Eppur si muove, come cambia l'export italiano* (Soveria Mannelli: Rubbettino).

Bugamelli, M., P. Cipollone and L. Infante (2000), 'L'internazionalizzazione delle imprese italiane negli anni novanta', *Rivista Italiana degli Economisti*, No. 3.

Bugamelli, M. and L. Infante (2003) 'Sunk Costs of Exports', Economic Working Papers of the Bank of Italy, No. 469, Rome.

Bugamelli, M. and A. Rosolia (2006) 'Produttività e concorrenza estera', *Rivista di Politica Economica*, September–October, pp. 55–87.

Buglione, E., (1999) 'Istituzioni e autonomia finanziaria in Italia', in E. Buglione and Vincenzo Patrizii (eds) *Governo e governi: Istituzioni e finanza in un sistema a più livelli* (Milan: Giuffrè).

Camera dei Deputati (2007a) 'Strumenti e procedure di finanza pubblica', *Documentazione e ricerche*, No. 46, 13 February, Rome.

Camera dei Deputati (2007b) 'Documento di Programmazione Economico-Finanziaria 2008–2011', 9 July, Rome.

Cardarelli, R. and N. Sartor (2000) 'Generational Accounting for Italy', in Fiscal Sustainability, Papers Presented at the Banca d'Italia Workshop Held in Perugia, 20–22 January, Rome.

Castellino, O. and E. Fornero (2001) *La riforma del sistema previdenziale italiano* (Bologna, Il Mulino).

CER (2006) 'La democrazia del bilancio. trasparenza, procedure, struttura dei bilanci pubblici', *Rapporto CER*, No. 4, Rome.

CER, IRS, Prometeia (2000) 'I DPEF della seconda metà degli anni novanta', *Rapporto al CNEL*, 11 May.

Chaney, E. (2006) 'Enough Italy Bashing', *European Economics*, Morgan Stanley Research, 24 October.

Chiarlone, S. and R. Helg (2002) 'Il modello di specializzazione internazionale italiano e le economie emergenti dell'Estremo Oriente', in L. Paganetto and G. P. Galli (eds) *La competitività dell'Italia: le imprese*, Il Sole 24 Ore.

Cimbolini, L. (2008) 'Progressività del disavanzo di parte corrente e stabilità dell'avanzo d'amministrazione: una preoccupante anomalia della finanza locale italiana', at: http://amcorteconti.it/articoli/cimbolini%20finanza%20locale.htm

Ciocca, P. (2003) 'L'economia italiana: un problema di crescita', report to the 44th annual scientific meeting of the Società italiana degli economisti, published in *Bollettino Economico*, 41, Banca d'Italia.

Ciocca, P. (2004) *Il tempo dell'economia* (Turin: Bollati Boringhieri).

Cipollone, P. and A. Guelfi (2006) 'The Value of Flexible Contracts: Evidence from an Italian Panel of Industrial Firms', Banca d'Italia, *Temi di discussione*, No. 583, March.

Commissione per l'analisi delle compatibilità macroeconomiche della spesa sociale (1997), 'Relazione Finale', 28 February.

Commissione Tecnica per la Finanza Pubblica (2007a) *Libro verde sulla spesa pubblica* (Rome: Ministero dell'Economia e delle Finanze).

Commissione Tecnica per la Finanza Pubblica (2007b), *Rapporto intermedio sulla revisione della spesa* (Rome: Ministero dell'Economia e delle Finanze).

Conference Board and Groningen Growth and Development Centre (2007) 'Total Economy Database', available at: www.conference-board.org/economics

Connolly B. (2005) 'Europe's Italy Problem', *The International Economy*, Spring.

Conway, P. and G. Nicoletti (2006), 'Product Market Regulation in the Non-manufacturing Sectors of OECD Countries: Measurement and Highlights', OECD Economics Department Working Papers, No. 530.

Conway, P., D. De Rosa, G. Nicoletti and F. Steiner (2006) 'Regulation, Competition and Productivity Convergence', OECD Economics Department Working Papers, No. 509.

Conway, P., V. Janod and G. Nicoletti (2005) 'Product Market Regulation in OECD Countries: 1998 to 2003', OECD Economics Department Working Papers, No. 429.

Costantini, M. and S. de Nardis (2007) 'Estimates of Structural Changes in the Wage Equation: Some Evidence for Italy', ISAE, *Documenti di lavoro*, No. 86.

Cotis, J-P. (2006) 'Comments on "Global Economy and Competitiveness"', SACE Conference on Global Competition: Challenges and Opportunities for Italy, Milan, 9 November.

Crescenzi, A. (ed.) (2007) *I Documenti di Programmazione* (Rome: Luiss University Press).

Daveri, F., and C. Jona-Lasinio (2005) 'Italy's Decline: Getting the Facts Right', *Giornale degli Economisti e Annali di Economia*, 64 (4), pp. 365–410.

Daveri, F. (2006) *Innovazione Cercasi* (Rome/Bari: Laterza).

De Cecco, M. (1989) 'The Italian Public Debt Conversion of 1906', in R. Dornbusch and M. Draghi (eds) *Public Debt Management: Theory and History* (Cambridge: CEPR/Cambridge University Press).

De Cecco, M. (2007) 'Consolidamento del debito e patrimonio pubblico: una via non percorribile', in in U. Mattei, E. Reviglio and S. Rodotà (eds) *Invertire la rotta* (Bologna: Il Mulino), pp. 179–85.

De Joanna, P. (1993) *Parlamento e spesa pubblica* (Bologna: Il Mulino).

De Nardis, S. (2007) 'Ristrutturazione industriale italiana nei primi anni duemila: occupazione, specializzazione, imprese', in 'Trasformazioni dell'industria italiana', *ISAE Quaderni di discussione*, October.

De Nardis, S. and C. Pensa (2004) 'How Intense Is Competition in International Markets of Traditional Goods? The Case of Italian Exporters', ISAE Working Papers, No. 45, May.

De Nardis, S., and F. Traù (2005) *Il modello che non c'era. L'Italia e la divisione internazionale del lavoro* (Soveria Mannelli: Rubettino).

De Nardis, S.and C. Pappalardo (2007) 'Attività di esportazione e di invesimento delle imprese italiane nel periodo 2000-06: un'analisi sui dati delle inchieste ISAE', in *L'Italia nell'economia internazionale – Rapporto ICE 2006–2007*.

Decressin, J. (2000) 'Puzzling Out Italy's Growth Performance', IMF Staff Country Report, 00/82, July, pp. 6–27.

Decressin, J., H. Faruqee and W. Fonteyne (2007) 'Integrating Europe's Financial Markets' (Washington DC: International Monetary Fund).

Degni, M., N. Emiliani, F. Gastaldi, G. Salvemini and C. Virno (2001) 'Il riequilibrio della finanza pubblica negli anni novanta', Studi e Note di Economia, *Quaderni*, No. 7.

Dell'Aringa, C. (2006) 'Una regia nazionale per la pubblica amministrazione', *La Voce*, 27 November, available at: www.lavoce.info/articoli/pagina2466.html

Docquier, F. and A. Marfouk (2004) 'Measuring the International Mobility of Skilled Workers', Policy Research Working Paper, No. 3381 (Washington DC: World Bank).

Draghi, M. (2007) 'Consumo e crescita in Italia', 48a Riunione Scientifica Annuale, Torino, 26 October.

ECB (European Central Bank) (2007) *Annual Report*, Frankfurt am Main

Esposito, M. (2003) *Chi paga la devolution?* (Bari, Laterza).

European Commission (1993) 'Debt, Deficit and Fiscal Adjustment', by L. Pench, in *The Economic and Financial Situation of Italy*, European Economy – Reports and Studies, No. 1.

European Commission (1999) *Italy's Slow Growth in the 1990s – Facts, Explanations and Prospects*, Directorate General for Economic and Financial Affairs, European Economy, No. 5 (Luxembourg: Office for Official Publications of the EC).

European Commission (2006a) *Public Finances in EMU – 2006*, Directorate General for Economic and Financial Affairs, European Economy, No. 3/2006 (Luxembourg: Office for Official Publications of the EC).

European Commission (2006b) *The EU Economy: 2006 Review. Adjustment Dynamics in the Euro Area – Experiences and Challenges*, Directorate General for Economic and Financial Affairs, European Economy, No. 6 (Luxembourg: Office for Official Publications of the EC).

European Commission (2007a) *Public finances in EMU – 2007*, Directorate General for Economic and Financial Affairs, European Economy, No. 3/2007 (Luxembourg: Office for Official Publications of the EC).

European Commission (2007b) *The EU Economy: 2007 Review – Moving Europe's Productivity Frontier*, Directorate General for Economic and Financial Affairs, European Economy, No. 5 (Luxembourg: Office for Official Publications of the EC).

European Commission (2007c) *Report on the Retail Banking Sector Enquiry*, Commission Staff Working Document accompanying the Communication from the Commission [COM (2007) 33 final] (Brussels: EC).

European Commission (2008) *EMU@10 – Successes and Challenges after 10 Years of Economic and Monetary Union*, Directorate General for Economic and Financial Affairs, European Economy, No. 2 (Luxembourg: Office for Official Publications of the EC).

European Commission Economic Policy Committee (2006) 'The Impact of Aging on Public Expenditure: Projections for the EU25 Member States on Pensions, Health Care, Long-term care, Education and Unemployment Transfers (2004–2050)', European Economy, Special Report No. 1 (Brussels: European Commission); available at: http://ec.europa.eu/economy_finance/publications/european_economy/2006/eesp106en.pdf

Fabiani, S., F. Schivardi and S. Trento (2003) 'Quale impresa italiana investe in tecnologie digitali?', in S. Rossi (ed.) *La Nuova economia. I fatti dietro il mito* (Bologna: Il Mulino).

Fabrizio, S. and A. Mody (2007) 'Breaking the Impediments to Budgetary Reforms: Evidence from Europe', paper presented at the DG ECFIN Workshop on Achieving and Safeguarding Sound Fiscal Positions, Brussels, 17 January.

Fachin, S. and A. Gavosto (2007) 'The Decline in Italian Productivity: A Study in the Estimation of Long-Run Trends in Total Factor Productivity with Panel Cointegration Methods', LLEE Working Document, No. 50.

Faini, R. (2004) 'Fu vero declino? L'Italia negli anni novanta', in G. Toniolo and V. Visco (eds) *Il declino economico dell'Italia* (Bologna: Bruno Mondadori Editori, Il Mulino).

Faini, R. (2004) 'Fiscal Policy and Interest Rates in Europe', in Banca d'Italia, *Public Debt*, Rome.

Faini R. (2006) 'Europe: a Continent in Decline?' in P. Rhode and G. Toniolo (eds) *The Global Economy in the 1990s: A Long-run Perspective* (Cambridge: Cambridge University Press).

Faini, R. (2007) *Il mondo in rosso e nero. Cronache di politica economica 2003-2007* (Pirola: Il Sole 24 Ore).

Faini, R., G. Galli, P. Gennari and F. Rossi (1997) 'An Empirical Puzzle: Falling Migration and Growing Unemployment Differentials among Italian Regions', *European Economic Review*, 41 (3–5), pp. 571–79.

Faini, R. and S. Gagliarducci (2005) 'Competitività e struttura dell'economia italiana: un'anatomia del declino', in L. Torchia and F. Bassanini (eds) *Sviluppo o declino: Il ruolo delle istituzioni per la competitività del paese* (Florence: Passigli), pp. 9–38.

Faini, R., S. Giannini, D. Gros, G. Pisauro and F. Kostoris Padoa Schioppa (2006) *I conti a rischio* (Bologna: Il Mulino).

Faini, R. and A. Sapir (2005) 'Un Modello Obsoleto? Crescita e Specializzazione dell'Economia Italiana', in T. Boeri, R. Faini, A. Ichino, G. Pisauro and C. Scarpa (2005) *Oltre e Declino* (Bologna: II Mulino), pp. 19–77.

Fausto, D. (2003) 'Il federalismo fiscale nel paese del dualismo', in A. Fossati (ed.) *La nascita del federalismo italiano* (Milan: Franco Angeli).

Fausto, D. and F. Pica (2000) *Teoria e fatti del federalismo fiscale* (Bologna: Il Mulino).

Ferrera, M. and E. Gualmini (1999a) *Salvati dall'Europa?* (Bologna: Il Mulino).

Ferrera, M. and E. Gualmini (1999b) 'Rescue from Without? Italian Social Policies 1970-1999 and the Challenges of Internationalisation', European University Institute Working Papers, No. 13.

Ferro, P., S. Lo Faso and G. Salvemini (1999) 'L'azione della pubblica amministrazione per la competitività internazionale in presenza di vincoli di finanza pubblica', in M. Bordignon and D. da Empoli (eds) *Concorrenza fiscale in un'economia internazionale integrata* (Milan: Franco Angeli), pp. 236–80.

Fornero, E. (2006) 'Una nuova riforma? . . . no, meglio applicare quella approvata', *AREL Europa Lavoro Economia*, November.

Francese, M. and A. Pace (2007) 'Il debito pubblico italiano dall'unità ad oggi', Banca d'Italia, mimeo.

Franco, D. (1993) *L'espansione della spesa pubblica in Italia* (Bologna: Il Mulino).

Franco, D. (2002) 'Italy: A Never-ending Pension Reform', in M. Feldstein and H. Siebert (eds) *Coping with the Pension Crisis – Where Does Europe Stand?* (Chicago: Chicago University Press).

Franco, D. (2005) 'Il consolidamento interrotto', in M. C. Guerra and A. Zanardi (eds) *La finanza pubblica italiana – Rapporto 2005* (Bologna, Il Mulino), pp. 253–78.

Franco, D. and M. Marè (2002) 'Le pensioni: l'economia e la politica delle riforme', *Rivista di Politica Economica*, XCII, July–August, pp. 197–276.

Franco, D. and M. R. Marino (2003) 'The Role of Forecasts in Social Security Policy', *Giornale degli economisti e annali di economia*, 61 (2), December.

Franco, D. and N. Sartor (2005) 'Notional Defined Contribution in Italy: Unsatisfactory Present, Uncertain Future', in R. Holzmann and E. Palmer (eds) *Pension Reform – Issues and Prospects for Non-Financial Defined Contribution (NDC) Schemes* (Washington DC: World Bank).

Franco, D., G. Messina and S. Zotteri (2004) 'Fiscal Federalism in Italy: An Unfinished Agenda', *Wirtschaftspolitische Blätter*, No. 4.

Franco, D., J. Gokhale, L. Guiso, L. J. Kotlikoff and N. Sartor (1994) 'Generational Accounting: The Case of Italy', in A. Ando, L. Guiso and I. Visco (eds) *Saving and the Accumulation of Wealth* (Cambridge, Cambridge University Press).

Franco, D., M. R. Marino and P. Tommasino (2008) 'Pension Policy and Poverty in Italy: Recent Developments and New Priorities', *Giornale degli economisti*, forthcoming.

Galeotti, G., A. Petretto and G. Pisauro (1998) 'Razionalizzazione e semplificazione dei documenti e delle procedure contabili', Commissione Tecnica per la Spesa Pubblica – Raccomandazione, No. 5 (Rome: Ministero del Tesoro).

Galí, J. (1999) 'Technology, Employment, and the Business Cycle: Do Technology Shocks Explain Aggregate Fluctuations?', *American Economic Review*, 89, pp. 249–71.

Galli, G. and F. Giavazzi (1992) 'Tassi di interesse reali e debito pubblico negli anni ottanta: interpretazioni, prospettive, implicazioni per la politica di bilancio', in Ente Einaudi (ed.) *Il disavanzo pubblico in Italia: natura strutturale e politiche di rientro* (Bologna: Il Mulino).

Garibaldi, P., L. Pacelli and A. Borgarello (2003) 'Employment Protection Legislation and the Size of Firms', IZA Discussion Papers 787, Institute for the Study of Labor (IZA).

Giannini, S. and M. C. Guerra, (2000) 'Dove eravamo e dove stiamo: il sistema tributario dal 1990 al 2000', in L. Bernardi (ed.) *La finanza pubblica italiana – Rapporto 2000* (Bologna: Il Mulino).

Giannini, S. and P. Onofri (eds) (2005) *Per lo sviluppo. Fisco e welfare* (Bologna: Il Mulino).

Giarda, P. (2003) 'Sull'incompletezza del sistema di federalismo fiscale proposto dalla nuova Costituzione: ci sono rimedi?', *Rivista Internazionale di scienze Sociali*, CIII, No. 2.

Giarda, P., A. Petretto and G. Pisauro (2005) 'Elementi per una politica di governo della spesa pubblica', in T. Boeri, R. Faini, A. Ichino, G. Pisauro and C. Scarpa (eds) *Oltre il declino* (Bologna, Il Mulino), pp. 223–76.

Giavazzi, F. and L. Spaventa (1988) *High Public Debt: the Italian Experience* (Cambridge: Cambridge University Press).

Giavazzi, F. and L. Spaventa (1989) 'Italy: the Real Effects of Inflation and Disinflation', *Economic Policy*, No. 8, pp. 133–71.

Giovannini, A. (1988) 'Capital Controls and Public Finance: the Experience of Italy', in F. Giavazzi and L. Spaventa (eds) *High Public Debt: the Italian Experience* (Cambridge, Cambridge University Press), pp. 177–211.

Grilli, V., D. Masciandaro and G. Tabellini (1991) 'Political and Monetary Institutions and Public Financial Policies in the Industrial Countries', *Economic Policy*, No. 13, pp. 341–392.

Grillo, M. (2004) *Alle radici di una Economia che non gira* (Bologna: Il Mulino).

Gronchi, S. (1998) 'La sostenibilità delle nuove forme previdenziali ovvero il sistema pensionistico tra riforme fatte e da fare', *Economia Politica*, Vol. 15, No. 2.

Gronchi, S. and S. Nisticò (2005) 'Implementing the NDC Theoretical Model: A Comparison of Italy and Sweden', in R. Holzmann and E. Palmer (eds) *Pension Reform – Issues and Prospects for Non-Financial Defined Contribution (NDC) Schemes* (Washington DC: World Bank).

Gros D. (2006) 'Will EMU Survive 2010?', *CEPS*, 17 January.

Gros, D. (2007) 'Italy on the Brink?', Centre for European Policy Studies, *Thinking Ahead for Europe*, 7 February.

Grossman, G. and E. Rossi-Hansberg (2006) 'Trading Tasks: A Simple Theory of Offshoring', August 2006, available from: www.princeton.edu/~grossman/offshoring.pdf

Guarino, G. (2007) 'Vincoli europei, finanza e patrimonio pubblico. Ovvero il problema del debito pubblico e una proposta per la sua risoluzione', in U. Mattei, E. Reviglio and S. Rodotà (eds) *Invertire la rotta* (Bologna: Il Mulino), pp. 157–78.

Hallerberg, M. (2004) *Domestic Budgets in a United Europe* (Ithaca: Cornell University Press).

Høj, J., M. Jimenez, M. Maher, G. Nicoletti, and M. Wise (2007) 'Product Market Competition in the OECD Countries: Taking Stock and Moving Forward', OECD Economic Department Working Paper No. 575.

Ichino, P. (2006) *I nullafacenti* (Milan: Mondadori).

International Monetary Fund (2004) 'Fostering Structural Reforms in Industrial Countries', *World Economic Outlook*, Washington DC, April.

International Monetary Fund (2005) *Italy: Selected Issues*, IMF Country Report, No. 05/41, Washington DC, February.

International Monetary Fund (2006) *Italy – 2006 IMF Article IV Consultation Preliminary Conclusions of the Mission*, at: www.imf.org/external/np/ms/2006/111306.htm

International Monetary Fund (2007a) *Italy: Report on the Observance of Standards and Codes*, IMF Country Report, No. 07/87, Washington DC.

International Monetary Fund (2007b) *Italy: Selected Issues*, IMF Country Report, No. 07/65, Washington DC.

International Monetary Fund (2007c) *Italy: 2006 Article IV Consultation – Staff Report; Public Information Notice on the Executive Board Discussion; and Statement by the Executive Director for Italy*, IMF Country Report No. 07/64, February 2007, available at: www.imf.org/external/pubs/cat/longres.cfm?sk=20447.0

International Monetary Fund (2007d) *Regional Economic Outlook, Europe*, 'Strengthening Financial Systems', Washington DC, November.

International Monetary Fund (2007e) *Italy: Budget System Reforms*, Fiscal Affairs Department, June, available at: www.tesoro.it/web/apri.asp?idDoc=17723.

ISAE (2003) *Rapporto annuale sull'attuazione del federalismo*, Rome.

ISAE (2005) *Rapporto previsionale sull'economia italiana*, Rome, February.

ISAE (2007a) *Le previsioni per l'economia italiana – L'Italia nell'integrazione europea*, Rome, March.

ISAE (2007b) *Finanza pubblica e istituzioni*, Rome, May.

ISTAT (2005) *National Accounts*, Rome.

ISTAT (2006a) *Indicatori demografici*, Rome.

ISTAT (2006b) *Previsioni demografiche nazionali*, Rome.

ISTAT (2006c) *La misura dell'economia sommersa secondo le statistche ufficiali*, Rome, December.

Istituto per il Commercio Estero (2002) 'L'Italia nell'economia internazionale', *Rapporto ICE 2001–2002*, Rome.

Istituto per il Commercio Estero (2007) 'L'Italia nell'Economia Internazionale', *Rapporto ICE 2006–2007*, Rome.

Jappelli, T. and Pistaferri, L. (2000) 'The Dynamics of Household Wealth Accumulation in Italy', *Fiscal Studies*, 21 (2) (London: Institute for Fiscal Studies).

Jonung, L. and M. Larch (2006) 'Improving Fiscal Policy in the EU: the Case for Independent Forecasts', *Economic Policy*, July, pp. 491–529.

Kamps, C. (2004) 'New Estimates of Government Net Capital stock for 22 OECD Countries 1960-2001', IMF Working Paper, No. 04/67.

Kopits G. (2001) 'Fiscal Rules: Useful Policy Framework or Unnecessary Ornament?', in Banca d'Italia, *Fiscal Rules*, Rome.

Kopits, G. and S. Symanski (1998) 'Fiscal Policy Rules', IMF Occasional Paper, No. 162 (Washington DC: International Monetary Fund).

Kostoris Padoa Schioppa, F. (2001) 'Budgetary Policies and Administrative Reform in Contemporary Italy', *Daedalus*, 130 (2), pp. 115–38.

Kremer, J., C. R. Braz, T. Brosens, G. Langenus, S. Momigliano and M. Spolander (2006) 'A Disaggregated Framework for the Analysis of Structural Developments in Public Finances', ECB Working Paper, No. 579.

Krueger, D. and K. Krumar (2003a) 'Skill-specific Rather than General Education: a Reason for US-Europe Growth Differences?', NBER Working Paper, No. 9408 (Cambridge: NBER).

Krueger, D. and K. Krumar (2003b) 'US-Europe Differences in Technology Driven Growth: Quantifying the Role of Education', NBER Working Paper, No. 10001 (Cambridge: NBER).

Lamieri, M. and A. Lanza (2006) 'La ripresa passa attraverso la qualità: un'analisi del potere di mercato delle imprese italiane', *Imprese e territorio*, No. 1.

Lanza, A., and B. Quintieri (2007) 'Quote di mercato e qualità delle esportazioni italiane: il quadro generale', in A. Lanza and B. Quintieri (eds) *Eppur si muove, Come cambia l'export italiano* (Soveria Mannelli: Rubbettino).

Larch, M. (2004) 'Relegated to the League of Laggards? Roots of Italy's Slow Potential Growth Creation', *ECFIN Country Focus,* Vol. I, Issue 8 (Brussels: European Commission, Directorate General for Economic and Financial Affairs).

Larch, M. (2005) 'Stuck in the Rut? Italy's Weak Export Performance and Unfavourable Product Specialization', *ECFIN Country Focus*, Vol. II, Issue 9 (Brussels: European Commission, Directorate General for Economic and Financial Affairs).

Leibfritz, W. (2000) 'Generational Accounting Around the World', in Fiscal Sustainability, papers presented at the Banca d'Italia workshop held in Perugia, 20–22 January, Rome.

Lissovolik, B (2008) 'Trends in Italy's Nonprice Competitiveness', IMF Working Paper No. 08/124 (Washington DC: International Monetary Fund).

Locarno, A. and A. Staderini (2008) 'Le entrate tributarie in Italia: sviluppi recenti e dinamiche di medio periodo', mimeo.

Lotti, F., and F. Schivardi (2005) 'Cross Country Differences in Patent Propensity: a Firm Level Investigation', *Giornale degli Economisti e Annali di Economia*, 64 (4), pp. 469–502.

Mandrone, E. and N. Massarelli (2007) 'Quanti sono i lavoratori precari', *La Voce*, 21 March, available at: www.lavoce.info

Marchetti, D. J. and F. Nucci, (2005) 'Price Stickiness and the Contractionary Effect of Technology Shocks', *European Economic Review*, 49, pp. 1137–63.

Marchetti, D. J. and F. Nucci, (2007) 'Pricing Behavior and the Response of Hours to Productivity Shocks', *Journal of Money, Credit and Banking*, 39, pp. 1587–11.

Marino, M. R., S. Momigliano and P. Rizza (2008) 'A Structural Analysis of Italy's Fiscal Policies After Joining the European Monetary Union: Are We Learning From Our Past?', *Public Finance and Management*, special issue on Public Finance in Europe, forthcoming.

Martinez-Mongay, C., Maza Lasierra, L. A. and Yaniz Igal, J. (2007) 'Asset Booms and Tax Receipts: The Case of Spain, 1995–2006', European Economy, Economic Papers No. 293 (Brussels: European Commission).

Messori, M. (ed.) (2006) *La previdenza complementare in Italia* (Bologna: Il Mulino).

Micco, A., E. Stein and G. Ordoñez (2003) 'The Currency Union Effect on Trade: Early Evidence', *Economic Policy*, 37, pp. 317–56.

Ministero del Tesoro (1988) *Il debito pubblico in Italia 1861–1987*, Rome.
Ministero del Tesoro (1998) *Italy's Convergence Towards EMU*, Rome.
Ministero dell'Economia e delle Finanze (2001) *Documento di programmazione economico-finanziaria per gli anni 2002–2006*, Rome.
Ministero dell'Economia e delle Finanze (2006) *Relazione generale sulla situazione economica del Paese*, Rome.
Ministero dell'Economia e delle Finanze (2004) *Conto patrimoniale delle Amministrazioni pubbliche. Stime 2001–2003*, Rome.
Ministero dell'Economia e delle Finanze (2006a) *Documento di programmazione economico-finanziaria per gli anni 2007–2011*, Rome.
Ministero dell'Economia e delle Finanze (2006b) *Le tendenze di medio-lungo periodo del sistema pensionistico e socio-sanitario*, Rapporto n. 8, Rome.
Ministero dell'Economia e delle Finanze (2007a) *Documento di programmazione economico-finanziaria per gli anni 2008–2011*, Rome.
Ministero dell'Economia e delle Finanze (2007b) *Italy's Stability Programme – November 2007 Update*, Rome.
Ministero dell'Economia e delle Finanze (2008) *Documento di programmazione economico-finanziaria per gli anni 2009–2013*, Rome.
Ministero dell'Economia e delle Finanze and Ministero della Pubblica Istruzione (2007), *Quaderno bianco sulla scuola*, Rome.
Moëc, G. (2007) 'Italy's Growth Prospects: Accelerando to Moderato', Bank of America Economic Brief, 25 May.
Momigliano, S. and P. Rizza (2007) 'Temporary Measures in Italy: Buying or Losing Time?', in G. P. Kiss (ed.) *Temporary Measures and Off-budget Activities* (Budapest: Magyar Nemzeti Bank).
Momigliano, S. and S. Siviero (2002) 'Appraising the Effects of the Budget on the Economy with an Econometric Model: The Italian Fiscal Adjustment in the Nineties', in Banca d'Italia, *The Impact of Fiscal Policy*, Rome.
Monorchio, A. (ed.) (1996), *La finanza pubblica italiana dopo la svolta del 1992* (Bologna: Il Mulino).
Montanino, A. and S. Nicoletti Altimari (2007) 'Per spendere meglio ripartiamo dal bilancio', *La Voce*, 16 October, available at: www.lavoce.info/articoli/-conti_pubblici/pagina1000068.html
Monti, P. (2005) 'Caratteristiche e mutamenti della specializzazione delle esportazioni italiane', Temi di Discussione della Banca d'Italia, no. 559.
Morcaldo, G. (1993), *La Finanza Pubblica in Italia*, Il Mulino, Bologna.
Morcaldo, G. (2005) *Una politica economica per la crescita* (Milan: Franco Angeli).
Morcaldo, G. (2006) 'Pensioni: necessità di una riforma', *Economia italiana*, 2007 (2).
Morcaldo, G. (2007) *Intervento pubblico e crescita economica: un equilibrio da ricostruire* (Milan: Franco Angeli).
Muraro, G. (2003) 'Federalismo fiscale e sanità nella crisi dello Stato sociale', in D. Franco and A. Zanardi (eds) *I sistemi di welfare tra decentramento regionale e integrazione europea* (Milan: Franco Angeli).
Nardozzi, G., (2004) *Miracolo e declino. L'Italia tra concorrenza e protezione* (Bari: Laterza).
Ng, F. (2004) 'Tariff Data on Trade and Import Barriers', World Bank Trade Website (econ.worldbank.org) (Washington DC: World Bank).
Nicoletti, G. and S. Scarpetta (2003) 'Regulation, Productivity and Growth: OECD Evidence', OECD Economics Department Working Paper, No. 347.

Nicoletti, G. and S. Scarpetta (2005) 'Product Market Reforms and Employment in OECD Countries', OECD Economics Department Working Paper, No. 472.
OECD (1994) *The OECD Jobs Study: Facts, Analysis, Strategies*, Paris.
OECD (2001) *Economic Outlook*, No 70, Paris.
OECD (2002) *Economic Surveys of Italy*, Paris.
OECD (2003) *Economic Surveys of Italy*, Paris.
OECD (2004) 'Ciclo economico e finanza pubblica', in M. C. Guerra and A. Zanardi (eds), *La finanza pubblica italiana – Rapporto 2004* (Bologna: Il Mulino).
OECD (2005) *Economic Survey of Italy*, Paris.
OECD (2006) *Employment Outlook*, Paris.
OECD (2007a) *Education at a Glance*, Paris.
OECD (2007b) *Economic Survey of Italy*, Paris.
OECD (2007c) *Going for Growth*, Paris.
OECD (2007d) *OECD Economic Survey: United Kingdom*, Paris.
Onida, F. (1999) 'Quali prospettive per il modello di specializzazione internazionale dell'Italia?', in *Economia italiana*, 3, pp. 573–629.
Onofri, P. (2001) 'La lunga fase di risanamento dell'economia italiana: 1992–2000', in C. D'Adda (ed.) *Per l'economia italiana* (Bologna: Il Mulino).
Padovano, F. and L. Venturi (2001) 'Wars of Attrition in Italian Government Coalitions and Fiscal Performance: 1948–1994', *Public Choice*, 109 (1/2), October, pp. 15–54.
Paesani, P. and G. Piga (2002) 'Cause e gestione del debito pubblico in Italia dal 1970 al 1990', in M. Bagella and L. Paganetto (eds) *Politiche macroeconomiche, gestione del debito pubblico e mercati finanziari* (Bologna: Il Mulino), pp. 217–63.
Pagano, P. and F. Schivardi (2003) 'Firm Size Distribution and Growth', *Scandinavian Journal of Economics*, 105 (2), pp. 255–74.
Paiella, M. (2004) 'Does Wealth Affect Consumption? Evidence for Italy', *Temi di discussione*, No. 510, July (Rome: Banca d'Italia).
Pammolli, F. and N. C. Salerno (2006) 'Spesa sanitaria, demografia e governance istituzionale', *Quaderno CERM*, No. 2/06.
Papp, T. K. and E. Takats (2008) 'Tax Rate Cuts and Tax Compliance – The Laffer Curve Revisited', IMF Working Paper, WP/08/7.
Pedone, A. (2005) 'La politica monetaria tra vincoli monetary ed esigenze di sviluppo produttivo', in G. Acquaviva (ed.) *La politica economica italiana negli anni ottanta* (Venice: Marsilio), pp. 25–49.
Peracchi, F. and N. Rossi (1998) 'Nonostante tutto, è una riforma', in F. Giavazzi, A. Penati and G. Tabellini (eds) *La costituzione fiscale* (Bologna: Il Mulino).
Petretto, A. (2003) 'Le entrate delle Regioni e degli enti locali secondo il nuovo art. 119 della Costituzione', *IRPET Interventi, note e rassegne*, Florence.
Pisauro, G. (2003) 'Un caso particolare di applicazione dell'art. 81: la legge finanziaria', in G. Salvemini (ed.) *I guardiani del bilancio* (Venice: Marsilio), pp. 141–56.
Presidenza del Consiglio dei Ministri (2007) *Lisbon Strategy National Reform Programme – Second Implementation Report*, October, Rome.
Quintieri, B. (2007), 'Qualità e differenziazione verticale nella teoria del commercio internazionale', in A. Lanza and B. Quintieri (eds) *Eppur si muove, Come cambia l'export italiano* (Soveria Mannelli: Rubbettino).
Rae, D. and M. Sollie (2007) 'Globalisation and the European Union: Which Countries Are Best Placed to Cope?', OECD Economics Department Working Papers, No. 586 (Paris: OECD).

Reviglio, E. (2007) 'Il conto patrimoniale delle Amministrazioni pubbliche', in U. Mattei, E. Reviglio and S. Rodotà (eds) *Invertire la rotta* (Bologna, Il Mulino), pp. 239–82.
Reviglio, F. (1977) *Spesa pubblica e stagnazione dell'economia italiana* (Bologna: Il Mulino).
Reviglio, F. (1998) *Come siamo entrati in Europa (e perché potremmo uscirne)* (Turin: UTET).
Reviglio, F. (2006a) 'Grazie alla finanza straordinaria siamo rimasti in Europa. Solo con l'abbattimento del debito vi resteremo', *Economia Pubblica*, No. 1–2.
Reviglio, F. (2006b) *Per restare in Europa* (Turin: UTET).
Rodrik, D. (2004) 'Industrial Policy for the Twenty-First Century', CEPR Discussion Paper, No. 4767 (London: CEPR).
Romani, F. (1980) 'Crisi dello stato democratico? Alcune riflessioni sulle finanze pubbliche italiane negli anni settanta', *Note Economiche.*
Rose, A. (2000) 'One Money, One Market: Estimating the Effects of Common Currencies on Trade', *Economic Policy*, 30, pp. 7–46.
Rosolia A. (2007) 'Notes on Undeclared Work in NAs and the Regularisations of Illegal Immigrants', mimeo, March.
Rosolia, A. and R. Torrini (2007) 'The Generation Gap: Relative Earnings of Young and Old Workers in Italy', Temi di Discussione della Banca d'Italia, No. 639.
Rossi, N. (1997) *Meno ai padri più ai figli* (Bologna: Il Mulino).
Rossi, N. (2002) *Riformisti per forza* (Bologna, Il Mulino).
Rossi, N. and G. Toniolo (2004) 'L'università italiana: autonomia o decadenza', *Italiani europei*, 1, pp. 61–74.
Rossi, S. (2007) *La politica economica italiana 1968–2007* (Bari: Laterza).
Rostagno, M. (1996) 'Il percorso della riforma: 1992–1995. Nuovi indicatori di consistenza e sostenibilità per il FPLD', in F. Padoa Schioppa Kostoris (ed.) *Pensioni e risanamento della finanza pubblica* (Bologna: Il Mulino).
Salvati, M. (1984) *Economia e politica in Italia dal dopoguerra a oggi* (Milan: Garzanti).
Salvati, M. (2000) *Occasioni mancate. Economia e politica in Italia dagli anni '60 a oggi* (Bari: Laterza).
Salvemini, G. (2003) *I guardiani del bilancio* (Venice: Marsilio).
Sapir, A. (ed.), with P. Aghion, G. Bertola, M. Hellwig, J. Pisani-Ferry, D. Rosati, J. Viñals, and H. Wallace (2004) *An Agenda for a Growing Europe: The Sapir Report* (Oxford: Oxford University Press).
Sartor, N. (ed.) (1998) *Il risanamento mancato. La politica di bilancio nella seconda metà degli anni ottanta* (Rome: Carocci Editore).
Sartor, N. (ed.) (2001) 'The Long-run Effects of the Italian Pension Reforms', *International Tax and Public Finance*, 8 (1), pp. 83–111.
Schivardi, F. and R. Torrini (2004) 'Firm Size Distribution and Employment Protection in Italy', Banca d'Italia, Servizio Study, Temi di Discussione, No. 504.
Sgherri, S. (2006) 'Regaining Competitiveness: A Challenge Made in Italy', pp. 7–25, Selected Issues 06/59, International Monetary Fund, available at: www.imf.org/external/pubs/cat/longres.cfm?sk=18925.0
Spaventa, L. (1988) 'Introduction: is There a Public Debt Problem in Italy?', in F. Giavazzi and L. Spaventa (eds) *High Public Debt: the Italian Experience* (Cambridge: Cambridge University Press), pp. 1–24.
Spaventa, L. and V. Chiorazzo (1999) 'The Prodigal Son or a Confidence Trickster? How Italy Got into EMU', in D. Cobham and G. Zis (eds) *From EMS to EMU: 1979 to 1999 and Beyond* (Basingstoke: Macmillan Press), pp. 129–55.

Spaventa, L. and V. Chiorazzo (2000) *Astuzia o virtù? Come accadde che l'Italia fu ammessa all'Unione Monetaria* (Rome: Donzelli).

Staderini, A. (2001) 'Tax Reforms to Influence Corporate Financial Policy: the Case of the Italian Business Tax Reform of 1997–98', Temi di discussione della Banca d'Italia, No. 423.

Steve, S. (1978) 'Conclusioni al Convegno di Pavia sulla spesa pubblica del 7–8 ottobre 1977', in E. Gerelli and F. Reviglio (eds) *Per una politica della spesa pubblica in Italia* (Milan: Franco Angeli).

Strauch, R., M. Hallerberg and J. von Hagen (2004) 'Budgetary Forecasts in Europe: the Track Record of Stability and Convergence Programmes', ECB Working Paper Series, No. 307, February.

Subramanian, A. and S. Wei (2003) 'The WTO Promotes Trade: Strongly, But Unevenly', IMF Working Paper, 03/185.

SVIMEZ (2007) *Rapporto Svimez 2007 sull'Economia del Mezzogiorno* (Il Mulino: Bologna).

Tabellini, G. (1988) 'Monetary and Fiscal Policy Coordination with High Public Debt', in F. Giavazzi and L. Spaventa (eds) *High Public Debt: the Italian Experience* (Cambridge: Cambridge University Press), pp, 92–126.

Tanzi, V. (1980) 'Inflationary Expectations, Economic Activity, Taxes, and Interest Rates', *American Economic Review*, 70, pp. 12–21.

Tanzi, V. (2006) 'Fiscal Policy: When Theory Collides with Reality', CEPS Working Document, No. 246, June.

Tanzi, V. (2007) *Questione di tasse: La lezione dall'Argentina* (Università Bocconi Editore).

Tanzi, V., M. Blejer and M. Teijeiro (1987) 'Inflation and the Measurement of Fiscal Deficits', *IMF Staff Papers*, 34 (4), pp. 711–38.

Toniolo, G. (1988) *Storia economica dell'Italia liberale 1850-1918* (Bologna: Il Mulino).

Toniolo, G. and V. Visco (eds) (2004) *Il declino economico dell'Italia* (Bologna: Bruno Mondadori Editori, Il Mulino).

Unioncamere and Istituto Tagliacarne (2007) *Le piccole e medie imprese nell'iconomia italiana – Rapporto 2007* (Milan: Franco Angeli).

Verzichelli, L. (1999) *La politica di bilancio* (Bologna: Il Mulino).

Visaggio, M. (1997) *Politiche di bilancio e debito pubblico* (Roma: Nuova Italia Scientifica).

Von Hagen, J. and I. Harden (1996) 'Budget Processes and Commitment to Fiscal Discipline', IMF Working Paper, No. 78 (Washington DC: International Monetary Fund).

Von Hagen, J., A. Hughes Hallet and R. Strauch (2002) 'Budgetary Institutions for Sustainable Public Finances', in M. Buti, J. von Hagen and C. Martinez-Mongay (eds), *The Behaviour of Fiscal Authorities* (Basingstoke: Palgrave), pp. 94–112.

Zaghini, A. (2001) 'Le recenti teorie di politica fiscale: uno studio empirico del caso italiano', in A. Verde (ed.) *Temi di finanza pubblica* (Bari: Cacucci Editore).

Index